Web 25

Steve Jones
General Editor

Vol. 112

The Digital Formations series is part of the Peter Lang Media and Communication list.
Every volume is peer reviewed and meets
the highest quality standards for content and production.

PETER LANG
New York • Bern • Frankfurt • Berlin
Brussels • Vienna • Oxford • Warsaw

Web 25

Histories from the First 25 Years
of the World Wide Web

Edited by Niels Brügger

PETER LANG
New York • Bern • Frankfurt • Berlin
Brussels • Vienna • Oxford • Warsaw

Library of Congress Cataloging-in-Publication Data

Names: Brügger, Niels, editor.
Title: Web 25: histories from the first 25 years
of the World Wide Web / edited by Niels Brügger.
Description: New York: Peter Lang, 2017.
Series: Digital formations; vol. 112 | ISSN 1526-3169
Includes bibliographical references.
Identifiers: LCCN 2017008861 | ISBN 978-1-4331-3270-4 (hardcover: alk. paper)
ISBN 978-1-4331-3269-8 (paperback: alk. paper) | ISBN 978-1-4331-4064-8 (ebook pdf)
ISBN 978-1-4331-4065-5 (epub) | ISBN 978-1-4331-4066-2 (mobi)
Subjects: LCSH: World Wide Web—History.
Classification: LCC TK5105.888 W36745 2017 | DDC 025.042—dc23
LC record available at https://lccn.loc.gov/2017008861
DOI 10.3726/b11492

Bibliographic information published by **Die Deutsche Nationalbibliothek.**
Die Deutsche Nationalbibliothek lists this publication in the "Deutsche
Nationalbibliografie"; detailed bibliographic data are available
on the Internet at http://dnb.d-nb.de/.

Table OF Contents

List OF Figures

List OF Tables

Introduction

Histories from the first 25 years of the World Wide Web

NIELS BRÜGGER

Web 25: Histories from the first 25 years of the World Wide Web celebrates the 25th anniversary of the web. Since the beginning of the 1990s the web has played an important role in the development of the internet as well as in the development of most societies at large, from its early grey and blue web pages introducing the hyperlink for a wider public, to today's uses of the web as an integrated part of our daily lives, of politics, of culture, and more.

Taking as point of departure that the World Wide Web was born between 1989 and 1994 (cf. Brügger, 2016, pp. 1061–1062), this volume presents some of the histories of how the web started and how it has developed. In 2010, in the epilogue "The future of web history" web scholars were encouraged to "engage in discussions about the theoretical and methodological foundations of web historiography" and to "launch concrete studies of the history of the web" (Brügger, 2010, p. 349). The contributors to *Web 25: Histories from the first 25 years of the World Wide Web* have taken up this challenge, and the book constitutes one of the first book-length steps towards the establishing of web history as a research field, and it is the first to look back at 25 years of web history.[1]

However, the volume does by no means pretend to be either exhaustive or comprehensive. Rather it comprises a number of probes into the vast and multifaceted past of the web, some of the first digs hopefully to be followed by other studies within the emerging field of web history.

Although the volume is not comprehensive, it is broad in scope in more respects. First, it features contributions about a variety of topics, from the birth of the web, the spread of the early web, and its introduction to the general public in mainstream media, to blogs, literature, and traditional media going online. Second, case studies are presented alongside with methodological reflections and accounts of how one of the most important source types is provided, namely the archived web. And, third, whereas a number of the chapters are transnational in nature the volume covers web histories from a large number of countries, from Australia, the UK and the US, to China, Denmark, Germany and Italy.

In Section 1—The early web—four chapters focus on the history leading up to the emergence of the World Wide Web as well as on how the web was narrated and understood in its early beginnings.

In "Connecting textual segments: A brief history of the web hyperlink" Niels Brügger investigates the history of one of the most fundamental features of the web: the hyperlink. Based on the argument that the web hyperlink is best understood if it is seen as another step in a much longer and broader history than just the years of the emergence of the web, the chapter traces the history of how segments of text have deliberately been connected to each other by the use of specific textual and media features, from clay tablets, manuscripts on parchment, and print, among others, to hyperlinks on stand-alone computers and in local and global digital networks.

In Chapter 2, Simone Natale and Paolo Bory employ the notion of 'biography of media' in their analysis of the history of the web, claiming that the biographies of Tim Berners-Lee and that of the invention of the web follow an identical narrative structure. Narratives regarding the invention, the diffusion and the institutionalization of the web can be framed through the hero 'monomyth', as described by Joseph Campbell in his seminal book *The Hero with a Thousand Faces*. The authors argue that biographies of media provide a trajectory through which we represent and imagine the impact of media in our societies and everyday lives.

Chapter 3 by Jean Marie Deken investigates how the SLAC National Accelerator Laboratory (then Stanford Linear Accelerator Center) became a very early adopter of the World Wide Web. The chapter is an account of the development and early history of the SLAC website that was not only the first outside of the European Centre for Nuclear Research (CERN) where the web was invented, it also delivered what the web's inventor, Tim Berners-Lee, has deemed the 'killer app' that showed the world the broader value and possibilities of the new tool.

Marguerite Barry, the author of Chapter 4, tells the story about the introduction of the World Wide Web to the general public. This chapter presents a picture of how international news reported on this new technology. Examining the earliest articles on the 'World Wide Web' from 1992 to 1994, it shows public discourse shifting from instrumental explanation, to commercial/utopian potential and conflict over structure to increasing availability and domestication. Barry explores different narratives anchored in events that illustrate the social, cultural and political context around its 'birth', arguing that comets, cats and Kurt Cobain did as much to introduce the web to the public as formal narratives around its birth.

Section 2—The web of culture and media—is composed of three chapters each of which tells the story of a cultural phenomenon on the web in three different national settings.

In Chapter 5, Michel Hockx provides a brief overview of the development of the World Wide Web in China since the late 1990s. The emphasis is on the wide range of cultural production happening on China's web, to counterbalance discourses about the 'Great Firewall of China' that underestimate the richness of online cultural life in the People's Republic of China. A case study is presented of online literature, a practice which, unlike in other countries, constitutes one of the most popular forms of online activity in China.

Chapter 6 by Elisabetta Locatelli investigates the early years of the diffusion of blogs in Italy (2001–2008) considering them as cultural objects. The chapter examines how blogs' technological, cultural, economic, and institutional dimension changed over time and contributed to define blogs as a multi-faceted phenomenon. In addition, it is argued that to fully understand the development of blogging in Italy one must include both the continuity between the origins of blogging in the USA and the peculiarities of the Italian blogosphere, such as the adoption of blogging like an online diary or the creation of online and offline micro-communities.

Sybil Nolan's Chapter 7 tells the story of the creation of the Age Online in 1995. The Age Online was the first major newspaper website in Australia, and Nolan relates the website's creation and the first year and more of its life, drawing on company reports, the newspaper archive, and especially on interviews with five employees who played a key role in the website or its management at that time. The chapter argues that the struggle for survival of Fairfax Media, the owner of the *Age*, forms part of the larger history of how 25 years of the web have changed (and are still changing) human sociality in ways that are negative as well as positive.

The three chapters in Section 3—Methodological reflections—take a methodological approach to web historiography, either by focusing on web data in general, or by using concrete cases to unlock questions of method.

In Chapter 8, Matthew S. Weber examines key research problems that have challenged researchers working with web data in the past, and outlines potential pitfalls for researchers engaging with web data today. The chapter identifies core challenges, and provides an overview of the main streams of web data-based research moving forward. Focus is on web data as an object of study, although some consideration is given to the use of tools to collect web data. Factors such as the size, time, validity and reliability of web data are considered.

In Chapter 9, Anne Helmond proposes to reconceptualize the study of websites by moving the focus of analysis from the content of websites to their context, thus supplementing web historiography with historical website ecology analyses. The website is seen as an ecosystem filled with third-party content and technology, and this ecosystem can be detected by examining the website's source code in which the connections with third-parties have become inscribed. By illustrating the changing composition of a website's ecosystem, namely that of *New York Times* between 1996 and 2011, the chapter highlights how transformations in the techno-commercial configurations of the web changes over time.

In their Chapter 10, Anwesha Chakraborty and Federico Nanni investigate how prominent scientific institutions, science museums, develop and update their websites over a period of time to communicate better with their visitors. The chapter presents and discusses a methodology for using websites as primary sources to trace and examine activities of scientific institutions through the years. First, snapshots of web pages of select museum websites found in the Internet Archive are analysed diachronically, second these analyses are combined with interviews of the current website managers and with resources available on the live web.

The four chapters in Section 4—Web archives as historical source—all revolve around the impact that the preservation of the web has for its use as a historical source in web historiography.

In Chapter 11, Peter Webster surveys the history of large-scale archiving of the web at length for the first time. By looking at each of the major institutional configurations in which web archiving has occurred it is shown how particular institutions with distinctive remits and cultures have interacted with their surrounding environments, and thus how their resulting activities can be understood. The chapter argues that as is always the case with any archive, it is key that the end users understand the way in which the archive they wish to use came into being, and that this is very poorly understood in the case of web archives.

Paul Koerbin's Chapter 12 considers archived web artefacts from the perspective of a web archive curator. It focuses on early archived materials to reveal curatorial processes that determine how and in what form and context artefacts enter the archive. It is argued that the web may be understood as an oral culture while web archiving records the preserved texts for historical study. Drawing on case studies from the National Library of Australia's PANDORA Archive the chapter illustrates that web archive curation thus contributes to what the author characterises as a taphonomic process whereby biases and actions determine the state in which individual artefacts are formed, preserved and received.

In Chapter 13, Ditte Laursen and Per Møldrup-Dalum look back on the first 10 years of archiving the Danish web. More specifically, the archive's development is investigated from three different perspectives, namely the legal, the technical, and the curational. Based on data and behind-the-scenes stories from the Danish web archive, it is shown how the three perspectives frame how web archives develop over time and will continue to develop. Based on these historical analyses it is contended that a web archive's history is as pertinent to all users and uses as is its content.

In Chapter 14, Camille Paloque-Berges suggests that understanding Usenet legacy and heritage can with advantage adopt a 'layered' approach to its data, metadata, and re-archiving in web software environments. The chapter presents a genealogy of how Usenet archives came to be searched and used through the web and reflected upon by internet services and audiences from 1995 to the 2000s, and in continuation of this two archival initiatives are analyzed: the Google groups stock and the Internet Foundation stock. It is argued that the use and analysis of Usenet archives can unlock the constraints of their hosting information systems for a cultural critique of the web as service economy.

ACKNOWLEDGEMENTS

I would like to thank the two editors without whom this book would never have been published: Senior Acquisitions Editor Mary Savigar at Peter Lang Publishing, and Series Editor Steve Jones—thanks for having supported the project from the very beginning. In addition, all authors deserve to be thanked, not only for having contributed excellent chapters, but also for having reviewed the chapters of their fellow authors.

Permissions to reprint the illustrations that appear throughout the book is gratefully acknowledged:

Chapter 7: Figures 7.1 and 7.2 © Fairfax Media Ltd. Used with permission of the publisher.

Chapter 10: Figure 10.1, Deutsches Museum, Munich, front page of http://www.deutsches-museum.de, 1998, Munich © Reprinted by permission of the publisher. All rights reserved.

Figure 10.2, Museo della Scienza e della Tecnologia, Milan, snapshot of the page dedicated to the virtual museum "Leonardo Virtuale" http://www.museoscienza.org/leonardo/leonardovirtuale/default.asp, 1999, Milan © Reprinted by permission of the publisher. All rights reserved.

Figure 10.3, The board of trustees of the Science Museum, London, snapshot of the front page of http://www.sciencemuseum.org.uk/, 2007, London © Reprinted by permission of the publisher. All rights reserved.

REFERENCES

Brügger, N. (2010). Epilogue: The future of web history. In N. Brügger (Ed.), *Web history* (pp. 349–352). New York, NY: Peter Lang Publishing.

Brügger, N. (2016). Introduction: The web's first 25 years. *New Media & Society*, *18*(7), 1059–1065. doi:10.1177/1461444816643787

Brügger, N., & Milligan, I. (Eds.). (in press). *Sage handbook of web history*. London: Sage.

Brügger, N., & Schroeder, R. (Eds.). *The web as history: Using web archives to understand the past and the present*. London: UCL Press.

Burns, M., & Brügger, N. (Eds.). (2012). *Histories of public service broadcasters on the web*. New York, NY: Peter Lang Publishing.

NOTES

1. Other web history books exist, but their focus is not on the first 25 years of the web's history (Burns and Brügger, 2012; Brügger and Schroeder, 2017; Brügger and Milligan, 2018 (forthcoming)).

The early web

CHAPTER ONE

Connecting textual segments

A brief history of the web hyperlink

NIELS BRÜGGER

Links are intrinsic to documents, and have been for millennia.

TED NELSON (1992, pp. 2/23)

THE HYPERLINK—A DEFINING FEATURE OF THE WEB

When looking back on the first 25 years of World Wide Web history, it is relevant to reflect on what has characterized the web during the entire period.[1] The web has undergone a number of technological changes in terms of hardware and software, and these shifts have taken place in a close interplay with a great variety of emerging forms of use such as blogs, RSS feeds, wikis, and social media. However, a set of fundamental web features have transcended these changes, namely the technological system that enables the transfer of web files from one computer to another, and the format in which these files are written. The HyperText Transfer Protocol (HTTP), the Uniform Resource Locator/Identifier (URL/URI), and the HyperText Mark-up Language (HTML) are the closest one gets to the bolts and nuts of the web. Although these features that enable the transfer, addressing, and writing/reading of web files have also developed during the last 25 years, they have been there as such all the time, in one form or another, thus enabling the web to run and develop 'on top' of the internet with its interconnected computer networks and protocols.

But from the very beginning, and in addition to HTTP, URL and HTML, the web has had one defining feature that we tend to overlook today, because it has become so intuitive and natural that it goes unnoticed. This feature is the web hyperlink, which enables a web user to click on one piece of text on one computer and thereby jump to another piece of text on another computer, from one web page to another.[2] The hyperlink was a key feature of the World Wide Web in Tim Berners-Lee's initial proposal (Berners-Lee, 1989 p. 1); and compared to what was possible in other computer networked software systems at the beginning of the 1990s, this feature was an eye-opening revolution to internet users. This is illustrated by the fact that the click-jump of a hyperlink had to be explained and learned, as can be seen in the many 'How to' books that were published in the early 1990s. In one of the first popular books about the internet, Ed Krol's successful and influential *The Whole Internet: User's Guide & Catalog*, published in 1992 by media company O'Reilly & Associates, one could read the following about how this new, almost experimental software system called the World Wide Web worked:

> You traverse the network by moving from one document to another via 'links'. [...] On a graphic browser, the links would 'highlight' words; to follow a link, just click on a word. [...] There are no rules about which documents can point where—a link can point to anything that the creator finds interesting. [...] A link can even point to a relevant sentence in the middle of an article. (Krol, 1992, pp. 229–231)

The functionality of the web hyperlink still needed to be explained in the book's second edition in 1994, which was extended with an introduction to the recently released graphic browser Mosaic, where buttons on the browser, document title, scroll bar, etc. have to be explained in detail (Krol, 1994, pp. 295–296). And even in the 1999 edition, the characteristics of the web hyperlink still needed to be explained (Conner-Sax & Krol, 1999, pp. 107–110).[3]

Although the hyperlink is strictly speaking not a necessity to constitute the web in the same way as HTTP, URL and HTML, it is *de facto* a defining feature. To illustrate and understand the fundamental importance of the clickable hyperlink for the functionality of the web, one just has to remove it. The only way of navigating the web would then be to insert the full URL address in the browser's address field, and press 'Enter' every time one wanted to go to another web page. It would not even be possible to use a search engine to get from one web page to another, partly because search engines are dependent on the hyperlink since search results are based on analyzing in-links, and partly because a search result page would be very hard to use if it only displayed URLs which then had to be copy-pasted in the user's address field instead of being clickable. It is therefore fair to maintain that hyperlinks are the threads that weave the web, and if it was not for the hyperlink the web would be composed of isolated islands of individual web pages.

In addition, it is worth noting that the hyperlink is not only an indispensable feature to support the frictionless and easy use of the web, but also important for the collecting and analyzing of the web, either by cultural heritage institutions, or by scholars or companies. For instance, when the web is archived by the use of so-called web crawlers, this is done by following links from a number of start URLs.[4] Network analyses of relations between web entities—images, pages, etc.—are by and large based on analyzing hyperlink structures, and the index that search engines use as the basis for presenting search results is also generated from hyperlinks.

Since the hyperlink is so fundamental to the functionality of the web, it will in many cases be a necessary analytical element in histories of the web, and it is therefore pivotal to get a deeper understanding of what characterizes the web hyperlink, not only as a technical software phenomenon, but also as a textual entity.

This chapter is based on the argument that the web hyperlink is best understood if it is seen as another phase in a much longer and broader history than just the years of the emergence of the web, namely the history of how segments of text are deliberately and explicitly connected to each other by the use of specific textual and media features. It has long been recognized within the literature about the web and hypertext that the linking of pieces of text has a long history. Introductions to Tim Berners-Lee's ideas for the World Wide Web often include an outline of the web hyperlink's predecessors, such as the footnote in printed books (Kirschenbaum, 2000, pp. 123–124), commentaries in the Talmud (Turow, 2008, p. 2), and quotation and citation (Halavais, 2008, p. 40), just to give a few examples. References to Vannevar Bush's Memex and Theodor (Ted) Nelson's ideas about hypertext are almost always mentioned in this connection, as well. However, since in most cases these brief mentions are not elaborated, a detailed and systematic examination of the history of connecting segments of text, including the web hyperlink is lacking.

As will also be shown in the following, Bush and Nelson undoubtedly played a key role in conceptualizing what later became the web hyperlink; but identifying the continuities as well as the breaks between earlier forms of connecting pieces of text as they have been used throughout a much longer media history is one way to shed new light on our understanding of the hyperlink's specific way of connecting text on the web. This chapter will give a brief outline of how we can understand the quotation with which this chapter started: "Links are intrinsic to documents, and have been for millennia" (Nelson, 1992, p. 2/23).

UNDERSTANDING INTENDED CONNECTIONS BETWEEN SEGMENTS OF TEXT

Creating a hyperlink basically involves creating an intended connection between segments of text; and as indicated above, this has been done for centuries.[5] To guide the historical analysis of the hyperlink, a systematic approach is needed. The reflections below on connections between segments of text, and on the relation between text and medium, will provide a recurring analytical grid in the historical analysis (see Brügger, 2009, pp. 118–122).

Textuality

From a textual point of view, connections between chunks of text can be established on three different levels: the semantic, the formal, and the physically performative levels. A semantic connection is established when the meaning of one segment of text refers to another segment. For instance, the sentence 'Read more page 7' establishes a semantic relation to whatever can be found on page 7. A formal connection is established by the use of means of expression, such as lines, arrows, colors, font types, length of lines, position on a page, and the like, for instance a small numeral in superscript placed after a word indicates 'footnote'. Finally, a physically performative connection is established when physical movement between elements is carried out, such as turning pages in a book or newspaper, scrolling up/down or left/right, or clicking/jumping via a hyperlink on the web. In most cases, all three levels of connection are present at the same time, but the distinction between them is relevant for analytical purposes when investigating the shifts in how semantic, formal, and physically performative connections take place.

Mediacy

The way in which the three types of connection can be established in practice depends largely on the materiality of the media type in which they are embedded. Each media type comes with a specific media-ness, a set of "relatively fixed features" that "make the medium physically, psychologically, and socially different from other media and from face-to-face interaction" (Meyrowitz, 1994, p. 50). And these media-specific features open up an array of possible forms of use with regard to the forms of content and expression they can convey and how they can be interacted with.[6] A printed book or a newspaper can be leafed through, but it cannot convey sound or moving images. A television program, on the other hand, is constituted by a flow of sound, moving images, and possibly writing, but it cannot be leafed through like a book.[7]

Thus, connections between segments of text are best understood as a media-specific nexus between semantic, formal and physically performative levels. This implies that a connection is not only the actual physical connecting of textual elements, for instance the click-jump of the hyperlink, but also the semantic and/or formal expressions that constitute the start and the end point of the connection. An understanding of an entry word in a book's index must include the word in the index list (semantic/formal), the text to which it refers (semantic/formal), and the book that can be leafed through (physically performative); just as an understanding of the hyperlink must include the text at the link source, the text at the link target, and the actual clicking and jumping from one to the other.[8]

Intended connections

A distinction needs to be introduced between intended and experienced connections, placed at opposite ends of the communicative circuit. On the one hand, one can focus on the intended connections between chunks of text, in other words the pieces of text that have been joined deliberately by the entity that has produced the text (man or machine). On the other hand, when reading, listening, watching, or browsing, a reader can connect any piece of text with any other piece of text, regardless of how the textual units were connected by the producer; and the thing that is actually connected in the reading process can be investigated by the use of a variety of reception analyses. The present study will investigate the intended connections, in other words how textual connections have been made available to a reader, viewer, listener, or user, and not how they were actually experienced in the process of reading, watching, listening, or using.[9]

Finally, it has to be stressed that the following historical account focuses primarily on forms of connecting and not on the function of the connections. Thus, the different textual forms are identified, but whether their function is to establish a reference, pass on a citation, enable navigation, attract attention, create a social tie, or anything else is not the primary focus point. Even so, it is worth pointing out that identifying the forms is a first step for a later study of the functions.

Three phases in the history of connecting textual segments

By re-interpreting the existing literature on media history with a focus on the connecting of segments of text, this chapter sets out to identify the continuities and the breaks between the different historical forms of linking text to text.

Throughout the history of communication and media, the need to connect textual elements has always been present, but it has been effectuated in various ways depending on the possibilities offered by the specific media types that were available. Three phases can be identified in the long history of connecting text, each characterized by one or more leading media type(s): non-digital media, digital computers as stand-alone, and digital computers as global networks.[10] As will be shown towards the end of the chapter it is worth noting that although the three phases are distinct there are a number of continuities between them.

TEXTUAL CONNECTIONS IN NON-DIGITAL MEDIA

In the following we shall see how the recurring need to intentionally connect textual elements arose before the advent of digital media, with a view to identifying the web hyperlink's ancestors. The focus is on clay tablets, handwritten manuscripts, printed books and newspapers, and on connections between different media types.[11]

Clay tablets, envelopes and their content

In *How writing came about* (1996), archaeologist Denise Schmandt-Besserat studies so-called tokens, which are small clay objects in various forms and with different markings, each representing a value. Tokens were used in the Near East as early as 8000 BC as counters to keep track of farming products, manufactured goods etc. Schmandt-Besserat's aim is to argue that tokens were the first step towards cuneiform writing on clay tablets; but her study can also be used to identify what is probably the first example of purposively connecting one piece of text to another, namely the markings on the outside of clay envelopes used for tokens in the early Mesopotamian civilizations.

Tokens represented an accounting system, and with a view to archiving them they were stored in an envelope in the form of a hollow clay ball, a *bulla* (measuring about 5–7 cm). Once the tokens were placed in the *bulla* it was closed and sealed (Schmandt-Besserat, 1996, pp. 7, 42). This practice was used from the early 4th millennium onward, but the "drawback of the envelopes was that they hid the enclosed tokens. Accountants eventually resolved the problem by imprinting the shapes of the tokens on the surface of the envelopes prior to enclosing them" (1996, p. 7; see also pp. 50–51). In other words: to keep track of what was inside the clay envelope once it was sealed without having to break the seal, signs were added to its outside indicating what it contained. In this way an intended connection was created between two textual entities: markings on the envelope's surface, and markings on the tokens inside the envelope.

As argued by Schmandt-Besserat, the "substitution of signs for tokens was a first step towards writing" (1996, p. 7; see also pp. 54–85), simply because accountants realized that once the nature of the tokens inside was written on the outside of the envelope, there was no need to actually store the tokens in the clay envelope. Thus, from approximately 3500 to 3100 BC the hollow clay tablets developed into solid clay balls with markings, thereby replacing the tokens by signs and paving the way for the development of clay tablets with signifying systems in their own right (first pictograms and later cuneiform writing).[12]

However, even though clay tablets with cuneiform writing became the most widespread way of storing information after 3000 BC, the use of clay envelopes still persisted. But instead of storing tokens, clay envelopes were used to store entire clay tablets, and this practice was used in a number of cases, including personal correspondence and business transactions. For instance, after a contract had been written on a tablet an extra layer of clay was wrapped around the tablet, thus forming an envelope, and on this the contract was written once more in identical terms. Since the envelope and its contents were identical, any tampering with the envelope could easily be discovered by breaking the envelope (Chiera & Cameron, 1939, pp. 70–73). Thus, it can be maintained that from a textual point of view a connection of identity was established between two segments of text: the text on the envelope, and the text on the tablet.

Finally, connections between segments of text also existed on the same clay tablet, in the main in lexical lists with translations from one language to another, one column with one language next to another column with the other language; in these cases there are no direct marks of connection except for the placing in lists in two columns next to each other.

Handwritten manuscripts on parchment, bound as codex

From approximately 4000 BC onward, papyrus was used as a writing medium in Egypt and other countries in the Mediterranean area. Papyrus books were named *volumen* and had the form of scrolls, that is sheets of papyrus glued together to form a horizontal band of sheets that could be scrolled, and that usually had writing on one side only. Papyrus was used for centuries, but between the second and 4th century AD parchment started to become the most widespread storing medium for writing, and this shift was accompanied by a new way of assembling sheets, namely the *codex*, with sheets being bound to form the type of book we know today.

The *codex* had a number of advantages over the *volumen*. For instance, it could store twice as much text since both sides of the sheet were used, and it was much simpler to navigate because it was easier to leaf through. It also made it possible to take notes, because one hand was free. During the Middle Ages these advantages were accompanied by the development of a number of features that made it easier to navigate the *codex*, such as illuminated or colored initials, words written with other ink colors (usually red), notes in the margins, and tables of contents. As argued by medievalist Paul Saenger in *Space between words: The origins of silent reading*, these new textual features were made possible by the introduction of space between words, thus allowing the reader to move his eyes more freely across the page by jumping around in a more complex textual structure than in manuscripts with continuous script (*scriptura continua*). And some of these textual features were also used for connecting segments of text.

In medieval manuscripts, notes were often added by the scribe or by readers in the margin of the page (Carruthers, 2008, pp. 135–152). They could have several forms, such as the *nota* sign, the letter N, or what Saenger (by borrowing from music) terms the 'tie note', which attached commentaries, annotations, explications, or corrections to the text to which they referred by the use of a graphical element, a tie, or sometimes even a *manucula*, a small pointing hand (cf. Saenger, 1997, pp. 75–76). From the 11th century onward, alphabetical sequential tie notes were widely used, and they constitute the "direct ancestors of the modern numbered footnote" (1997, p. 76; cf. also p. 260). In addition, notes could be in the form of *résumé* notes that "designated multiple points of entry into texts, thereby providing an alternative to reading texts from beginning to end". *Résumé* notes were often placed in boxes, and in addition to written text they could also have the form of schematic diagrams (e.g. depicting the logic of an argument from the body text) (1997, p. 79).

From the 12th century onward tables of contents started to be used in *codices*, thus establishing a connection between words in a list and a specific point in the manuscript where the corresponding text could be found.[13] In contrast to the note, the table of contents did not refer to text segments on the same page but to text segments on other pages, which made it very flexible since it could create a connection to segments of text placed anywhere in the book. From the 13th century the functionality of the table of contents was improved by the introduction of subdivisions of the text in so-called *distinctiones* with headings, involving smaller segments than chapters, which had until then been the smallest textual unit (Saenger, 1997, p. 259). However, since pagination was not in use yet, the table of contents referred to *folios* and not pages, that is to a sheet of parchment folded in half making two leaves (four pages) (cf. Saenger, 1997, p. 77).

Finally, two other types of connecting text in parchment *codices* deserve to be mentioned. First, a practice that was widely used in the British Isles from the 8th century, namely the simultaneous presence of two versions of the same text, each in their own language, positioned on the page either as alphabetical glossaries or as interlinear translation, where "each line of Latin was interpolated with a word-for-word vernacular translation" (Saenger, 1997, pp. 92–93). Second, connections between two types of semiotic systems, namely captions adding information to an image or other illustration placed in its vicinity (either below or elsewhere).

The connecting features mentioned above are all used to establish connections in the same book, but already in the 4th century references between books were used, and later they were refined by medieval scholars, in particular when universities were established (Grafton, 1997, p. 30). However, since the number of copies of each book was limited in the Middle Ages, referring between books often meant that if a scholar wanted to connect a reference with the text to which it referred he had to travel to the library where the book was to be found, as noted by Rhodes and Sawday:

Rather than texts circulating amongst communities of readers, it was the task of readers to circulate themselves around those centres where books were known to exist. Often, these travelling readers were uncertain about what, exactly, was to be found in the many scattered locations which they visited in search of books: their journeys were as much voyages of discovery into *terra incognitae* of the past as they were attempts at working with known collections of books and manuscripts. (Rhodes and Sawday, 2000, pp. 2–3)

Printed books and newspapers

As pointed out by historian Elizabeth Eisenstein, the invention of the printing press in the middle of the 15th century, based on paper and movable types, led to different forms of standardization. In the centuries following the advent of the printing press the different systems of connecting segments of text that were already in place in the Middle Ages were refined, expanded and standardized. In addition, the development of the newspaper added still more ways of connecting text.

The alphabetical notes in the margins of pages that were known in medieval books slowly developed into the system of numbered footnotes, and in particular in the 18th century these footnotes started to proliferate (cf. Grafton, 1997, pp. 107, 118, 221; Pollak, 2006, pp. 14–20; Zerby, 2003, p. 59). The table of contents was supplemented by the index, which became widespread from the late 15th century, and the alphabetical ordering of an index slowly became the standard (Eisenstein, 1993, pp. 65–73). And towards the end of the 19th century the referencing system with in-text references that referred to a list of references which referred in turn to other publications evolved (cf. Pollak, 2006, pp. 20–24). All these features were facilitated by the slow adaptation of pagination instead of foliation (the numbering of *folios*), which did not become widespread until the 16th century (Breton-Gravereau, 1998, p. 158). Finally, the references to other works that were already in place in the Middle Ages became much more widely used after the invention of the printing press, and in particular in the late 18th century. A major reason for this was the fact that there were many more copies of the same book available for more people, books became accessible much faster, and public libraries slowly started to emerge (cf. Rhodes & Sawday, 2000, pp. 3–4). Hence, the references between works became much easier to pursue, and therefore their use grew.

Shortly after the printing press was invented it was used to print publications on one single sheet, used to convey news, gossip, odd incidents, and songs, and to be sold in the streets or on market places, which eventually in the 17th century developed into a more formal system of periodical publications: newspapers. Throughout the history of newspapers new ways of connecting text were developed. As newspapers grew bigger in size and the layout became more complex, it became necessary to connect segments of text at different positions in the newspaper, which was done by the use of a table of contents or expressions such as 'Continued on page 5'. In addition, the periodicity of the newspaper opened up for temporally supported connections, either by connecting to past text—"as mentioned in yesterday's newspaper"—for instance in relation to the ongoing development of a news story (cf. Bell, 1995, p. 312; Bødker, 2016, p. 59), or by connecting to the future, seen most notably in the feuilleton novel by authors such as Charles Dickens and Eugène Sue in the 19th century, with a chapter in today's newspaper being connected to a chapter on the following day by the words 'to be continued', or something similar. With the newspaper the temporality of print publications was institutionalized by the widespread use of connections pointing back or leaping forward in time towards a text that had not yet been published.

Connections between different media types

The intended textual connections identified above all take place either within an individual copy of a medium or within the same media type, but connections have also existed between different media types. Three examples can illustrate the use of intermedia connections: a very simple example, the catalog file card on carton, and two more complex examples of which the first was partly realized—Belgian specialist in information science Paul Otlet's 'Mundaneum'—whereas the latter was only a vision, namely Vannevar Bush's 'Memex'.

One of the first examples of text in the form of an inventory referring to a collection of media is the *Pinakes*, Callimachus' catalog of the library of Alexandria in the 3rd century, which helped library staff to retrieve the book scrolls in the library (cf. Olesen-Bagneux, 2015, pp. 284, 288–290; Reynolds & Wilson, 1991, p. 7). But the *Pinakes* was itself written on scrolls, so the connecting of textual chunks took place within media of the same type. However, one of Callimachus' predecessors, Zenodotus, had invented a system to improve the functionality of the library of Alexandria which, in fact, was based on the creation of textual connections between different media types. The so-called *sillyboi* were small tags attached to the end of each scroll with information about its content, such as author, title and subject. This information told the library staff what was on the scroll without having to take it down from the shelf and unroll it (Philips, 2010, p. 9). The concept of a catalog like the *Pinakes*, and the string's very direct connection between the *sillyboi* and the scroll later merged into the catalog file card on carton (usually kept in a chest of drawers), that is a catalog with a file card, in many ways similar to the *sillyboi* tag, referring to a specific object in a collection (of books or other items) by numbers and/or text instead of by a string. It is worth noting that for one of the first library card systems, developed in France in the 1790s, paper was not considered robust enough. Therefore, a very specific type of card was used, designed so they could be shuffled and produced in a standardized format, namely playing cards. Initially these were only printed on one side (the idea of using playing cards had already been formulated in 1775 by Abbé François Rozier) (Krajewski, 2011, pp. 33, 45–47).

A more complex way of connecting textual chunks across different media types was formulated and partly realized by Paul Otlet. In his *Traité de Documentation* from 1934 he coined the idea of a global repository and knowledge sharing system that could handle all known media formats. His text was based on previous work, including the 1910 project entitled 'the Palais Mondial' (with Henri La Fontaine), and the ideas materialized in the 1920–1930s in the so-called Mundaneum (van den Heuvel, 2010, pp. 284–85). The Mundaneum was designed to gather all the world's knowledge independent of the medium in which it was to be found. And although it was only partly built and not all of Otlet's visons about it were realized, the Mundaneum did contain large collections of books, newspapers, posters, postcards, glass plates, and artefacts. In a drawing from 1937 Otlet imagined the Mundaneum as a number of repositories of different media types such as film, microfilm, gram-ophone, radio, and television, to which users could connect (van den Heuvel, 2010, pp. 286, 290). And a system of connector signs enabled the interlinking of textual elements in two different documents or between entire documents, regardless of media type. These links were created manually, but Otlet also imagined mechanical ways of linking (van den Heuvel, 2010, pp. 294–295).[14]

In contrast to Paul Otlet's Mundaneum, which was built in part, the visions of the American engineer Vannevar Bush regarding a 'Memory extender', a Memex presented in the article "As we may think" (originally published in *The Atlantic Monthly*, July, 1945), were never realized as such. But nevertheless these ideas re-mained very influential for later conceptualizations of the hyperlink in relation to the digital computer, in particular by Douglas Engelbart and Ted Nelson (cf. Barnet, 2014, pp. 11–12). The Memex was imagined as a machine that could be used to extend the human memory by storing information as well as the interconnections between bits and pieces of information. Bush's Memex was a child of its time be-cause it combined the media material solutions that were available—photoelectrical technologies in the form of an optical reader and microfilm—with the ideas about the human associative memory that were widespread in the 1930s. Based on this combination, Bush describes the Memex as a new type of desk:

> On the top are slanting translucent screens, on which material can be projected for con-venient reading. There is a keyboard and sets of buttons and levers. […] In one end is the stored material. The matter of bulk is well taken care of by improved microfilm. […] Most of the memex contents are purchased on microfilm ready for insertion. If the user wishes to consult a certain book, he taps its code on the keyboard, and the title page of the book promptly appears before him, projected onto one of the viewing positions. (Quoted in Nelson, 1992, pp. 1/50–1/51)

As this description shows, the reader does not have access to the different media types in their original form, but rather to media which have been transferred to and reproduced on a new and shared format, the microfilm (Bush mentions books, records, communications, pictures, periodicals, newspapers, and business correspondence, Nelson, 1992, p. 1/50). In addition to having all the information of the world at hand, what is key to Bush is that the Memex enables the simulation of human associative memory by the establishing of links, or what he calls 'trails', between two textual items. In Bush's own words, this is envisioned as taking place in the following way:

> When the user is building a trail, he names it, inserts the name in his code book, and taps it out on his keyboard. Before him are the two items to be joined, projected onto adjacent viewing positions […] The user taps a single key, and the items are permanently joined. […] It is exactly as though the physical items had been gathered together from widely separated sources and bound together to form a new book. It is more than this, for any item can be joined into numerous trails. (Nelson, 1992, p. 1/51)

Shifts in mechanical ways of connecting

The outline above has identified some of the most important ways of connecting segments of text in the non-digital era. Each of the available media types allowed for a variety of mechanical ways of creating links, and towards the end of the period photoelectric links were imagined.

A closer look at the spatial extension of connections as well as the number of media types to connect reveals several shifts. The first intended connections take place either on the same page or between pages, and they can thus be termed *intrapage* and *interpage* connections, respectively. They are later extended by the widespread use of relations between different works of the same media type and between different media types, i.e. *interwork* and *intermedia* connections. Interpage connections are seen with clay tablets, whereas intrapage, interpage, and interwork connections are realized in different constellations during the era of handwritten manuscripts, and later refined and standardized in print media, gaining a temporal dimension with newspapers and other periodicals. In parallel with the growing number of available media in the late 19th century, intermedia connections are envisioned, first Otlet's vision of actually connecting across different media types, and later the transforming of media types to a uniform medium, as illustrated with Bush's Memex.

The development on the textual level *per se*, i.e. the semantic, formal and physically performative connecting of segments of text, is characterized by continuity as well as breaks. In terms of semantics and form, each of the new ways of establishing connections marks a break, but these breaks occur against a backdrop of continuity since all connections are related to writing and still images positioned on pages, and in many cases the changes are mere refinings of already established forms such as the footnote and the table of contents in handwritten manuscripts and print.

The major breaks are on the physically performative level, where changes in media materiality enable new forms of realizing the connection between segments of text. From the most fundamental and simple ways of physically connecting—the breaking of the clay envelope and the ocular gestures across the page in the manuscript era (intrapage)—via the simultaneous movements of the eyes and of pages in the form of leafing (interpage), to the movement of the body within the same library or between libraries (interworks). At different points in the history of media, the last two of these are each made easier, the first by a semantic-formal development, pagination, and the latter with the spread of print, with books becoming cheaper to purchase and being made available in more places. If there is any continuity on the physically performative level, it is in the sense that already established practices are integrated in the next phases, thus accumulating the different forms of connecting.

THE DIGITAL COMPUTER—CONNECTIONS ON STAND-ALONE COMPUTERS

A new era starts when the interconnecting of pieces of text is no longer based on mechanically supported connections, but rather is combined with the digital computer, and in particular the computer with a screen as an input/output device, combined with a pointing device.

The digital computer

To understand this fundamental change it is worth digging deeper into how the digital can be conceptualized. The two entities that constitute a basis for the digital computer—1 and 0—are often understood as numbers, but a more fruitful approach is to regard them as the only two letters in a binary alphabet.[15] These two letters can be combined endlessly to form 'texts'—software code and the text treated by the software—but texts that are not understandable as such for the end user who reads a text or watches a video on a computer screen. In contrast to mechanical media that have only one layer of text, such as the writing and images we see on a page and which are made possible by the specific mediacy of each medium (clay, papyrus scroll, parchment, print on paper, etc.), digital media have an extra layer of text, namely the digital text below the text that can be experienced by the reader. Hence, because of the digital text the mediacy of digital media is partly textual. However, this does not entail that digital media are purely digital. They are also always non-digital, because the digital text is always embedded in a material artefact (mainframe computer, laptop, cables, wireless networks, etc.).[16]

With these reflections in mind, it becomes clear that the three manifest levels of a textual connection (semantic, formal, and physically performative) are doubled by the level of the digital text that (in combination with the media-material nature of each digital media type) enables the different forms of manifest textual connections. Therefore, the digital computer with a screen and a pointing device allows for the physically performative part of the connectedness to become the clickable link, followed by the jumping from one text element to another.

Connections on stand-alone computers

In late 1987 Apple computers were sold with a free version of the application HyperCard preinstalled, which, among other things, enabled hyperlinking. For the first time a wider public experienced digital hypertext, that is computer software that allowed users to click on words, sentences, images, or graphics that functioned as hotspots, after which they were 'transported' to another piece of text. Since HyperCard was still to be found on Apple computers for many years after 1987, it became *de facto* the archetype of what hypertext—and hyperlinking—was (cf. Barnet, 2014, p. xxii). However, HyperCard was not the beginning of digital hyperlinking, but rather the result of a number of previous visions, projects and experiments.

In the early and mid-1960s Ted Nelson, an American philosopher and specialist in information technology, developed the idea of hypertext and hyperlinking in relation to the digital computer. As explained by Nelson himself in the book *Literary machines*, he developed three designs, all revolving around how screen-based computers could work with text. In a 1965 paper this led to the idea of 'zippered lists', that is "sequences which could be linked together sideways" (Nelson, 1992, p. 1/27), the idea being that documents could link to one another on a computer screen, linking any segment in one document to any segment in another. In the same period Nelson coined the term 'hypertext', which appeared for the first time in print in two conference papers. It is also worth noting that in the same period Nelson started using the terms 'hyperfilm', 'hyperfile' and 'hypermedia' (Nelson, 1992, Erratum, p. 1/29), terms which were considered interchangeable with hypertext to indicate that hypertext refers not only to written text, but to any form of interlinked forms of expression.

Also in 1965 a computer scientist called Douglas Engelbart, working at Stanford Research Institute (SRI), experimented with links on a single computer; and Engelbart and his collaborator Bill English were able to demonstrate roughly how links could work on one computer in the form of clicking and jumping (Barnet, 2014, p. 51), which later led to Engelbart's revolutionary demonstration of the prototype of the oN-Line System (NLS) in 1968 (cf. below).

Nelson and Engelbart soon began to envision the hyperlink as part of a larger online environment where links could take the user from one computer to another (e.g. Nelson, 1992, p. 1/31). But although Nelson's visions as well as Engelbart's NLS system were moving increasingly towards hyperlinking in online computer networks, the available networks at the time made it less feasible to establish true global hyperlinking. Consequently, in the 1970s–1980s Nelson's and Engelbart's ideas had their biggest impact as guiding visions for the computer developing environments that were experimenting with hypertext on stand-alone computers, and later in small computer networks (cf. Barnet, 2014, pp. 8–9 about the relation between vision and technical prototype). Two such examples of hypertext systems that were not networked were the Hypertext Editing System (HES) and the File Retrieval and Editing System (FRESS) (Barnet, 2014, p. 92; see also pp. 91–114).[17]

THE NETWORKED DIGITAL HYPERLINK— CONNECTING GLOBALLY

In parallel with the development of hypertext and hyperlinking capabilities on individual computers, hyperlinking between computers in networks was also tested and developed. And visions of segments of text that could connect globally started to emerge and were eventually realized with the World Wide Web.

The NLS system

The first computer system to use hyperlinks was the above-mentioned NLS system. In continuation of Bush's "As we may think" (cf. Barnet, 2014, p. 41), Engelbart wanted to create a computer system that could augment human intellect and work more efficiently with knowledge. This ambition led Engelbart's team to a number of ground-breaking inventions, one of which was the clickable hyperlink on a computer screen, while others were word processing, computer windows, the mouse, and networked collaboration. A prototype of the NLS system's many components was demonstrated at a breathtaking event, often termed 'the mother of all demos', where Engelbart sitting in San Francisco communicated via a computer network with his associates sitting at a computer in Menlo Park some 30 miles south of San Francisco. The demonstration clearly illustrated that not only was it possible to connect segments of text on one computer, it was also possible to jump from a piece of text on one computer to a piece of text on another computer. However, although the demonstration of the NLS system was proof of a concept which would have a far-reaching and long-lasting impact on the development of computers in general and hypertext systems in particular in the following years, it was still a closed environment that was not connected to a wider network. So online jumping from computer to computer still remained within a confined local network with a limited number of nodes.[18]

Xanadu

The most extensive conceptualization of hyperlinks connecting segments of text between computers in a global network is Ted Nelson's project Xanadu. In the late 1960s Nelson started to think about how stand-alone computers could and should be networked (cf. Nelson, 1992, p. 1/31), thoughts which evolved during the following decades to become the Xanadu project. Despite the fact that Xanadu has never been built as a complete system (a prototype was online in 1987 (Nelson, 1992, Preface 1993, p. 0/5)), Nelson's ideas have proven to be very influential for the development of hypertext systems, including for Tim Berners-Lee when he was developing the World Wide Web (cf. below, and Berners-Lee, 1999, pp. 70–72).

As was the case with both Bush and Engelbart (Nelson, 1992, p. 1/5), Nelson's ideas about hypertext are embedded in a wider and more ambitious venture: the creation of a global hypertext system, based on hyperlinking, that would "change the face of literature and civilization" (1992, Preface to the 1993 edition) and support the "survival of humanity" (1992, p. 0/11).

To understand Nelson's Xanadu hyperlink, it is important to identify some of the characteristics of the context in which it is placed, namely the hypertext. Nelson understands hypertext as "non-sequential writing—text that branches and allows choices to the reader, best read at an interactive screen" (Nelson, 1992, p. 0/2; cf. pp. 0/2, 1/15, 1/17 for further characteristics of hypertext). In addition to this general characteristic, it is important to have the following three points in mind. First, that although Nelson's ideas were picked up by a number of literary scholars and theorists, his idea of 'literature' is broader than literature understood as an aesthetic genre of writing. To Nelson literature is not 'belles lettres', but rather literature on a subject, a system of interconnected writings (1992, p. 2/9), kept together by "a flux of invisible threads and rubber bands" (1992, p. 2/11). Second, hypertext is a general textual feature related to the arrangement of textual segments as such, no matter what type of media the text is found in. Thus, hypertext can also be seen in print magazine and newspaper layout (1992, pp. 1/15, 1/17), and therefore non-sequential writing does not emerge with the computer, but comes in new forms with it. Third, hypertext in the form of a global hypertext system is understood as a universal layer that can be used to connect different types of content and media, the "universal storage of all interactive media, and, indeed, all data" (1992, p. 0/6; cf. also p. 0/4), a unified system to overcome what Nelson terms the Balkanization of different systems for publishing and communicating, from videotext and videocable to email and different computer networks (1992, p. 1/9).

The hyperlink is just one element in this broader philosophical and cultural hypertext project, but it is a pivotal element since it is the fundamental glue that keeps everything together.[19] It is fair to maintain that Nelson's conceptualization of the Xanadu hyperlink (often just called 'link') constitutes one of the most extended descriptions of what computer hyperlinks can be.

According to Nelson, hyperlinks can link between all types of data: "There must be no restrictions as to data types […]. We believe you should be able to put footnotes and marginal notes and branching jumps on pictures, on music—on any forms of data" (Nelson, 1992, p. 2/28, cf. also p. 2/23). Not only can links connect any form of data, they can also link arbitrarily within or between documents or between sections of units (1992, pp. 0/6, 2/30). In addition, hyperlinks can be created in all documents by anyone, in the form of "comments, personal notes, or other connections" and then published or remain private (1992, Preface 1993). In terms of spatial reach Xanadu is conceived as a global linking system, a "system for the world" (1992, Preface 1993, cf. also pp. 0/10, 2/53–2/54).

A closer look at the Xanadu hyperlink as such reveals four important features. First, connections are understood as concrete, visible connections on a screen, for instance as lines, whereby the Xanadu link echoes the medieval tie note (Barnet, 2014, p. 65; Nelson, 1992, 4/76–4/78). Second, Xanadu will make it possible to be informed about which documents link to a document, revealing where in-links come from (Nelson, 1992, p. 2/47). Third, hyperlinks can be embedded and combined in documents to form so-called "compound text, where materials are viewed and combined with others" (1992, p. 1/15), or as Nelson also calls it 'windowing text': "a set of windows to original materials from the compound texts themselves" (1992, p. 1/15, cf. also p. 2/32). And fourth, users are allowed to arbitrarily label a hyperlink themselves by identifying it as a certain type of link (1992, p. 4/43–4/44), thus adding a third element to link source and link target, namely a textually manifested characteristic of the link.

THE WORLD WIDE WEB HYPERLINK

In 1989 the British computer scientist Tim Berners-Lee handed in a proposal to the management of CERN, the European Centre for Nuclear Research, where he was employed. The text was entitled 'Information Management: A proposal', in which Berners-Lee proposes the establishing of an information management system in the form of a hypertext system, and mentions Apple's HyperCard and Ted Nelson's ideas about hypertext as his sources of inspiration. With hypertext comes the hyperlink, so the proposed system is based on "the idea of linked information systems" because "a 'web' of notes with links (like references) between them is far more useful than a fixed hierarchical system" (Berners-Lee, 1987, p. 1).

As pointed out in a later iteration of the proposal, written with Robert Cailliau in 1990 (Berners-Lee & Cailliau, 1990), hypertext was different from the prevalent way of organizing information on computers at the time, namely in hierarchical trees. But hypertext was still quite new, so it needed to be explained:

> A hypertext page has pieces of text which refer to other texts. Such references are highlighted and can be selected with a mouse [...]. When you select a reference, the browser presents you with the text which is referenced: you have made the browser follow a hypertext link. [...] The network of links is called a web. The web need not be hierarchical, and therefore it is not necessary to 'climb up a tree' all the way again before you can go down to a different but related subject. [...] The texts are known as nodes. The process of proceeding from node to node is called navigation. Nodes do not need to be on the same machine: links may point across machine boundaries. Having a world wide web implies some solutions must be found for problems such as different access protocols and different node content formats. [...] Nodes can in principle also contain non-text information such as diagrams, pictures, sound, animation etc. The term hypermedia is simply the expansion of the hypertext idea to these other media. (Berners-Lee & Cailliau, 1990, pp. 2–3)

Although the proposal was only about the establishing of an information management system at CERN, Berners-Lee already imagined links pointing "across machine boundaries" in "a world wide web"; and the possibility of creating a global web is repeated towards the end of the 1990 version, in the section 'Future paths': "Work on efficient networking over wide areas, negotiation with other sites to provide compatible online information" (Berners-Lee & Cailliau, 1990, p. 7). The proposal was accepted by CERN, and at the beginning of the 1990s the World Wide Web, which the project was now called, was born. It rapidly became a global system (cf. Berners-Lee, 1999; Brügger, 2016a).

What is specific for the hyperlink on the World Wide Web is that it is embedded in a digital medium that allows the connection of any segment of text on one computer to any other segment of text on another computer, and that this can be done instantaneously and on a global scale. Thus, within the framework of the same medium one and the same digital feature—the HTML text of the web hyperlink—enables the creation of intrapage, interpage and interwork connections on the manifest textual level, and these connections can be realized immediately across space without having to move physically. Intermedia connections are also enabled in so far as the interconnected media can be 'transformed' to become part of the World Wide Web. Intrapage, interpage, interwork and intermedia connections all (co)existed already, but they can be combined and integrated with the web hyperlink.

The textuality of the World Wide Web hyperlink as such is both similar to and different from the forms known from previous media. On the semantic and formal level the segment of text which is the source of a web hyperlink can signal that it is, in fact, the first step in a connection in two ways. Either the link source is marked directly by the use of underlining, bold text, shadow, a different color or the like—as with other previous media. Or it can be marked only indirectly and switch from being invisible to becoming visible through mouse-over, which produces a pointing hand or other kind of highlighting, a feature that is not seen in previous media types (the indirect marking is also mentioned in Berners-Lee's proposal, where it is referred to as 'hotspots'). On the physically performative level, the web hyperlink as such allows different forms of linking, of which the click-jump link is the most widespread. But other important forms also exist, for instance pop-up windows or similar features that appear as a result of a mouse-over, or embedded content linking to content on another web server and showing the retrieved content without a user clicking anything (images, headings, feed, embedded video, etc.).[20] Click-jumping, pop-up windows and embedding are not known in previous media types. So when looking at the forms that characterize the textuality of the web hyperlink as such, continuity and breaks coexist simultaneously. Although a semantic-formal sign such as the *manucula*—the small pointing hand that is often used in handwritten manuscripts—is reintroduced with digital hyperlinks such as the web, it is embedded in a fundamentally different media environment where it does not appear before it is 'triggered' by a mouseover, and, in addition, it is physically and performatively 'alive' in the sense that it can actually be activated and will then take the reader to the segment of text towards which it points.

Building on these general textual characteristics of the World Wide Web hyperlink as such, the web allows a great variety of concrete ways of establishing connections. However, although the digital text allows new forms of connecting, the concrete realizations of web hyperlinks constitute a complex variety of continuities and breaks when compared to previous forms. In many cases, web hyperlinks repeat well-known practices almost unchanged. For instance, established features such as the table of contents, footnotes and references to other texts are widely used on Wikipedia pages. On the semantic-formal level they are very close to their ancestors, but obviously they differ in terms of physical performativity.

In other cases, well-known ways of connecting are reused in a reinterpreted form to fit the web. The index and the table of contents are also used on the web, but because of the nature of the web they often come in new forms, for instance as a search box, a site map, or a horizontal or vertical menu system, in many cases with 'drop-down' menus with hidden hyperlinks that unfold following a click or mouse-over.[21]

Finally, a number of ways of connection are specific to the web hyperlink, in the main based on the fact that any semantic-formal entity can function as a link source without communicating directly that it is a hyperlink (cf. above). For instance, in previous media types graphic elements could constitute the semantic-formal expression of a connection, such as the *manucula* or the tie on the tie note; but their graphic nature in itself conveyed some sort of indexicality such as 'pointing' or 'connecting with lines'. But what is new with the web (and other hypermedia systems) is the ability to use any form of expression, be it writing, images, graphics, or video, as a link source, without it having any indexicality. And even to do this without indicating it directly in cases where the link source (an image for example) does not reveal that it is a link source until the cursor is placed over the image. Furthermore, not even an entire image needs to constitute the link source, since any arbitrary fragment of an image can be enclosed to form a hotspot and thus function as a link source, as seen with tagging and hyperlinking in photographs or maps. In previous media types a part of an image could not in itself provide a connection. What is at play here is that the digital text beneath the manifest text enables the fragmentation and dissolution of semantic-formally recognizable objects (words, graphics, images, videos) as the determining entity for the link source, since the link can 'graft' anything onto the surface of what is shown in a web browser, independently of the semantic/formal structure of recognizable elements which ultimately makes the creation of textual connections very flexible.

This latter point indicates that in many cases the digital text, the HTML code, must be included in an understanding of the web hyperlink, since this is where the hyperlink connection actually materializes as a piece of code, and would not be identifiable by simply looking at a web page with its graphics, images and the like. Consequently, understanding the web hyperlink may involve the semantic, the formal and the physically performative levels in the manifest text that we see and interact with on our screen, as well as the digital level that we do not experience but which is the condition for what we see and that may hold information about the link otherwise hidden. The decision about which of these levels should be included in an analysis often depends on what one wants to know about the hyperlink, and it may also depend on whether the approach is a close or a distant reading of the web, to use the terminology of Franco Moretti (Moretti, 2000). In a close reading, aiming at understanding the visible web hyperlink as presented in a web browser, one can either focus on the manifest textual level or on the digital level, and in the first case possibly include the digital level to check the code that generates a specific piece of information or a feature if needed. But when scaling up to a distant reading of hyperlink connections, only the digital level is possible because of the scale, and automated methods have to be used. However, moving from the manifest to the digital text comes at the expense of losing the textualities of the link source and the link target, and the hyperlink is thus reduced to its HTML code.

MAJOR TRENDS IN THE HISTORY OF CONNECTING TEXTUAL SEGMENTS

As has been shown above, the need to establish intended connections between textual elements has existed for millennia, and complex landscapes of textual systems to support and enable these connections have been developed, each embedded in a media-specific array of semantic, formal and physically performative ways of connecting. The web hyperlink is just the latest phase in this history.

When seeing the shifts in how this need has been realized through the lens of emerging new media environments, each with its own impact on linking practices, it becomes clear that the major shift is that between non-digital and digital media. However, two things are worth noting in this respect. First, that this macro shift covers a number of smaller shifts within the non-digital and the digital era: the changing mechanical ways of creating links, and the envisioned photoelectric possibilities, and the shift from stand-alone computers to local and global networks, in parallel with the supplementing of mainframe computers with personal computers. Second, that although the advent of the digital computer establishes a radically new media environment than that of mechanical media, thus opening a new textual field of linking possibilities, an undertow of continuity underpins this break on the textual levels, since practices that have been known for centuries are either incorporated or reinterpreted, along with the fundamentally new linking features such as the click-jump.

With the web hyperlink as the temporary endpoint in the long history of connecting segments of text, it is possible to summarize developments by mapping some of the major trends of this history in terms of space, time, movement, and forms of expression.

Early in the mechanical era the spatial and temporal distance between the segments of text that can be connected and the movements that can realize the connections are tied to the movement of eyes, hands, and body: the segments on a single page are connected almost instantaneously by the movement of the eyes. Later segments scattered on different pages in the same book are connected by the leafing movement of the hand, or segments in different books spread over a wider area are connected even more slowly by the movement of the body. Later in the mechanical era, after the introduction of print, the time required for connection is reduced and the speed of the movement required is accelerated: pages become more standardized, and the same goes for books as such, which makes them faster to handle. In the later stages of the printing era, the increased accessibility to books decreases the time span required for connection and increases the speed of connecting. With the advent of the web, the already existing trend of the print era towards reducing the spatial and temporal distance between segments as well as increasing the speed of the movement is intensified: the click-jump compresses the connecting movement to a mouse-click and eyes moving on a screen, thus collapsing the spatial and temporal distance to zero. What was previously a here and there and a now and then is reduced to a here and now, and the movement becomes almost instantaneous. Concurrently with this, the forms of expression that can be connected expands by including more and more forms in the linking system, from writing and graphics to images, until the web tends to become so flexible that it allows the dissolution of the relation between a recognizable semantic-formal entity and the hyperlink. And since many of the trends above supplement each other instead of continuously disappearing or replacing each other—printed books and newspapers co-exist with the web—the linking system as such tends to become increasingly complex and to accumulate increasingly varied forms. In summary, the hyperlink is embedded in a history of compression of space and time, of accelerated speed, of increased dissolution and flexibility, and of growing complexity and accumulation.

UNDERSTANDING THE WEB HYPERLINK—NEXT STEPS

This brief history of the hyperlink and its ancestors can be used as a stepping stone for a variety of further studies, three of which will be mentioned here.

First, the brief history of the web hyperlink can be expanded by detailed studies of specific phases, visions, or media types, including some of the media types that have been left out, for instance electronic media such as radio and television.

Second, where this history ends—the emergence of the web hyperlink—new histories can start looking ahead with a view to understanding how the hyperlink has developed on the web and beyond. Such studies could examine major general changes in the functionality of the hyperlink, for instance, as argued by Helmond (2013), the important shift marked by the emergence of automated creation of hyperlinks as a supplement to manually created hyperlinks (see also Helmond, 2018, forthcoming). Alternatively, changes in specific hyperlink networks could be investigated, such as the historical development in hyperlinking practices in online newspapers (Karlsson, Clerwall, & Örnebring, 2015), or the development of a national blogosphere (Weltevrede & Helmond, 2012).[22]

And third, a more systematic study aimed at categorizing hyperlinks could be pursued, either as a history of hyperlink types or as a more general typology, or rather typologies, because one overarching typology is probably not possible or even useful (cf. Halavais, 2008, p. 43; Harries, Wilkinson, Price, Fairclough, & Thelwall, 2004, p. 441). Establishing hyperlink typologies has a history of its own, starting with Ted Nelson's "tentative listing of some link types" (Nelson, 1992, pp. 4/52–4/55, 2/23–2/40), followed by the first outline of web-specific hyperlink types in Tim Berners-Lee's first proposal (Berners-Lee, 1987, p. 4), to discussions by a number of scholars in the years following the advent of the web (e.g. Aguilar,

2009; Burbules, 1998, pp. 110–117; Landow, 1997, pp. 11–16; Thelwall, 2003; Tosca, 2000).

Regardless of which of these paths are taken in future studies of web hyperlinks, an inclusion of the long history of connecting textual segments can be helpful since it offers a catalog of past or existing forms of connecting in which present developments can be mirrored.

REFERENCES

Aguilar, S. U. (2009, April 1–3). The hyperlink as a form of reference: Beginning the process of classification of hyperlinks when used in referential relationships. 8th European Academy of Design Conference. Aberdeen: The Robert Gordon University.

Barnet, B. (2014). *Memory machines: The evolution of hypertext*. London: Anthem Press.

Bell, A. (1995). News time. *Time & Society, 4*(3), 305–328.

Berners-Lee, T. (1989). Information management: A proposal. Retrieved from https://www.w3.org/History/1989/proposal.html

Berners-Lee, T. (1999). *Weaving the web: The past, present and future of the World Wide Web by its inventor*. London: Orion.

Berners-Lee, T., & Cailliau, R. (1990). WorldWideWeb: Proposal for a HyperText project. Retrieved from http://www.w3.org/Proposal.html

Breton-Gravereau, S. (1998). *L'Aventure des écritures: Matières et formes*. Paris: Bibliothèque nationale de France.

Brügger, N. (2002). Theoretical reflections on media and media history. In N. Brügger & S. Kolstrup (Eds.), *Media history: Theories, methods, analysis* (pp. 33–66). Aarhus: Aarhus University Press.

Brügger, N. (2009). Website history and the website as an object of study. *New Media & Society, 11*(1–2), 127–144. doi:10.1177/1461444808099574

Brügger, N. (2010). *Website analysis. Elements of a conceptual architecture*. Aarhus: The Centre for Internet Studies.

Brügger, N. (2011). Web archiving—between past, present, and future. In M. Consalvo & C. Ess (Eds.), *The handbook of Internet studies* (pp. 24–42). Oxford: Wiley-Blackwell.

Brügger, N. (2016a). Introduction: The web's first 25 years. *New Media & Society, 18*(7), 1059–1065. doi:10.1177/1461444816643787

Brügger, N. (2016b). Digital humanities in the 21st century: Digital material as a driving force. *Digital Humanities Quarterly, 10*(3).

Brügger, N., & Finnemann, N. O. (2013). The web and digital humanities: Theoretical and methodological concerns. *Journal of Broadcasting and Electronic Media, 57*(1), 66–80.

Burbules, N. C. (1998). Rhetorics of the web: hyperreading and critical literacy. In I. Snyder (Ed.), *Page to screen: Taking literacy into the electronic era* (pp. 102–122). Abingdon: Routledge.

Bødker, H. (2016). The time(s) of news websites. In B. Franklin & S. Eldridge II (Eds.), *The Routledge companion to digital journalism studies* (pp. 55–63). Abingdon: Routledge.

Carruthers, M. (2008). *The book of memory: A study of memory in mediaval culture*. Cambridge: Cambridge University Press.

Chiera, E., & Cameron, G. G. (Eds.). (1939). *They wrote on clay: The Babylonian tablets speak to-day*. Cambridge: Cambridge University Press.

Conner-Sax, K., & Krol, E. (1999). *The whole Internet: The next generation.* Sebastopol, CA: O'Reilly & Associates.

De Maeyer, J. (2012). Towards a hyperlinked society: A critical review of link studies. *New Media & Society, 15*(5), 737–751. doi:10.1177/1461444812462851

Eisenstein, E. L. (1993). *The printing revolution in early modern Europe.* Cambridge: Cambridge University Press.

Finnemann, N. O. (1999). Modernity modernised: The cultural impact of computerisation. In P. A. Mayer (Ed.), *Computer, media and communication* (pp. 141–159). Oxford: Oxford University Press.

Grafton, A. (1997). *The footnote: A curious history.* London: Faber and Faber.

Halavais, A. (2008). The hyperlink as organizing principle. In J. Turow & L. Tsui (Eds.), *The hyperlinked society: Questioning connections in the digital age* (pp. 39–55). Ann Arbor, MI: the University of Michigan Press.

Harries, G., Wilkinson, D., Price, L., Fairclough, R., & Thelwall, M. (2004). Hyperlinks as a data source for science mapping. *Journal of Information Science, 30*(5), 436–447. doi:10.1177/0165551504046736

Helmond, A. (2013). The algorithmization of the hyperlink. *Computational Culture: A Journal of Software Studies, 3.*

Helmond, A. (2018, forthcoming). A historiography of the hyperlink: Periodizing the web through the changing role of the hyperlink. In N. Brügger & I. Milligan (Eds.), *Sage handbook of web history.* London: Sage.

Karlsson, M., Clerwall, C., & Örnebring, H. (2015). Hyperlinking practices in Swedish online news 2007–2013: The rise, fall, and stagnation of hyperlinking as a journalistic tool. *Information, Communication & Society, 18*(7), 847–863. doi:10.1080/1369118X.2014.984743

Kirschenbaum, M. G. (2000). Hypertext. In T. Swiss (Ed.), *Unspun: Key concepts for understanding the World Wide Web* (pp. 120–137). New York, NY: New York University Press.

Krajewski, M. (2011). *Paper machines: About cards and catalogs, 1548–1929.* Cambridge, MA: MIT Press.

Krol, E. (1992). *The whole Internet: User's guide and catalog.* Sebastopol, CA: O'Reilly & Associates.

Krol, E. (1994). *The whole Internet: User's guide and catalog.* Sebastopol, CA: O'Reilly & Associates.

Landow, G. P. (1997). *Hypertext 2.0: The convergence of contemporary critical theory and technology.* Baltimore, MD: The John Hopkins University Press.

Meyrowitz, J. (1994). Medium theory. In D. Crowley & D. Mitchell (Eds.), *Communication theory today* (pp. 50–77). Cambridge: Polity Press.

Moretti, F. (2000). Conjectures on world literature. *New Left Review, 1*(Jan–Feb), 56–58.

Nelson, T. H. (1992). *Literary machines 93.1.* Sausaliti, CA: Mindful Press.

Olesen-Bagneux, O. (2015). Mnemonics in the Mouseion: Considerations on spatial mnemonics as a tool for classification and retrieval. *Journal of Documentation, 71*(2), 278–293. doi:10.1108/JD-01-2014-0016

Phillips, H. (2010). The Great Library of Alexandria? *Library Philosophy and Practice,* paper 417.

Pollak, O. B. (2006). The decline and fall of bottom notes, op.cit., loc.cit., and a century of the Chicago Manual of style. *Journal of Scholarly Publishing, 38*(1), 14–30.

Reynolds, L. D., & Wilson, N. G. (1991). *Scribes and scholars: A guide to the transmission of Greek and Latin literature.* Oxford: Oxford University Press.

Rhodes, N., & Sawday, J. (2000). Introduction: Paperworlds: Imagining the Renaissance computer. In N. Rhodes & J. Sawday (Eds.), *The renaissance computer: Knowledge technology in the first age of print* (pp. 1–17). Abingdon: Routledge.

Robinson, A. (2000). *The story of writing: Alphabets, hieroglyphs and pictograms*. London: Thames & Hudson.

Saenger, P. (1997). *Space between words: The origins of silent reading*. Stanford, CA: Stanford University Press.

Schmandt-Besserat, D. (1996). *How writing came about*. Austin, TX: University of Texas Press.

Snyder, I. (1998). Beyond the hype: Reassissing hypertext. In I. Snyder (Ed.), *Page to screen: Taking literacy into the electronic era* (pp. 125–143). Abingdon: Routledge.

Thelwall, M. (2003). What is this link doing here? Beginning a fine-grained process of identifying reasons for academic hyperlink creation. *Information Research, 8*(3). Retrieved from http://informationr.net/ir/8-3/paper151.html

Tosca, S. P. (2000). *A pragmatics of links*. Paper presented at the Hypertext 2000, San Antonio, TX.

Turow, J. (2008). Introduction. In J. Turow & L. Tsui (Eds.), *The hyperlinked society: Questioning connections in the digital age* (pp. 1–18). Ann Arbor, MI: The University of Michigan Press.

Turow, J., & Tsui, L. (2008). *The hyperlinked society: Questioning connections in the digital age*. Ann Arbor, MI: The University of Michigan Press.

van den Heuvel, C. (2010). Web archiving in research and historical global collaboratories. In N. Brügger (Ed.), *Web history* (pp. 279–303). New York, NY: Peter Lang.

Weltevrede, E., & Helmond, A. (2012). Where do bloggers blog? Platform transitions within the historical Dutch blogosphere. *First Monday, 17*(2). Retrieved from http://firstmonday.org/ojs/index.ph

Zerby, C. (2003). *The devil's details: A history of footnotes*. New York, NY: Touchstone.

NOTES

1. In the following the terms 'World Wide Web' and 'web' are used synonymously.
2. In addition to the web hyperlink, the web browser can also be considered a defining feature since a web file does not make much sense without the browser to interpret it. This distinction between web content and browser was not natural to a user in 1992: "It's important to realize that the home page [...] and everything else that's available is not 'built-in' to your browser" (Krol, 1992, p. 230).
3. For descriptions of how the web works from a user's point of view with a line mode browser in 1992, with the graphic browser Mosaic in 1994, and with Netscape Navigator and Internet Explorer in 1999, see Krol (1992, pp. 227–242, 1994, pp. 287–323), and Conner-Sax and Krol (1999, pp. 107–143).
4. For an introduction to web archiving, including web crawling, see Brügger (2011).
5. In the following the term 'text' is used in a broad sense, including not only written text, but also any semiotic unit capable of conveying meaning, be it writing, sound, images, or moving images.
6. I use the term 'mediacy' for this media-ness (Brügger, 2002, pp. 44–52).
7. An understanding of hypertext (and thereby also of the hyperlink) with a focus on media materiality is found in Kirschenbaum (2000).
8. This approach also adds some of the contextuality that scholars have called for in relation to analyses of hyperlink networks (cf. De Maeyer, 2012, pp. 745–748; Halavais, 2008, p. 43).
9. Burbules (1998) is an early example of focusing on hyperlinks and reading.
10. Snyder (1998) also distinguishes between the hyperlink on stand-alone computers and in global networks such as the World Wide Web (p. 127).

11. Analog electronic media are not included in the following, although it would be relevant to do so. See Brügger (2010, pp. 26–31) for a brief discussion of some of the textual- and media-related differences between radio/televison and websites.
12. Schmandt-Besserat's hypothesis of tokens and envelopes as the precursor of cuneiform writing is debated, and some argue that tokens did not precede writing but accompanied its development (e.g. Robinson, 2000, pp. 60–62).
13. Carruthers maintains that similar systems were in use earlier and had been "known since antiquity as memorial schemes" (Carruthers, 2008, p. 129).
14. The relation between Otlet's Mundaneum and the World Wide Web is discussed in detail by Charles van den Heuvel (2010). More information on the Mundaneum can be found on the website http://www.mundaneum.org.
15. This approach to the digital is inspired by Finnemann (1999) (see also Brügger, 2009, pp. 118–119, 2016b, pp. 12–15; Brügger & Finnemann, 2013, pp. 68–69).
16. I use the term 'digitality' to identify the medium-specific ways in which different digital media combine the digital text with an artefact (cf. Brügger, 2016b, pp. 12–15).
17. Other hypertext systems in the 1980s were NoteCards, Office Workstations Limited's Guide, KMS, Microcosm, and Storyspace (cf. Barnet, 2014, xxii, pp. 115–136).
18. One example of a fully developed networked multiuser hypertext system running on a local network within a university was Intermedia, developed at Brown University. Among other things, Intermedia supported bidirectional links for text as well as graphics (cf. Barnet, 2014, pp. 111–112).
19. Another key concept in Nelson's Xanadu is transclusion, "that part of a document may be in several places—in other documents beside the original—without actually being copied there" (Nelson, 1992, Preface 1993).
20. The latter of these forms resonates Ted Nelson's way of describing 'windowing hypertext' (cf. Nelson, 1992, pp. 1/15–16).
21. The textuality of search boxes and search results is briefly discussed in Brügger (2010, pp. 42–43).
22. An overview of hyperlink studies can be found in De Maeyer (2012), and for examples of the understanding of the social meaning of a hyperlink, see Turow and Tsui (2008).

CHAPTER TWO

Constructing THE biographies OF THE web

An examination of the narratives and myths around the web's history

SIMONE NATALE AND PAOLO BORY

INTRODUCTION

Rather than being confined to the nebulous realm of the imagination, the way we understand and talk about a new medium of communication has important consequences at a cultural, social, political, and legal level. As pointed out by Susan Crawford (2007, p. 467), what we mean when we refer to particular media technologies helps determine "which actors' voices will be listened to, what arguments will be respected, and which goals will be considered legitimate." Studying the social and cultural imaginaries of the information age, therefore, not only provides an entry point towards contemporary cultures; it also helps to comprehend how and why particular institutional frameworks are erected around given technologies, and certain practices of governance are preferred over others (Mansell, 2012; Schulte, 2013). In this context, the question of which mechanisms contribute to the formation of the imaginary becomes crucial to the study of digital culture, as well as to attempts of unveiling the dynamics of media change.

Scholars in literature and critical theory have shown that one of the key ways through which we form our images, opinions, and understandings about reality is storytelling (Cavarero, 2000; Olney, 1972). Throughout our everyday life, narratives allow us to make sense of events and situations, representing a crucial mediator between our experiences and our worldviews. Yet, in the study of the media imaginary, few attempts have been made to disclose the role of narrative and storytelling in the formation of our ideas and views about media. Employing a theoretical approach called "biographies of media" (Natale, 2016), which looks at how the histories of particular media are built up through recurring narrative patterns, this chapter uncovers the particular imaginary hidden behind the story of the emergence and development of the World Wide Web. It argues that the history of the web has become a key context in which cultural, political, and ideological representations of the medium are constructed and negotiated within the public sphere. More broadly, the chapter aims to show that the stories we tell about technological systems such as the web are essentially similar to the stories we tell about people—in other words, to biographies in the strictest sense of the word. Drawing on literature exploring the archetypal structure of narratives and myths, we demonstrate that both biographical writings about the web's inventor, Tim Berners-Lee, as well as the "biographies" of the web follow quite closely the trajectory of the hero's journey, as sketched by Joseph Campbell (2004). Ultimately, this narrative pattern provides a familiar framework through which the story of the emergence of the web has come to make sense to us, contributing to the formation of particular claims and views about this medium's role in our societies and everyday life.

Studying the biographies of the web is important for three main reasons. First, it helps to comprehend why certain ways to imagine and represent this medium have been privileged over others, and how they influence its use and insertion within social environments. Second, since narratives are created, recounted and animated by particular individuals and groups, it helps to unveil how and why different agents invest in particular interpretations of the medium's role and impact. Technologies function not only through their material substance, but also according to the narratives they generate or into which they are adjusted. As Schulte (2013) aptly demonstrated by focusing on the case of the internet, policies are implemented also in relation and as a reaction to the emergence of particular narratives about new media. As a consequence, studying the biographies of the web allows to reconstruct the relationship between the level of the discourse and the level of power. Third, it provides insight into an aspect of the web's history which is relatively stable in time. One of the characteristics of biographies of media, in fact, is their persistence across time. The most influential anecdotes and stories become closely associated to the life cycle of a medium, circulating and being renovated in different places and times. This contrasts sharply with the inherent ephemerality of webpages, to which historians of the web have to respond by adopting particular approaches and methods (Brügger, 2013). Thus, looking at the biographies of the web reminds us that the fluctuating character of web contents is complementary to technical and discursive elements that are constant and far-reaching over longer, if still limited, periods of time.

BIOGRAPHIES OF MEDIA: A THEORETICAL APPROACH

Social anthropologists such as Armin Appadurai (1986) and Alfred Gell (1998) have pointed out that not only humans, but artifacts as well can be regarded as social agents. In Gell's words, "social agency can be exercised relative to 'things' and social agency can be exercised by 'things' (and also animals)." This also applies to media, which are depicted as agents in numerous social situations (Reeves & Nass, 1996). Media have social lives, and their meaning is continually negotiated through a process that informs technological change and shapes how they are inserted and domesticated within domestic and professional environment (Silverstone & Haddon, 1996). An important role in this negotiation process is played by the different narratives and anecdotes through which histories of different media are recounted in the public sphere, which can be called "biographies of media" (Natale, 2016). Like biographies of prominent people, in fact, these narratives are a form of contingent narrative that frames historical characters, places, events, and things into stories that are written, recounted, and circulated through numerous channels and in different ways.

As with all media, the narratives about the emergence of the World Wide Web have come to signify much more than its mere history. Its narratives have become a key component of the way we imagine and conceptualize the web's impact on our societies and cultures. Scholars in media and technology studies have showed that ideas and cultural representations inform not only how technologies are imagined, but also how they are designed and adopted (Flichy, 2007; Mosco, 2004; Nye, 1994). In the case of the web, narratives about its "birth" and development have played a paramount role in orienting the public's imagination towards positive elements such as plurality, openness, and creativity, which in turn facilitated its insertion into broader narratives of political, social and cultural change (Lesage & Rinfret, 2015). An example of this dynamic is the use of narratives about the web in the political message of groups such as the Pirate Parties in northern and central Europe or the 5-Star-Movement in Italy, which explicitly linked the rise of this medium with the emergence of new forms of democracies and politics (Natale & Ballatore, 2014).

It is important to note that the use of the plural form "biographies" is meant to underline the plurality of these narratives. Although there might be dominant narratives and less influential ones, there is never, in fact, a single biography referring to any single medium. One of the main aspects characterizing the stories we tell about media and technologies is the coexistence of different and often contrasting versions of how a medium was born, developed, became ubiquitous, or disappeared (see Natale, 2016). Indeed, some of these narratives are historically inaccurate or inexact: take, for instance, the anecdotes about the first spectators of the cinematograph escaping before the image of a coming train, whose apocryphal nature has been documented by film historians (Bottomore, 1999; Sirois-Trahan,

2004; Tsivian, 1994). Nevertheless, whether an anecdote is based on events that have or have not taken place, its social and cultural impact depends on the extent to which this story is reported, disseminated, and used by different agents, such as individuals and institutions. Thus, a fake or greatly exaggerated anecdote such as the one about early cinema's "train effect" has become a veritable founding myth for this technology, informing its representation as an illusory machine and contributing to its attractiveness for large audiences throughout the world (Loiperdinger, 2004).

The relationship between narratives, biographies and technological change has recently received increasing attention in media history. Merav Katz-Kimchi, for instance, compares some of the main biographies and narratives of internet pioneers (e.g. Hafner & Lyon, 1998; Salus & Vinton, 1995), arguing that popular stories on American engineers and inventors "cast the history of the internet into the mythopoetic form of the technological romance" (Katz-Kimchi, 2015, p. 160). Others, such as Erkki Huhtamo, underlined the recurrence of narrative tropes or 'topoi' in different moments of media history and in reference to different media and practices (Huhtamo, 2013). Our approach aims to extend and complement these perspectives by stressing how biographies of pioneers and inventors, and the narrative tropes according to which they are constructed, go hand in hand with the biographies of their inventions.

THE BIOGRAPHIES OF THE WEB AND ITS INVENTOR IN PARALLEL LINES

The analogy between the historical narratives regarding media and the biographical narratives regarding the life of people works not only at a metaphorical level. In fact, there is often a peculiar resemblance between the stories we tell about individuals and those we tell about media such as cinema, television, or the internet. Adriana Cavarero (2000) has shown that storytelling proceeds through trajectories that are embedded in the storyteller's life. Narratives are created by people, and bear the trace of narrative patterns retrieved from the people's lives. It is probably for this reason that biological and experiential events such as birth, maturity, aging, and death enter very often in narrative constructions through which we attempt to make sense of media change (Acland, 2007; Gaudreault & Marion, 2005). The idea that 'old media' might die as a consequence of the introduction—or birth—of 'new media' is an example of how much this dynamic enters into representations and narratives of media change (Ballatore & Natale, 2015).

The construction of biographies of the web, in this regard, is a particularly in-teresting case. Biographical narratives about its inventor, Tim Berners-Lee, conflate and become sometimes almost indistinguishable from the story of how the web emerged and developed. In Berners-Lee's autobiography, this association surfaces sometimes in illuminating ways: when he describes the creation of the first web browser/editor, for instance, he links the episode to the birth of his first child, stressing that "as amazing as it would be to see the web develop, it would never compare to seeing the development of our child" (Berners-Lee, 2000, p. 31). It is not by chance that Micheal L. Dertouzos starts his introduction to *Weaving the web* claiming that it "is a *unique* story about a *unique* innovation, by a *unique* inventor [...] he opens a rare window into the way a unique person invents and nurtures a unique approach that alters the course of humanity" (Berners-Lee, 2000, p. vii, our italics). In fact, the entire trajectory of Berners-Lee's biography provides a narrative line that also characterizes the biographies of the web.

In *The Hero with a Thousand Faces*, a classic work in narrative theory, Joseph Campbell demonstrates how a wide range of popular stories and myths from different cultural and linguistic traditions replicate a common narrative structure, which he calls 'monomyth.' As he points out:

> whether presented in the vast, almost oceanic images of the Orient, in the vigorous narratives of the Greeks, or in the majestic legends of the Bible, the adventure of the hero normally follows the pattern of the nuclear unit [...]: a separation from the world, a penetration to some source of power, and a life-enhancing return. (Campbell, 2004, p. 33)

In what follows, we show that not only the story of Berners-Lee's life and invention, but also the story of how the web emerged and came to play a key role in our society and everyday life follow the pattern of a narrative of the hero. Drawing on sources such as Berners-Lee's autobiography (Berners-Lee, 2000), as well as other histories of the web and its inventor (e.g. Gillies & Cailliau, 2000; McPherson, 2009), we show that Campbell's monomyth provides a useful resource to unveil how stories about the emergence of a new medium may be similar to the unfolding of stories about mythical characters. Looking at Berners-Lee and at the web's biographies in parallel lines, in this sense, helps uncover how the recurring narrative pattern of the hero applies to stories about individuals as well as about 'things,' such as media.

The departure

According to Campbell, the first stage in the narrative of the hero is the *departure*, where the hero receives his call to adventure. Through this call, destiny summons the hero, preparing him for entering into an unknown space of adventure and realization. Following a pattern that characterize many biographies of inventors (Ortoleva, 1996), a call to adventure can be found in the recounting of the life of Berners-Lee, as his vocation is located within his family heritage and his natural disposition. Berners-Lee's parents were both mathematicians and worked together at the Ferranti Mark I, the first computer sold commercially. In his autobiography, the inclination of the young Berners-Lee for computing is related to his educational path and his parents' teaching. Moreover, the premature passion for experimenting and problem solving foretells his destiny since the beginning. The first symptom of the fascination with the 'connectivity issue' is identified with a brief discussion between the young Berners-Lee and his father Conway:

> He was reading books on the brain, looking for clues about how to make a computer intuitive, able to complete connections as the brain did. We discussed the point [...] The idea stayed with me that computers could become much more powerful if they could be programmed to link otherwise unconnected information. (Berners-Lee, 2000, p. 4)

Similar episodes establish a twofold representation of inventorship as the result of both predestination and fortunate environmental conditions—a combination of natural gifts and chance.

Other anecdotes in his narrative point to the role of chance, such as the acquisition of the NeXT computer, a special 'gift' through which his supervisor Mike Sendall encouraged him to work on the web idea. Chance is a common characteristic of biographies of scientists and inventors, in which it often plays a paramount role in representing the nature of the creative act leading to innovation: think of the apple in the story of Newton realizing the principle of gravity, or the anecdotes about the chance discovery of X-rays by W.C. Röntgen (Dessauer, 1945). Such anecdotes tend to simplify the complexity of the act of invention, enforcing the existence of a veritable call of destiny (Gorman & Carlson, 1990). In Campbell's monomyth, this can be identified with the supernatural aid that prepares the hero for the initiation—which, in Berners-Lee's case, will be the invention of the World Wide Web.

The call to adventure may coincide with a particular episode: "an event, often happened seemingly by chance, activates the hero's adventure" (Campbell, 2004, p. 53). In the footsteps of Campbell's work, Christopher Vogler argues that "most stories take the hero out of the ordinary, mundane world and into a Special World, new and alien" (Vogler, 2007, p. 10). This "new and alien world" was, in Berners-Lee's journey, the European Organization for Nuclear Research (CERN), which he joined for the first time in 1980. The new environment is portrayed with mythical tones in Berners-Lee's autobiography as "an electronic engineer's paradise, with columns of oscilloscopes and power supplies and sequencing equipment, most of it built especially for or by the CERN" (Berners-Lee, 2000, p. 8).

To what extent does the call to adventure characterize not only the biography of the web's inventor, but also the 'biographies' of the web? In narrative recounting of the web's birth, one finds several traces of a similar call that prepares and anticipates the new medium's purported destiny as an egalitarian and democratic means for transmitting information. A similar dynamic is involved, for instance, in the construction of a lineage of precursors for the web such as Ted Nelson's Xanadu, but also hypertext programs like Apple's Hypercard, the narrative software Storyspace and Berners-Lee's Enquire, considered as the predecessor of the web. This lineage is inserted into canonical histories of the web (Banks, 2008; Gillies & Cailliau, 2000, pp. 11–46). Through the reference to a pre-history populated by visionary thinkers (e.g Bush, 1945; Engelbart, 1962; Nelson, 1987) who imagined the design and implications of technologies and systems yet to be, as well as enthusiastic early adopters, the preconditions to the web take the shape of a 'call for adventure' that ultimately supports claims about the revolutionary character of this medium. Additionally, as in the case of Berners-Lee's biography, the 'Special World' (Vogler, 2007, p. 10) where the emergence of the web is contextualized is CERN—an environment which is characterized by some of the same qualities, such as openness and cooperation, attributed to the web by mythical and imaginary constructions (Lesage & Rinfret, 2015; Mansell, 2012; Mosco, 2004; Natale & Balbi, 2014). The CERN, a collaborative scientific enterprise created under the auspices of European cooperation, based in "a city at the heart of Europe with a cosmopolitan heritage" such as Geneva (Gillies & Cailliau, 2000, p. 48), is represented as the ideal context where a medium like the web might originate and flourish. The destiny of the web is traced through a myth of origins that contrasts sharply with narratives about the emergence of the internet, according to which the idea for the structure of the network was conceived within a military mind frame, in order to counteract the effects of a potential nuclear attack. As Tung-Hui Hu recently pointed out, the latter narrative is historically inaccurate, and yet continues to be kept alive, also due to the deeper ideological implications that this myth of origins implies for representations of the internet (Hu, 2015, pp. 8–10). In contrast, the web's origins in CERN tell a different story, one preparing and supporting arguments about the web's decentralized and egalitarian character.

The constant parallelism between anecdotes about Berners-Lee's life and anecdotes on the development of the web shows how the hagiography of the inventor contributes to the hagiography of the medium. According to the narrative, it is not by chance that, when Berners-Lee became an expert programmer and was hired by CERN, some relevant technological events were occurring too. In the late 1980s new powerful computers like the NeXT were commercialized, hypertext-based software spread in Western countries, and CERN had just decided to adopt the TCP/IP protocol, a keystone for the web's success. Berners-Lee himself claims that, unlike his unlucky predecessors, his walk of life coincided with the time in which the web could finally occur: "Unfortunately, just like Bush and Nelson, Doug (Engelbart) was too far ahead of time. [...] I happened to come along with time, and the right interest and inclination, after hypertext and the internet had come of age. The task left to me was to marry them together" (Berners-Lee, 2000, p. 6). Similarly, the emergence of the web is grounded within a context of social and technological foundations that make it not only possible, but also to a certain extent inevitable (Lesage & Rinfret, 2015). The inescapable destiny of the departure, in this sense, is a narrative trope that underpins the biographies of both the medium and its inventor.

The initiation

In Campbell's monomyth the departure is followed by the second phase, the *initiation*, in which the hero transcends the threshold to the unknown world in which the core of the adventure takes place. This stage includes the hero overcoming several trials and finally completing his quest, for which he might receive a reward. Translating this pattern into the biography of Berners-Lee, this phase corresponds to the invention of the World Wide web and the initially uncertain pattern of institutionalization and diffusion for the new invention. Biographical recountings of Berners-Lee's life underline the struggles and trials he had to endure in this phase. At the beginning, the CERN community did not entirely grasp the implications of Berners-Lee's idea. His supervisor, Mike Sendall, wrote a famous remark on the first web project proposal defining it 'vague but exciting' (Berners-Lee, 1989, p. 1). Promoting the web at CERN was therefore the first trial Berners-Lee and Robert Cailliau—his 'allied,' to use the term employed to describe another archetypal character in narratives of the hero (Vogler, 2007)—had to face.

In his proposal, Berners-Lee argued that CERN is a "model in miniature of the rest of world in a few years time" (Berners-Lee, 1989, p. 1). The fluid environment of this institution, characterized by the constant exchange of international researchers and the consequent problem of information loss, was in Berners-Lee's narrative an element that also characterized larger challenges the new information society would face. The parallelism made by Berners-Lee between the CERN's organizational structure (which represented a micro-structure of the new society) and the need for a new system of information management (the web) hinted at the idea that technological and social change were following the same path, or in other words, that the same 'biographical' transitions would occur both in the media landscape and in everyday life.

Berners-Lee knew that promoting the web meant first of all persuading expert users to adopt the new system (Bory, Benecchi, & Balbi, 2016). Besides CERN, the major step towards the evangelization of the web was to convince the hypertext community that hypertext and the internet could be matched and used together. For this reason, in 1991 Berners-Lee and Cailliau joined the Hypertext Conference in San Antonio. Even though their paper proposal was rejected because of a lack of references to the field, they asked to give a demonstration of their project. However, as Berners-Lee put it, "the Hypertext community was so separated from the internet community that we couldn't get any kind of connectivity at all" (Berners-Lee, 2000, p. 51). Thanks to the hacking skills of Cailliau and to the creativity of Berners-Lee, the demonstration finally took place, with the hero overcoming several trials: "Several obstacles stood on their way. First they needed a telephone outlet to hook up their modem. [...] They had to dismantle the modem, rewire it, and put it together with a soldering iron. Then they still needed a way for the modem to get internet access" (McPherson, 2009, p. 59).

Further attempts to promote the web and demonstrate its usefulness are described by Berners-Lee as a series of trials, such as stopping the attempt by NCSA to rename the WWW as Mosaic (Berners-Lee, 2000, p. 70), or negotiating funding and resources for the development of the project, demonstrating the usefulness of the web to editors and companies (Berners-Lee, 1992). As in the case of the departure stage, the same pattern of initiation can be fruitfully applied also to the 'biographies' of the emergence of the World Wide Web. Narratives of the web's emergence, in fact, also underline the many trials and difficulties involved in establishing the World Wide Web as a functional system, and in keeping the spirit of its foundations (e.g Gillies & Cailliau, 2000, pp. 172–201).

According to Campbell, when the hero completes her quest and therefore her initiation, she might reach an apotheosis that makes her closer to a godlike state— which is, however, never to be fully reached, as the story of Prometheus teaches us (Campbell, 2004, 127–47). Berners-Lee's apotheosis coincides with the sacrifice of his invention's intellectual property. Many authors and scholars have acknowledged the heroism of Berners-Lee. The story of the inventor who renounced richness and power to protect the public mission of an invention is a recurrent trope in biographies of inventors, and has shaped popular representations of figures such as Daguerre or Röntgen. A video interview given by media scholar Andrew Keen to the website C-Span is an apt example of how this contributes to the hagiography of the web's inventor:

> In my view, Tim Berners-Lee is a hero. He was a typically publicly-spirited scientist who did this out of love. No one was paying him. He essentially gave it away. He could have owned the World Wide Web. He could have put all sorts of IP around it and would have become an incredibly rich man, but he didn't. He was very publicly-spirited. (Lamb, 2015)

Along similar lines, an article of the *Time* defines Berners-Lee as "the unsung—or at least undersung—hero of the information age. Even by some of the less breathless accounts, the World Wide Web could prove as important as the printing press. That would make Berners-Lee comparable to, well, Gutenberg, more or less" (Wright, 1997, p. 64).

As Marcel Mauss has shown in a classic essay (Mauss, 1990), every gift brings along the donor's identity. In this regard, the sacrifice of Berners-Lee and the gift of the web to society is a "personal renunciation that nourishes social forces" (Hubert & Mauss, 1964, p. 102) reinforcing at the same time the characterization and the identity of the hero. More broadly, the refusal of getting money or any other advantage from his invention, which coincides with the sacrifice of the hero, does not only contributes to the hagiography of Berners-Lee; it also strengthens the analogy between the web's inventor and the web itself, portrayed as a neutral space also in terms of economic interests and power. This is, in fact, one of the most common myths about the web: as some point out, "the web is Franciscan, anti-capitalistic" (Casaleggio & Grillo, 2011, p. 8; see Natale & Ballatore, 2014, p. 114). Such ideological representation contrasts sharply with the actual role of commerce and money in the web (Brunton, 2013). The recent call for a "Magna Carta for the web" (Berners-Lee, 2014) is only one example of how this tension between contrasting visions of the web is playing a central role in the trajectory of Berners-Lee and the web's journey.

The return and reintegration with society

In the third and last stages of Campbell's monomyth, the hero returns to his own world:

> The full round, the norm of the monomyth, requires that the hero shall now begin the labor of bringing the runes to wisdom, the Golden Fleece, or his sleeping princess back into the kingdom of humanity, where the boon may redound to the renewing of the community, the nation, the planet, or the ten thousand worlds. (Campbell, 2004, p. 167)

This might involve new difficulties as the hero is reluctant to return, or overcomes further trials before reaching his goal.

In Berners-Lee's biographical narrative, the foundation and governance of the World Wide Web Consortium (W3C) at the MIT corresponds to the return stage in Campbell's myth. Once the web has spread globally, and Berners-Lee has accomplished his main mission, new responsibilities and trials emerge as the hero struggles to protect his invention from new powers threatening the public domain of his invention, as well as to preserve the message that the web conveys through the mythological narrative inscribed in its biographical path. Within the W3C, the hero becomes the guardian of his treasure. Rather than representing the end of the adventure, Berners-Lee's return coincides with a new call to adventure where the inventor has to safeguard his heritage, also by making people aware of the importance of web neutrality. Additionally, Berners-Lee's late conversion to the Unitarian Universalist church (UU)—a religious community that lists among its principles the "respect for the interdependent web of all existence of which we are a part" (Unitarian Universalist Association, n.d.)—also stress the new quest of the hero. In the FAQ page of his website and in the final chapter of his autobiography (Berners-Lee, 2000, pp. 207–209), Berners-Lee compares the web and the UU, claiming that "web and the UU concept of faith are similar in that both serve as a place for thought, and the importance of the quest for truth, but without labelling any one true solution" (Berners-Lee, 1998). Covering the same biographical path, the institutionalization of the web as a global medium goes hand in hand with the foundation of a new supervising institution, the W3C, and the promotion of a religious association, the UU: two different but concomitant expressions of the universalist vision behind the technical structure of the web. As Berners-Lee himself points out, "the parallels between technical design and social principles have recurred throughout the web's history" (Berners-Lee, 2000, p. 207).

As for the other stages in the hero's path, the return phase applies well also to the construction of biographical narratives related to the web as a medium. Crucially, the preservation of web neutrality is ensured through a process that involves continuity and change at the same time. In this context, paradigmatic shifts in the conventions and uses of the medium are offered as biographical narratives through which the web's participatory and neutral ideology is preserved even in the process of change. This is the case, for instance, of the passage between Web 1.0 and Web 2.0, which represents one of the key narratives through which the recent history of the medium has been told and constructed. According to such narratives, the shift in the definition of the web reproduces the same values of its origins, such as authenticity, openness, the relinquishing of control, the sharing of code, and the building on the efforts of others (Scholz, 2008). As Megan Sapnar Ankerson has recently shown, the shift to Web 2.0 not only involved the emergence of new technologies and practices, but perhaps even more crucially, the construction of a new narrative through which the history of the medium was connected to broader cultural imaginaries. As this narrative became dominant, other potential narratives carrying different and potentially disruptive implications and meanings were pushed to the margins—to give an instance, the crisis of the internet-based sector in the late 1990s, known as dot-com bubble, was ultimately overshadowed by competing narratives celebrating the rise of the web (Ankerson, 2015).

The history of the web, as a result, becomes a field through which particular representations of the medium and its impact are produced and preserved. Like a hero's journey, the passing of the web through different technical and cultural frameworks is portrayed as a path where different trials are overcome to safeguard what is imagined as the true essence of the medium—its open, participatory nature.

CONCLUSION

Biographies of inventors are a highly standardized subgenre, characterized by common patterns and narrative tropes (Ortoleva, 1996). Not unlike biographies of other classes of individuals, such as artists (Kris & Kurz, 1979) or entrepreneurs (Godelier, 2007), the life stories of inventors from different ages and places include recurring anecdotes that help define the limits and possibilities of issues such as geniality and invention. A similar discourse applies, as the case of the web contributes to show, to biographies of media. Rather than being isolated narratives about single technologies and media, these stories should be regarded as a particular genre with its own recurring patterns and tropes. Looking at these patterns helps unveil the levels of meaning that are embedded in the stories we tell about media technologies.

Biographies of media, in fact, are not 'mere stories': they should be regarded as one of the ways in which cultural, social and ideological representations of media are created and disseminated (Natale, 2016). By following familiar narrative patterns such as Campbell's monomyth, they provide a trajectory through which we represent and imagine the impact of media in our societies and everyday lives. In this respect the imaginary associated to the biographies of media, rather than being relegated to the status of a 'mirror metaphor' (Castoriadis, 1987), actively contributes to the shaping and institutionalization of the role of specific media in our society. While biographies of inventors are useful sources to comprehend how inventorship is defined and culturally approached in a society, narratives about the emergence and development of new media such as the web are access points to the particular representations concerning innovation, technology, and communication that circulate across societies. Built around the familiar narrative pattern of departure, initiation, and return, the 'biography' of the web becomes therefore a field through which particular definitions and understandings of the new medium are constructed, reproduced, and disseminated.

REFERENCES

Acland, C. R. (2007). *Residual media*. Minneapolis, MN: University of Minnesota Press.

Ankerson, M. S. (2015). Social media and the 'Read-Only' web: Reconfiguring social logics and historical boundaries. *Social Media and Society, 1*(2), 1–12. doi:10.1177/2056305115621935

Appadurai, A. (1986). *The social life of things: Commodities in cultural perspective*. Cambridge: Cambridge University Press.

Ballatore, A., & Natale, S. (2016). E-readers and the death of the book: Or, new media and the myth of the disappearing medium. *New Media & Society, 18*(10), 2379–2394. doi:10.1177/1461444815586984

Banks, M. A. (2008). *On the way to the web: The secret history of the internet and its founders*. Berkeley, CA: Apress.

Berners-Lee, T. (1989). *Information management: A proposal*. Retrieved January 20, 2016 from http://www.w3.org/History/1989/proposal.html

Berners-Lee, T. (1992). Electronic publishing and visions of hypertext. *Physics World, 5*(6), 14–16.

Berners-Lee, T. (1998). *The World Wide Web and the "Web of Life."* Retrieved January 20, 2016 from https://www.w3.org/People/Berners-Lee/UU.html

Berners-Lee, T. (2000). *Weaving the web: the original design and ultimative destiny of the World Wide Web by its inventor*. New York: Harper Collins.

Berners-Lee, T. (2014). *A Magna Carta for the web*. Retrieved January 20, 2016 from http://www.ted.com/talks/tim_berners_lee_a_magna_carta_for_the_web

Bory, P., Benecchi, E., & Balbi, G. (2016). How the web was told: Continuity and change in the founding fathers' narratives on the origins of the WWW. *New Media & Society, 18*(7), 1066–1087.

Bottomore, S. (1999). The panicking audience?: Early cinema and the "train effect." *Historical Journal of Film, Radio and Television, 19*(2), 177–216.

Brunton, F. (2013). *Spam: A shadow history of the internet*. Cambridge, MA: MIT Press.

Brügger, N. (2013). Web historiography and internet studies: Challenges and perspectives. *New Media & Society, 15*(5), 752–764. doi:10.1177/1461444812462852

Bush, V. (1945). As we may think. *The Atlantic Monthly, 176*(1), 101–108.

Campbell, J. (2004). *The hero with a thousand faces*. Princeton, NJ: Princeton University Press.

Casaleggio, G., & Grillo, B. (2011). *Siamo in guerra. Reverse* (1st ed.). Milano: Chiare Lettere.

Castoriadis, C. (1987). *The imaginary institution of society*. Cambridge: Polity Press.

Cavarero, A. (2000). *Relating narratives: Storytelling and selfhood*. Abingdon: Routledge.

Crawford, S. (2007). Internet think. *Journal on Telecommunications and High Technology Law, 5*, 467–486.

Dessauer, F. (1945). *Wilhelm C. Röntgen: Die Offenbarung einer Nacht*. Frankfurt am Main: Josef Knecht.

Engelbart, D. C. (1962). *Augmenting Human Intellect: A Conceptual Framework. Summary Report AFOSR-3223 under Contract AF 49 (638)-1024, SRI Project 3578 for Air Force Office of Scientific Research*. Stanford, CA: Stanford Research Institute.

Flichy, P. (2007). *The internet imaginaire*. Cambridge, MA: MIT Press.

Gaudreault, A., & Marion, P. (2005). A medium is always born twice. *Early Popular Visual Culture, 3*(1), 3–15.

Gell, A. (1998). *Art and agency: An anthropological theory*. Oxford: Clarendon Press.

Gillies, J., & Cailliau, R. (2000). *How the web was born: The story of the World Wide Web*. Oxford: Oxford University Press.

Godelier, E. (2007). "Do you have a garage?" Discussion of some myths about entrepreneurship. *Business and Economic History Online, 5*, 1–20.

Gorman, M. E., & Carlson, W. B. (1990). Interpreting invention as a cognitive process: The case of Alexander Graham Bell, Thomas Edison, and the Telephone. *Science, Technology & Human Values, 15*(2), 131–164. doi:10.1177/016224399001500201

Hafner, K., & Lyon, M. (1998). *Where wizards stay up late: The origins of the internet*. Boston, MA: Simon and Schuster.

Hu, T.-H. (2015). *A prehistory of the cloud*. Cambridge, MA: MIT Press.

Hubert, H., & Mauss, M. (1964). *Sacrifice: Its nature and functions*. Chicago, IL: University of Chicago Press.

Huhtamo, E. (2013). *Illusions in motion: Media archaeology of the moving panorama and related spectacles. Leonardo book series*. Cambridge, MA: MIT Press.

Katz-Kimchi, M. (2015). "Singing the strong light works of [American] engineers": Popular histories of the Internet as mythopoetic literature. *Information & Culture, 50*(2), 160–180.

Kris, E., & Kurz, O. (1979). *Legend, myth, and magic in the image of the artist: A historical experiment*. New Haven, CT: Yale University Press.

Lamb, B. (2015). Q&A with Andrew Keen. Retrieved January 20, 2016 from http://www.c-span.org/video/?323814-1/qa-andrew-keen&start=1973

Lesage, F., & Rinfret, L. (2015). Shifting media imaginaries of the web. *First Monday, 20*(10). doi:10.5210/fm.v20i10.5519

Loiperdinger, M. (2004). Lumière's arrival of the train: Cinema's founding myth. *The Moving Image, 4*(1), 89–118.

Mansell, R. (2012). *Imagining the internet: Communication, innovation, and governance*. Oxford: Oxford University Press.

Mauss, M. (1990). *The gift*. Abingdon: Routledge.

McPherson, S. (2009). *Tim Berners-Lee: Inventor of the World Wide Web*. New York, NY: Twenty-First Century Books.

Mosco, V. (2004). *The digital sublime: Myth, power, and cyberspace.* Cambridge, MA: MIT Press.

Natale, S. (2016). Unveiling the biographies of media: On the role of narratives, anecdotes and storytelling in the construction of new media's histories. *Communication Theory, 26*(4), 431–449. doi:10.1111/comt.12099

Natale, S., & Balbi, G. (2014). Media and imaginary in history: The role of the fantastic in different stages of media change. *Media History, 20*(2), 203–218. doi:10.1080/13688804.2014.898904

Natale, S., & Ballatore, A. (2014). The web will kill them all: New media, digital utopia, and political struggle in the Italian 5-Star Movement. *Media, Culture & Society, 36*(1), 105–121. doi:10.1177/0163443713511902

Nelson, T. H. (1987). *Computer lib: Dream machines.* Redmond, WA: Tempus Books of Microsoft Press.

Nye, D. E. (1994). *American Technological Sublime.* Cambridge, MA: MIT Press.

Olney, J. (1972). *Metaphors of self: The meaning of autobiography.* Princeton, NJ: Princeton University Press.

Ortoleva, P. (1996). Vite geniali: Sulle biografie aneddotiche degli inventori. *Intersezioni, 1*, 41–61.

Reeves, B., & Nass, C. I. (1996). *The media equation: How people treat computers, television, and new media like real people and places.* Stanford, CA: CSLI Publications.

Salus, P. H., & Vinton, G. (1995). *Casting the net: From ARPANET to internet and beyond.* Boston, MA: Addison-Wesley Longman.

Scholz, T. (2008). Market ideology and the myths of Web 2.0. *First Monday, 13*(3). doi:10.5210/fm.v13i3.2138

Schulte, S. R. (2013). *Cached: Decoding the internet in Global Popular Culture.* New York, NY: New York University Press.

Silverstone, R., & Haddon, L. (1996). Design and the domestication of information and communication technologies: Technical change and everyday life. In R. Mansell & R. Silverston (Eds.), *Communication by design: The politics of information and communication technologies* (pp. 44–74). Oxford: Oxford University Press.

Sirois-Trahan, J.-P. (2004). Mythes et limites du train-qui-fonce-sur-les-spectateurs. In V. Innocenti & V. Re (Eds.), *Limina: Le soglie del film* (pp. 203–216). Udine: Forum.

Tsivian, Y. (1994). *Early cinema in Russia and its cultural reception.* Abingdon: Routledge.

Unitarian Universalist Association. (n.d.). *7th principle: Respect for the interdependent web of all existence of which we are a part.* Retrieved January 20, 2016 from http://www.uua.org/beliefs/what-we-believe/principles/7th

Vogler, C. (2007). *The writer's journey. Mythic structures for writers.* Studio City, CA: M. Wiese Productions.

Wright, R. (1997). The man who invented the web. *Time Magazine, 149*(20), 64–68.

CHAPTER THREE

THE web's first 'Killer App'

SLAC National Accelerator Laboratory's World Wide Web site 1991–1993

JEAN MARIE DEKEN

INTRODUCTION

In the late 1960s, high energy physicists had an unusual problem: with Federal funding for physics research flowing into laboratories around the world, and experimental results proliferating at an ever-increasing rate, scientists now faced a logjam in communicating and analyzing theories and experimental results.[1] In 1968, W. K. H. 'Pief' Panofsky, director of the two-year old Stanford Linear Accelerator Center (SLAC),[2] along with Art Rosenfeld of the venerable Lawrence Radiation Laboratory, initiated an effort to address this vexing problem.

Panofsky, newly elected chairman of the Division of Particles and Fields (DPF) of the American Physical Society (APS) and newly elected Division Secretary Rosenfeld formed an alliance with three SLAC librarians—Louise Addis, Bob Gex and Rita Taylor. Together they would address the communications gridlock of accessing hardcopy pre-publication draft papers, or 'preprints' in the field of particle physics. This small group met headlong the insistent demands of the worldwide high energy physics community for near instantaneous access to the field's preprints, would be instrumental not only in the creation of the first world wide website in North American, but would also lead to the 'killer app,' (T. Berners-Lee, personal communication, April 11, 1997) that helped ignite the spread of the web beyond the boundaries of high-energy/particle physics.

The confluence of the group's timing, location, and community of practice were coincidental, yet critical to the success of their efforts. They began their collaboration at a decisive time in the evolution of electronic communications and information technology. Additionally, they were located in the heart of the technologically innovative Stanford research community and adjacent to the equally innovative start-ups of Silicon Valley. They themselves were important players within an international high energy/particle physics community poised to exploit new developments in communication for research and scholarly purposes.

WHY DO WE CARE/SHOULD WE CARE TODAY?

I embarked upon research into this history the day that a television reporter asked me, more than a bit incredulously; why it was that it was SLAC that had installed the first world wide website outside of Europe. At the time we were standing in the SLAC Archives and History Office storage area looking at the NeXT machine on which the web software had been mounted back in 1991, and the reporter's question caught me a bit off-guard. Why indeed? The laboratory is very proud of its status as a web pioneer, and as the laboratory archivist, I had become well acquainted with the local story of how and when the world wide web had come to SLAC, but up until then I had not thought about the 'why' of it in any detail. The history of the creation of the world wide web has been written about at length by the web's inventor and his colleagues (Berners-Lee, 1999; Gillies & Cailliau, 2000) but that history has tended to focus narrowly on the actions of a few individuals, and on developments and conditions at only a few locations. The reporter's question and my curiosity led me to investigate the wider context of the development of the world wide web and its early arrival at SLAC, and to look into concurrent and prior research and developments in Europe and in the United States. What I found tells an interesting and nuanced story about how widespread research and related innovations at that time pushed communications and publishing developments forward and helped place SLAC in position to take advantage of both.

METHODOLOGY AND SOURCES

I began with thorough readings of the web inventor's and his colleagues' accounts, and then delved into the accounts written by the SLAC group known as the 'World Wide Web Wizards' (Addis, 2002; Cottrell, 1994; Johnson, 1994; Kunz,1999; White, 1998; Winters, 1996). I also interviewed those Wizards still locally available: Louise Addis (personal communication, February 2, 2016) and Tony Johnson (personal communication, March 21 and 25, 2016). The SLAC Web Wizards' accounts led me investigate the communications research of Edward Parker (Parker, 1969, 1970). Parker's work in turn led me to investigate the ecology of information, communications, and publication services research from the 1960s through the time of the web's invention (Bourne & Bellardo, 2003; Lancaster & Owen, 1976; Wu, 2010). In keeping this account focused on the placement of SLAC in the larger information and publications context, I have necessarily only scratched the surface of developments in this fascinating area. Further work could well be done studying the many efforts at innovation in communications and publishing and analyzing the reasons why a few efforts have flourished over the long-term while many others have not.

STANFORD, SLAC AND SPIRES

Even before SLAC's official opening in 1966, research on the Stanford campus was underway to investigate ways to use computers to improve scholarly communication. Communications professor Edwin B. Parker, who had arrived at Stanford in 1962 from the University of Illinois, began studying the effects of communication media on human behavior by using the cohort of Stanford University physicists as his research subjects. The 5-year National Science Foundation (NSF)-funded project, entitled "Information Retrieval in High-Energy Physics," included all of the Stanford physicists busy with linear accelerators on campus, including those working on the blossoming SLAC project. The main outcome of Parker's efforts would be the Stanford Physics Information Retrieval System, soon known across the campus as SPIRES.

As he pursued his own research, Parker was well aware of the other online information retrieval research projects then underway. Parker and researchers at MIT working on the Intrex project were in contact with and influenced by each others' developments. Parker was also very aware of MIT's work on TIP (Technical Information Project), Harvard's on the SMART project (initially System for the Mechanical Analysis and Retrieval of Text); and other concurrent and predecessor university online information research projects (Bourne & Hahn, 2003). Parker's effort, however, utilized pre-existing electronic databases selected to be responsive to user needs, and he focused on the development of robust software and applications programming that did not rely on any manual indexing.

Despite its strong behavioral science approach, the SPIRES project also took an interest in the needs of scientists. "It is presumed that within the present (third) generation of computers and the present generation of communication satellites, that each of several scientific disciplines, including physics, will continue the development of national information systems" (Parker, 1967).

Parker's goal was to create something that scientists would not only actively use but could continue to develop. His choice of research subjects was inspired; he found a ready and willing collaborator in Louise Addis at SLAC. Addis, responsible for technical and public services for the SLAC Library, was keen to improve both, and she saw her collaboration with Parker as a means toward those ends. Parker saw the collaboration with Addis, whom he viewed as an influential science librarian who was also enthusiastic about technology and highly attuned to the needs of her patrons, as one of the key elements that distinguished his communications information system research project from the others (Parker, 1967).

The SPIRES project prioritized organization of both SLAC's growing preprint collection and use of the existing High Energy Physics Index (DESY-HEP) of Germany's Deutsches Elektronen Synchrotron (DESY). These were thought to most closely meet the goals of providing specialized users with access to the latest physics information (preprints) as well as to a relevant specialized database large enough to permit exhaustive retrospecive searches (Parker, 1970).

A FEW WORDS ABOUT 'PREPRINTS'

As early as the late 1950's, when Stanford still referred to its proposed two-mile linear accelerator as 'Project M,' Panofsky instructed his library staff to quickly acquire and catalog all high-energy physics preprints, regardless of the authors' institutional affiliations. With initial guidance and assistance from Luiselle Goldschmidt-Clermont, pre-print librarian at the European high-energy physics laboratory (CERN), the newly established SLAC library had succeeded in setting up a robust system for acquiring, cataloging and announcing preprints to the particle physics community, as well as a procedure of routinely discarding from the preprint collection those papers that had made their way into publication (Addis, 2002; Goldschmidt-Clermont, 2002; Vigen, 2002).

Although many disciplines circulate papers prior to their publication, preprints (or grey literature) are singularly important to high-energy physicists. CERN began its efforts to organize preprints in the 1960's under the leadership of Goldschmidt-Clermont (Vigen, 2002), who noted at the time that the importance of preprints in high-energy physics could be traced to high-energy physics' "rapidly developing science requiring large capital investments to carry out its experimental programs, relatively small number of laboratories involved but with world-wide geographical dispersion [and] traditional code of ethics widely accepted by the scientific community." (Goldschmidt-Clermont, 2002) Also lending itself to the importance of preprints in physics is that fact that, as has been noted elsewhere, physics theorists "live in a state of accelerated time that shapes their reading and publishing practices around a 24-hour cycle" (DelFanti, 2016).

In 1969, through the advocacy of Panofsky and Rosenfeld, the APS began subsidizing the weekly preparation, publication, and mailing of a new, hardcopy SLAC serial, *Preprints in Particles and Fields* (PPF). The goal of PPF was to quickly disseminate to an international mailing list the efforts of the preprint project, including brief citations of new preprints. PPF was wildly successful from the start; hundreds of physicists from around the world paid a modest annual subscription fee in order to receive their weekly copies via regular U.S. mail or airmail.

Contributing to the popularity of PPF, and perhaps even requiring it as a necessity, were several facts. No other indexing service at that time addressed itself to preprints, and those services that handled publications did not index beyond the first two or three authors' names. As a consequence, because authors were listed in alphabetical order, established physicists whose last names came toward the latter half of the alphabet (for example, Panofsky and Rosenfeld) as well as early-career physicists participating in a large experimental collaboration could be quite prolific writers and important contributors to physics papers, but never appear in the indexes of the discipline's literature. If an individual was not one of the first authors (hence, an indexed author) on a paper that had already been published (a process that took months), one could not find their work via a name search in the published indexes.

PPF neatly solved these problems, and the high-energy physics community's demand for its speedy and detailed information was insatiable. However, PPF almost immediately ran in to a bit of controversy. While PPF allowed physicists around the world to quickly acquire full citation information for unpublished papers relevant to their own current research, they began complaining that it was often difficult and sometimes impossible to obtain the full-text preprint papers. Physics journal publishers also complained, fearing that PPF would cut into their business, but they were somewhat mollified by the introduction in PPF of an 'Anti-Pre-Prints' section which listed full citations of papers now published and readily available to subscribers of the relevant journals. SLAC staff and visitors in residence enjoyed a distinct advantage over their non-local colleagues, since the locals' copies of PPF were received in the mail immediately, and the full-text preprints cited were available in hardcopy in the SLAC library stacks, centrally located at the lab.

A COMMUNITY OF TECHNOLOGY BUILDERS

As Segal has noted in his investigation into why the web came out of high-energy physics, the "community, run by physicists and engineers, is not afraid of taking a leading role to develop technologies that it considers essential." (Segal, 2012). I would further add that this community, in order to meet its own pressing needs, does not hesitate to quickly adopt new technologies developed by others. For example, since their publications rely heavily on mathematical notation, the high-energy physics community was an early, enthusiastic adopter of the robust notation-enabling typesetting program TeX, created by Stanford computer science professor Donald Knuth in the early 1980's (Knuth, 1984).

One among the many at SLAC on the cutting edge of technology useful to physics was Paul F. Kunz. Kunz received his PhD in physics from Princeton University in 1968 and came to SLAC in 1974. During his intial post-doctoral appointment with Professor David Leith's Experimental Group B, Kunz quickly addressed himself to the intersection of experimental physics and computer technology, studying the problems created by the mismatch between the rapid speed and high volume of experimental physics data generation and the relatively limited capacities of top-of-the-line mainframe computers then available.

His partial solution, implemented for SLAC's Large Aperture Solenoid Spectrometer (LASS) experiment, was an IBM mainframe emulator (168/E) designed to provide fast pre-processing of data by emulating an IBM 370/168. As fast as the mainframe IBM computer was at processing data (100 milliseconds per event), the rate of data generation and recording to tape by the LASS experiment was even faster (a new event every 10 milliseconds). Kunz's invention sat between the experimental data acquisition system and the mainframe and preprocessed the events "so as to cut down significantly the amount of computer time required to support a LASS experiment." He went on to note that, "with the advent of large detectors and relatively inexpensive read-out electronics, the problem of computer support for the data analysis in LASS is becoming a familiar one faced by many experimenters in high energy physics." (Kunz, 1976).

As Kunz suspected, the emulator he developed proved useful internationally to many high-energy physics experiments. As is typical of the community, physics labs continuously improved on the original emulator over the next few years, freely sharing their designs, specifications, and software for it.

Throughout the late 1970's and 1980's, Kunz remained deeply involved in developing and refining main-frame emulators, microcircuits, and software for physics. In the mid 1980's he also turned his attention to issues involving computer architecture and the proliferation of computer networking protocols (Kunz, 1984; Breidenbach,1988). He and his SLAC colleagues also acquired an early NeXT computer, and they undertook a project to develop a program for it for use in high-energy physics analysis (Atwood, 1990). The presence of several powerful NeXT machines at the lab, and the interest of lab staff in using them, proved important in the later installation of the web at SLAC.

W3 CROSSES THE POND

At the same time that Paul Kunz was busy at SLAC, Tim Berners-Lee was busy at CERN, where he played a somewhat parallel role. Berners-Lee's career at CERN and his invention of what became the world wide web are recounted in full detail elsewhere (Berners-Lee, 1999; Gillies & Cailliau, 2000). What is relevant to recount here is that Berners-Lee and Kunz knew each other through their independent work at their respective laboratories on the software and systems for high-energy physics data analysis, and through their mutual interest in using NeXT machines. They also each knew that the other was actively working on developing computer software and applications to enhance productivity in all aspects of their respective laboratories' experimental efforts.

While Berners-Lee had an undergraduate degree in physics, he had an established career as a computer scientist when he first came to CERN in 1980 as a microprocessor software developer for the lab's Proton Synchroton (PS) complex. It was during his first stint at CERN, as a contractor, that he began writing the documentation management program he named 'Inquire Within Upon Everything' (Gillies & Cailliau, 2000). During his subsequent tenure as a CERN employee, he further developed the software into a tool called the 'world wide web' (W3). While Berners-Lee was grappling with the electronic seeking, sharing and management of information at CERN, Kunz began assisting in SLAC's efforts to make high-energy preprints more easily and equitably available.

SPIRES-HEP DEBUTS

Addis continued to work with Parker on the SPIRES project and with her counterparts at CERN and DESY, and in 1974 spearheaded development of the new 'SPIRES-HEP' electronic database of high-energy physics preprint and publication citations, made freely available on-site at SLAC to anyone with a SLAC computer account. This electronic version of PPF was a breathtaking advance in speed of access to preprint information by local users, and further widened the advantage of SLAC practitioners over their remote colleagues both in the U.S. and abroad.[3] As the departures of post-docs, visiting and sabbatical physicists became imminent, they became increasingly reluctant to give up their SLAC email accounts—and with them the enhanced access to SPIRES-HEP that the accounts provided.

Abetted by Kunz, Addis initiated a significant enhancement to electronic access to the database in the mid 1980's when SLAC migrated to an IBM VM/CMS system capable of creating 'servers.' As a result, George Crane of SLAC's Computing Group developed the 'Remote SPIRES' software and set up a 'QSPIRES' (Query Spires) server on Bitnet, the cooperative national university computer network.[4] Based on an idea proposed by Kunz, this configuration, using both Bitnet and QSPIRES, made it possible for someone to query the SPIRES-HEP database without having an account on the SLAC computer system. Anyone who registered also could send a message or email to the QSPIRES server and receive a system-generated email response.

QSPIRES was an immediate success, and at its peak was responding to inquiries from 662 nodes in 44 countries. This setup dramatically improved remote access and leveled the home location playing field; it also satisfied, at least temporarily, the exponentially increasing demand for rapid and complete access to SPIRES-HEP. It was, as yet, less than ideal. The process of registering and managing the nearly 5,000 non-SLAC users was cumbersome and time-consuming for the SLAC Library staff to administer, in addition to their many other duties (Addis, 2002).

In the meantime, Addis had taken on a second job in 1988 with the newly created U.S. Superconducting SuperCollider (SSC) laboratory being built in Waxahatchie, Texas. Addis' SSC assignment was to assist the laboratory in the rapid establishment of their own research library. Many of the systems and services developed by and in use at SLAC could be imported wholesale to the new SSC Library, but technical difficulties were encountered in setting up a much-desired remote interface to the SLAC instance of SPIRES. On Addis' advice, SSC hired a University of California-Berkeley programmer familiar with SPIRES (and available to consult locally at SLAC with both Kunz and Johnson) to write an X-Windows interface for SSC. The effort proved to be difficult (L. Addis, personal communication, February 5, 2016).

Such was the state of affairs when Kunz finally accepted one of Berners-Lee's several invitations to visit his office at CERN to see a demonstration of the world wide web program. Kunz had previously been too busy, too disinterested in 'documentation management,' and too distracted by other priorities, to follow up until his visit to CERN in September 1991 (Severance, 2006). "Like me, he was an early NeXT enthusiast," Berners-Lee wrote about the demonstration to Kunz, "and he had come to CERN to work on some common NeXT programs. Since he had the right computer, he was in a position to use the web directly, and he loved it" (Berners-Lee, 1999; Severance, 2006).[5]

Kunz immediately saw how this tool would solve many of the issues facing Addis in providing networked access to the very demanding users of SPIRES-HEP (Severance, 2006). Kunz brought a copy the W3 program back to SLAC that September, and when he demonstrated it to Addis, she enthusiastically agreed that the web should be adopted to provide online access to SPIRES-HEP. Since Berners-Lee had developed the W3 software on a NeXT computer, they decided that the most effective approach would be to set up one of the SLAC NeXT machines with the W3 browser software and use SLAC's IBM VM mainframe as the server. There was a bit of delay in configuring the setup, but both were up and running on Thursday, December 12, 1991, with the browser installed on a NeXT machine located in an office in SLAC's Central Lab Building, around a corner and down the hall from the SLAC Library.

The next day, December 13, 1991, Berners-Lee sent an announcement to two of the CERN electronic mail lists, announcing the first U.S. website, stating: "There is an experimental W3 server for the SPIRES High energy Physics preprint database, thanks to Terry Hung, Paul Kunz and Louise Addis of SLAC" (SLAC AHO 2000-072B1f10). Addis and Kunz quickly realized that the world wide web could also be used to deliver SPIRES-HEP to the Library at the SSC, so the floundering effort to develop an X-Windows interface for that use was speedily abandoned (L. Addis, personal communication, February 5, 2016).

At this point, the W3 experimental server project could be thought of as indistinguishable from many other cutting-edge internet or document indexing and search projects then underway internationally. It was what happened over the next few months that, in large part, set this project apart from now lesser-known, less-long-lived peers. Because of the new enthusiasm for the web at SLAC, Berners-Lee and his CERN colleagues began to promote the web more aggressively (Berners-Lee, 1999).

Only one month after the SLAC server went live, while at a workshop of the High Energy Physics computing group held in January of 1992 in southern France, Berners-Lee concluded his presentation on the web by live-connecting to the SLAC SPIRES-HEP database (Kunz was attending the workshop, but did not know of the planned demonstration). The demonstration electrified the attendees, who quickly spread the word to their home institutions that access to SPIRES-HEP was now significantly easier to obtain. Just a few years later, Berners-Lee, in his keynote address to the 'Web History Day' of the Sixth International WWW Conference, told the assembly that the SPIRES-HEP database had proved to be the web's 'killer app' by providing a compelling use for this new technology. It also catalyzed users to expand the extent and reach of the web, and to employ the web in ways unanticipated by its creator (Berners-Lee, 1997).

The two years after the installation of SLAC's server saw rapid spread of use and new developments of the world wide web. By June 1992, web servers were running at three other physics laboratories: Fermi National Accelerator Laboratory (FNAL) near Chicago, Illinois; the Nationaal Instituut voor Kern- en Hoge Energie Fysika (NIKHEF) in the Netherlands; and the Deutsches Elektronen Synchrotron (DESY) in Germany. By October of the following year, there were more than 200 web servers around the world (Connolly, 2000).

New tools called 'web browsers' were quickly developed to facilitate web searching. The Viola browser, by Pei Wei of O'Reilly Associates, was reviewed favorably by Berners-Lee as early as May 1992; the MIDAS browser was released by SLAC physicist Tony Johnson in the fall of 1992; and the National Center for SuperComputing Application's (NSCA) Mosaic browser came out in February 1993. The first commercial web browser, Mosaic Netscape 0.9, followed in October 1994 (Zook, 2005).

World wide access to the web technology was dependent upon the internet, which had come into being out of U.S. government research projects on wide area networking, beginning with the ARPANET (1969–1990) and its spin-off networks. ARPANET originated with the Defense Department, but as time went on additional federal agencies became heavily involved in wide-area networking research, and in the early 1980's these agencies began creating their own networks. As early users of the government's wide-area networks, academics and government researchers had access to some of the most advanced computer wide-area networks of the time, but because they were government-funded projects, early use of the internet was limited to non-commercial activities. The March 1993 re-interpretation by the National Science Foundation of the internet's Acceptable Use Policy (AUP) opened the world wide web to commercial use. This announcement was followed a month later by CERN's decision to share the W3 technology at no cost.

Spurred on by the opportunities provided by the web, and encouraged as always by the persistent physics community, the SLAC Library obtained its own NeXT computer, along with a 1.3 gigabyte disk. Library staff began routinely converting and compressing full-text physics papers, also requesting that the papers' figures and illustrations be faxed by the authors directly to the library's new NeXT fax. The library staff converted such figures to Encapsulated PostScript (EPS) format and posted them, along with the papers' text, to the SLAC PostScript server (preprint. slac.stanford.edu). This enhanced workflow procedure meant that by June of 1993, for the first time the SPIRES-HEP could be searched using a Viola, MidasWWW, or Mosaic browser on an X-terminal. Users now could access more than the original simple citation; the full-text article, complete with equations (and often figures) could be displayed on the screen or printed by any user, around the world.

A mere eight weeks later, by August of 1993, SPIRES-HEP was handling 38,000 queries a month, of which, 15,000 were transacted via the web. The SPIRES-HEP electronic transition was completed when PPF ceased altogether its hard-copy publication in October 1993. The last hard-copy issue, published on October 1, announced the end of the line with an oversized text-box message on the cover page that read: "LAST ISSUE (PPF is continuing but in electronic edition only)." All of the information that was provided in the mailed hard-copy issues of PPF could now be provided much more rapidly via the SPIRES-HEP world wide website. That November, SLAC mounted its first official laboratory-wide web home page, with links to the growing number of pages produced by units across the lab and including the much-used SPIRES-HEP search page.

CONCLUSION

Dr. Louis Pasteur famously stated that "chance favors only the prepared mind." (Pasteur, 1854). There were many 'prepared minds' at work in the processes that ultimately brought the world wide web to SLAC and made the laboratory the site of the web's 'killer app.' The international preeminence of Panofsky and Rosenfeld in the field of high energy physics research, and their influence at their respective laboratories, gave them leverage to advocate effectively for faster and more efficient access to physics research information, in as close to real-time as possible.

The connection between Panofsky and Addis at SLAC ensured that the SLAC Library's participation in the international physics preprint project would flourish with robust support. Parker's Stanford University communications research project made an early and valuable connection with SLAC, and Parker's collaboration with Addis advanced the goals of both his research and her preprint indexing and dissemination efforts.

SLAC's original SPIRES-HEP database, just one outcome of Parker's project, was enthusiastically embraced by the physics community. It built upon the foundation of work with preprints at CERN, DESY, and SLAC, and took the hard-copy PPF into a digital environment where the amount of information provided and the timing of the communication of that information were greatly expanded and enhanced. While the physics community embraced the web-delivered SPIRES-HEP effort, they continued to agitate for more, faster, and fuller information. Addis and her team responded to this need by continually improving and expanding content, and by speeding up access, as quickly as technological developments and local resources allowed.

Kunz and Berners-Lee, active members of the physics research community, brought an impressive array of skills to bear on problems of computer access to information at their respective labs. As he worked on other SLAC projects, Kunz consulted with the SLAC Library team and became very familiar with the technological issues they faced. Berners-Lee, while also working on science projects at CERN, developed an elegant solution to the problems of access to distributed electronic documentation and information, although it would not be until 1991 that he could convince CERN's administration of the value of his world wide web.

Timing, location, and research community coalesced when Berners-Lee made his September 1991 demonstration to Kunz, and Kunz then realized that the utility of the web to help Addis take PPF and SPIRES-HEP to the next level. The newly empowered SPIRES-HEP database revealed to its avid users the elegance and power of the world wide web. As they had in the past with other technologies, the physics community responded with enthusiasm for this useful new tool, and again insisted on enhancements for a faster, more widely accessible, and yet more detailed level of information. Unafraid of taking a leading role in developing essential technologies, the high-energy physics community embraced the world wide web—and immediately set about expanding its reach and depth for their own uses. Onlookers and colleagues from related fields, as well as physicists themselves, participated in disseminating the use of the web outside the confines of high energy physics.

By extending the well-known concept of hyper-text from within the boundaries of a single machine to across the connections between machines, the world wide web brought the internet out of the small community of computer adepts and into the public sphere. The international high-energy physics community, along with the SLAC laboratory, served as a cold-frame nursery, or perhaps a petri dish, for the early germination and nurturing of the world wide web by happy circumstance and by design due to the unique information demands and advanced technical skills of these communities.

The SLAC website went live in December of 1991; Tim Berners-Lee electrified an audience of physicists with a live demonstration of the SPIRES-HEP killer-app web interface in January of 1992. By the start of 1993, two web browsers, Viola and Midas, had been developed and disseminated and there were 50 known HTTP servers in the world. Less than a year later there would be over 500 active HTTP servers; by June 1994 the number of HTTP servers would jump to an astounding 1,500 (Johnson, 1994).

As early as 1994, Tony Johnson described the world wide web as "the most significant development to have sprung from the world of high energy physics in the last few years" because "the web is able not only to access the entire spectrum of information available on the internet, but also to present it to the user using a single consistent easy-to-use interface." (Johnson, 1994). The enormity of this achievement may elude the 'digital native' individual of the present-day, but it shook the world in the early 1990s.

ACKNOWLEDGEMENTS

The author would like to thank Louise Addis, James Axline, George Crane, Tony Johnson, Roxanne Nilan, and James Reed, for their careful reading and helpful suggestions for improvements of this manuscript. Work on this manuscript has been supported by Department of Energy contract DE-AC02-76SF00515. Any errors, misstatements or opinions herein are the author's own, and are no reflection on the reviewers or the US DOE.

REFERENCES

Addis, L. (2002). *A brief and biased history of preprint and database activities at the SLAC library 1962–present*. Retrieved from http://www.slac.stanford.edu/spires/papers/history.html

Atwood, W. B. (1990). *The reason project*. Retrieved from http://www.slac.stanford.edu/cgi-wrap/getdoc/slac-pub-5242.pdf

Berners-Lee, T. (1997) Keynote Talk, W3C @ WW6. [Powerpoint slides] Retrieved from https://www.w3.org/Talks/9704WWW6-tbl/

Berners-Lee, T., & Fishetti, M. (1999). *Weaving the web*. New York, NY: Harper Collins.

Breidenbach, M. (1988) Status Report on the SLD Data Acquisition System SLD Collaboration. *IEEE Transactions in Nuclear Science*. 36 (1989) 23–28 SLAC-PUB-4786, C88-11-09 DOI: 10.1109/23.34395

Bourne, C. P., & Bellardo Hahn, T. (2003). *A history of online information services, 1963–1976*. Cambridge, MA: MIT Press.

Connolly, D. (2000). *A little history of the world wide web*. Retrieved from http://www.w3.org/History.html

Cottrell, R. (1994). *Networking with China*. Retrieved from http://slac.stanford.edu/pubs/slacpubs/6250/slac-pub-6478.pdf

DelFanti, A. (2016). Beams of particles and papers: The role of preprint archives in high energy physics. Retrieved from https://arxiv.org/ftp/arxiv/papers/1602/1602.08539.pdf

Gillies, J., & Cailliau, R. (2000). *How the web was born*. New York, NY: Oxford University Press.

Goldschmidt-Clermont, L. (2002) Communication patterns in high-energy physics, *High Energy Physics Libraries Webzine*, 6. Retrieved from http://library.cern.ch/HEPLW/6/papers/1/

Johnson, T. (1994). Spinning the world wide web. *Beam Line*, Fall/Winter *24*(3/4), 2–9.

Knuth, D. (1984) *The T_EX Book*. Menlo Park, CA: Addison Wesley.

Kunz, P. (1976) The LASS Hardware Processor. *Nuclear Instruments and Methods* 135 (p. 435). SLAC-PUB-1723; DOI: 10.1016/0029-554X(76)90056-2

Kunz, P. (1984) The 3081/e Processor. SLAC-PUB-3332, CERN/DD/84/4. Retrieved from http://inspirehep.net/

Kunz, P. (1999) *Bringing the web to America*. [Video]. Retrieved from Interlab99: http://web.archive.org/web/20030824115014/http:/www-conf.slac.stanford.edu/interlab99/program/kunz-web-to-america.htm

Lancaster, F., & Owen, J. (1976). Information retrieval by computer. In D. Hammer (Ed.), *The information age: Its development and impact* (pp. 1–33). Metuchen, NJ: Scarecrow Press.

Parker, E. B. (1969) Developing a campus based information retrieval system. *Proceedings, Stanford conference on collaborative library systems development* (p. 213–30). SU Libraries: ERIC document number ED 031 281

Parker, E. B. (1970). *SPIRES (stanford physics information retrieval system) 1969–1970 annual report to the National Science Foundation*. Stanford, CA: Institute for Communication Research.

Parker, E. B. (1971). *Requirements for SPIRES II: An external specification for the stanford public information retrieval system*. Stanford, CA: University Computation Center (NSF Report).

Pasteur, L. (1854). Lecture, University of Lille, December 7. Retrieved from *Wikiquote*: https://en.wikiquote.org/wiki/Louis_Pasteur

Segal, B. (2012). Why HEP invented the web? In R. Brun, F. Carminati, & G. Gall-Carminati (Eds.), *From the web to the grid and beyond: Computing paradigms driven by high-energy Physics* (pp. 55–67). Berlin: Springer-Verlag.

Severance, C. (Interviewer) (2006, November 5). Sakai video report. *Internet and web pioneers: Dr. Paul Kunz SLAC the first web server in America*. Retrieved from https://www.youtube.com/watch?v=lOgqP2yoKwc

Vigen, J. (2002). New communication channels: Electronic clones, but probably the first steps towards a new paradigm. *High Energy Physics Libraries Webzine*, 6 (March). Retrieved from http://webzine. web.cern.ch/webzine/6/papers/2/

White, B. (1998). The world wide web and high-energy physics. *Physics Today*, *51*, 30–36.

Winters, J. (1996). Designing the SLAC information architecture: A workplace for users. *In Interlab '96*. Retrieved from http://www.slac.stanford.edu/grp/scs/net/talk/ilab96/winters/index.htm

Wu, T. (2010). The master switch: The rise and fall of information empires. New York, NY: Vintage.

Zook, M. A. (2005). *The geography of the internet industry: Venture capital, dot-coms, and local knowledge.* Oxford: Blackwell Publishing.

NOTES

1. The idea for a two-mile linear accelerator at Stanford University was conceived in 1956, proposed in 1957, and authorized by Congress in 1961. Initially called 'Project M,' the venture was renamed the 'Stanford Linear Accelerator Center' (SLAC) in August of 1960, and again renamed 'SLAC National Accelerator Laboratory' in October 2008. Further information about the history of SLAC can be found at http://www.slac.stanford.edu/history/history.shtml.

2. In 1953 the total U.S. federal government spending on research was $20.2B; by 1963 it rose to $106.3B (National Science Foundation, National Patterns of R&D Resources survey data (http://www.aas.org/page/historical-trends-federal-rd))

3. Addis and Parker won the 1983 Special Libraries Association Physics-Astronomy-Mathematics Division Award for SPIRES-HEP, the first time the award was given for an online database, rather than a print publication (Addis, 2002).

4. 'Because It's Time' network. Founded in 1981 by Ira Fuchs at CUNY and Greydon Freeman at Yale for academic institutions across the United States. Corporation for Research and Educational Networking (CREN). A Brief History of BITNET. Bit.net. Retrieved January 19, 2016.

5. Kunz puts date of visit as September, Berners-Lee as May of 1991.

CHAPTER FOUR

Untangling THE threads

Public discourse on the early web

MARGUERITE BARRY

If you're interested in using the code, mail me. It's very prototype, but available by anonymous FTP from info.cern.ch. It's copyright CERN but free distribution and use is not normally a problem [...]. The WWW project was started to allow high energy physicists to share data, news, and documentation. We are very interested in spreading the web to other areas, and having gateway servers for other data. Collaborators welcome!"[1]

INTRODUCTION

When Tim Berners-Lee sent an email to the alt.hypertext newsgroup in August 1991, describing the 'WWW project', little did he expect it would later be regarded as marking the birth of the web.[2] It was not a formal announcement of a major technological breakthrough, but just a reply to a query on work in progress, offering access for the first time to the hypertext community outside CERN to its experimental communication network. However, his informal language and collaborative spirit set the tone for how the web would subsequently be disseminated and received.

The description of a 'very prototype' project suggests an early iteration, a stage designed to study the feasibility of a technical process (Beaudoin-Lafon & Mackay, 2009). A request for expressions of interest is the logical next step in testing feasibility. But testing through "free distribution and use" rather than further internal iterations mirrors an unusual project goal of sharing data. The www project would be made 'available' using FTP protocols from the CERN server, in other words, to those with the knowledge and means to do so. The implied institutional support ("not normally a problem") also matched the project aims, allowing researchers to access protocols and configure more servers to allow 'other data' beyond high-energy physics, to be shared. A final salute welcoming 'collaborators' celebrates the shared spirit of research, which was itself being increasingly mediated by the internet (see Flichy, 2007). Although supportive, CERN management were also conflicted about allocating further resources to the project (Gillies & Cailliau, 2000), thus compelling researchers to turn to their external community. To succeed, this project would have to be released from the constraints of the research lab into the wild.

A different historical narrative could tell of a press release announcing "Invention of World Wide Web!" with formal language and a structured release, establishing intellectual property rights and so on. Media reports would cement this language in public discourse and its availability would be circumscribed. But instead, the inclusive tone of the email characterised the conditions in which the web would grow from being *available* to selected experts to becoming universally *accessible*. This distinction is important for understanding how the web trickled out into the public domain—it would not be an overnight process. The 'web' as an entity did not appear in international print media until December 1992, well over a year after the Berners-Lee email. The 'world wide web' was born but had to take unpredictable paths outside its domestic origins, becoming a 'feral' technology (after Fuller & Matos, 2011) for a while at least. Its journey would yield an alternative and more utopian ecology for expansion.

PUBLIC INTEREST AND PUBLIC DISCOURSE ON THE WEB

The history of the web has been well documented from engineering and technical perspectives (Gillies & Cailliau, 2000), through personal narratives (Berners-Lee & Fischetti, 1999), in accounts of web cultures, industries and historiographical challenges (Brügger, 2012) and in its social production through influential US discourses (Flichy, 2007). The inherent 'public interest' in such a global communication network (Mansell, 2012) and aspects of governance, access and competition have been the focus of much historical analysis (see Braman, 2011; Denardis, 2009). Yet we have little information about how the web entered general public discourse. When did the first reports emerge and what did they describe? Did they recognise this revolution in communication technologies?

Public discourses contain a wide variety of perspectives on the early web that are concurrent with its diffusion and thus historically valuable. Print news anchors public discourse in a particular time and place, relating it to key events that illustrate the social, cultural and political context in documents of record. Discourses around the web often communicate utopian visions for what it could be; indeed conflicting discourses around such new technologies are also an integral part of their development as systems (Flichy, 2007). Yet public discourse is less controlled and shaped than formal concurrent or retrospective narratives, utopian or otherwise. It allows for contradictions and unforeseen associations, which help us understand how the web arrived and whether the early vision for it remained—free distribution and use, sharing information, availability—or if the focus shifted. Public discourse also reveals geographical and cultural differences and the discourse communities visible in the coverage which shape and influence discussion. The findings reveal a dynamic set of narratives from early articles capitalising the 'Web' and explaining its operation, to differing perspectives on its structure and scale, to visions of its commercial vs. utopian potential towards a growing recognition of its ordinary domesticated uses in society.

Why discourse analysis?

The news media reflect how journalists (and others) represented the early web, how they thought readers should be informed about it and what they considered to be in the public interest, comprising a valuable historical record. Texts, whether news or otherwise, are not neutral but are sites of struggle that show traces of different discourses and ideologies competing for dominance. Critical discourse analysis frequently uses print media, and considers it "very rare that a text is the work of only one person" (Wodak & Meyer, 2009, p. 10). News texts often have a double structure or purpose, telling a *story* while also making an *argument*, often through "judicious" editing (Van Leeuwen, 2008, p. 352).

This study adopts a descriptive discourse analysis approach (Gee, 2014) to pick apart the language around the early web. It is not a search for truth or a critique of other histories but aims to widen discussion (Jorgensen & Phillips, 2002), towards understanding its subsequent reception. Tracking both the quantity and quality of discourses during the web's early years provides insights into its reception and evaluation. For example, Braman's (2011, 2012) analyses of discourses in the Requests for Comments (RFC) series on the early internet, highlight the value of bringing different discourses together as a contribution to understanding our "shared sociotechnical space" (2011, p. 307). Similarly, this analysis presents the variety of commentary in public discourses as a collective real time negotiation of the many threads weaving the early web.

ANY NEWS? STUDYING THE BIRTH

To get a sense of the scope and style of early web coverage, a mixed method content and discourse analysis was implemented. The sample was obtained from a keyword search for 'world wide web' from 1991 to 1994, in the LexisNexis 'Major World publications (English)' source, containing 193 international titles regarded as reliable for content reliability and accuracy of reporting.[3] Of these, 30 titles, which contain complete archives for the timeframe, returned results for the search, representing North America, Europe and Asia and delivering a total of 412 articles for analysis. Although it is not possible to state the total sample possibly available from other archive sources, this is greater than the sample size stated to be required in comparable longitudinal research in the literature on content analysis sampling (see Lacy, Riffe, Stoddard, Martin, & Chang, 2001). For the discourse analysis, 25 articles were chosen according to a number of criteria including frequency of keywords, relevance of keywords to discussion and intertextual discourse material available, following a methodological approach in similar public discourse studies (Barry, 2012; Barry & Doherty, 2016).

References to 'www' in print media

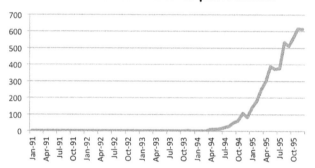

Figure 4.1: No. of articles making reference to the 'world wide web' in major (English language) international newspapers on a monthly basis from August 1991 to December 1995 (Source: LexisNexis search results)

Table 4.1: Number of articles per month for each year from 1991 to 1995 referencing the 'world wide web' in international newspapers.

	1991	1992	1993	1994	1995
January	0	0	0	2	141
February	0	0	1	2	181
March	0	0	1	0	251
April	0	0	0	11	299
May	0	0	0	12	388
June	0	0	0	14	373
July	0	0	0	22	377
August	0	0	0	31	535

	1991	1992	1993	1994	1995
September	0	0	1	51	512
October	0	0	0	64	565
November	0	0	5	108	617
December	0	1	2	83	613
Total	0	1	10	401	4852

The 'world wide web' received no mention in 1991 and only appears once in international print media in 1992, for the first time on December 27th in *The Washington Post*. It then appears in just ten articles in 1993, finally gaining traction from April 1994 onwards (see Table 4.1). The total figure rises to 401 articles in 1994 and reaches almost 5000 in 1995, which, while not part of the analysis, indicates that in quantitative terms, the web had arrived.

Table 4.2: Number and percentage of articles from 1992 to 1994 by geographic location.

Location	No. of articles 1992–1994	% 1992–1994
UK	130	31.6%
US	128	31.1%
Australia	94	22.8%
Canada	30	7.3%
Hong Kong, Singapore, Japan	21	5.1%
Ireland	5	1.2%
Scotland	4	1%

From 1992 to 1994, most of the coverage arose in UK and US publications (c. 31% each), followed by Australia (22%) with some notable coverage from Canada (7%) and Asia (5%)—see Table 4.2. In terms of individual publications during that period, the *Guardian* (UK) has largest number of articles referencing the web (92), following by *The Age* (Australia) at 62 and the *New York Times* at 38.

The following discourse analysis examines selected coverage from 1992 to 1994 in key publications and locations, through a detailed inspection of language, references, genre of writing, use of metaphor and so on, with a particular focus on recurring and/or conflicting themes. It examines 25 articles in detail (see Appendix B) but includes many more in describing overall tone and style in coverage, generating discourse themes that include: early descriptions of the web and its 'content'; a procedural 'how to' style of reporting; limited availability and increased accessibility; commercial vs. utopian discourses around access; claims over 'parenthood' of the web; conceptualisation of users; concerns around science communication; cats on the web and the (re)domestication of the web in the home.

1992: First impressions

The first article to mention the 'web' quite appropriately concerns a pending birth, reporting on a pregnant woman who joined an "electronic forum […] because she was overdue and felt like 'the Goodyear blimp'". The article explains where to find such a 'forum':

> The Internet, the world's largest collection of computer networks, was begun by the federal government in the mid–1980s as a research tool, and now is growing so fast that even federal officials aren't exactly sure what resources are on it. Its newest programs include […] a growing database called the World Wide Web, which offers easy access to information about the sciences, arts, politics and geography. Specialists who use the Internet say its most valuable resource may be the people connecting to it […]. (*Washington Post*, December 27, 1992)

This report reflects a common 'technology in society' discourse (see Barry, 2001) by introducing a human 'problem' (pregnant, concerned) and its technological 'solution' (the web). Although merely a 'database' on the internet, the web is 'new', growing beyond 'federal' governance and gives 'easy access' to information—an irresistible combination for any human problem. This characterisation reflects public interest concerns over governance at the time (Mansell, 2012), yet the lack of structure might also offer the only route to innovation (Barlow, 1996, see also "How John Perry Barlow views", 2016). Unnamed 'specialist' users make some prescient observations on its social potential but elaborate no further.

This explanatory style of reporting continues into 1993, where each article offers a definition of the web, clearly not yet a familiar term for readers, for example: "[…] the World Wide Web, makes available physicists' research from many locations" (*New York Times*, February 1993); "[…] the World-Wide Web is an attempt to link textual data that sits on hundreds of machines using hypertext" (*The Age*, March, 1993). It reappears only in September where the *Guardian* reports on the "World Wide Web […] the name of a point-and-click Internet access program developed at CERN and placed in the public domain earlier this year". This is a key development in the story of the web, ensuring free access to the source code, protecting the web from commercial control. However, its significance is not yet realised, as reporters perhaps do not imagine 'physicists' research' and 'hypertext' will catch on. Public domain does not yet equate with public discourse.

1993: Who's daddy?

By November, the 'Business Technology' section of the *New York Times* (*NYT*) still has little expectation of familiarity among readers, but seeks to generate interest in the web because:

> [...] at the National Center for Supercomputer Applications [NCSA] [...] a new service that answers requests to an electronic library called the World Wide Web, has seen the number of daily queries explode [...]. (*NYT,* November, 1993)

This report is significant in a number of respects. First, it links the web with the NCSA, where the first graphical browser Mosaic was being developed, reflecting complex background events. Berners-Lee and Fischetti (1999) recall being suspicious that the NCSA "were attempting to portray themselves as the centre of Web development and to basically rename the Web as Mosaic" (*ibid.*, p. 75). Parenthood of the web was under question in public discourse.

Secondly, this report introduces the first transport metaphor in public discourse, describing access to the web as 'gridlock', like 'rush hour' and having to "sit in the car and wait [...]" This early critique of web hype suggests something problematic in its structure and governance. Readers not yet familiar with the web might even be disinclined towards it. The article quotes 'experts' saying changes are needed in its "disorganized and largely voluntary system" and makes clear which experts are heard:

> Economists who have studied the Internet say one potential way to ease the approaching gridlock will be to charge for services, thereby generating the capital to meet the required performance upgrades.

The article follows these economists with a series of quotes from network administrators, ISP providers, an IBM/MCI joint venture executive, a university economist and the founder of Infoseek, who observes: "the more customers we have using information [...] the more money we have to spend to handle the load." The *story* of this article may be about growth and scale, but the structure of its supporting quotes presents an *argument* for regulation and commercialisation of the web. Over the space of five articles in less than 12 months, public discourse (in the US at least) has moved from how the web "offers easy access to [...] sciences, arts, politics and geography" (*Washington Post*, December 27 1992) to the need for "rethinking free information" (*NYT,* November 3 1993). Both its parenthood and free availability are under threat.

A week later, parenthood is reclaimed in the UK—"the Internet-based World Wide Web (WWW or W3) project stems from CERN", (*Guardian* November 11, 1993). Readers are asked to "imagine a system that links all the text, data, digital sounds, graphics and video on all the world's computers into a single interlinked hypermedia 'web'". If readers have to 'imagine' it, they have possibly not yet seen it and even the system's name remains enigmatic. The article continues:

[…] any (authorised) person should be able to access it from anywhere in the world, using one simple program. The system allows for different information formats so that existing and future information need not be especially tailored to be accessible […].

Although access 'should' be possible for anyone, the notion of authorisation implies access as *permission*. The issue is not just commercialisation versus freedom of information, but the potential for different levels of access to the web—political, economic and physical. This, the article resignedly admits, will 'inevitably' lead to a system where "information providers can charge users for information". It then offers instructions:

To access the World Wide Web, telnet to info.cern.ch (128.141.201.74). This will bring up a simple text-based query system with pointers to information on the Web. Mosaic is available by anonymous ftp from ftp.ncsa.uiuc.edu […].

Such access details, found more frequently in UK articles than elsewhere, make for striking reading. It reflects how web access was still a technical operation, but moving within reach of individual 'dial-up' users, a rich potential market for the web and a valuable new demographic among newspaper readers.

Front-end innovation vs. back-end frustration

In a year-end financial feature, the *New York Times* invites readers to "Think of it as a map to the buried treasures of the Information Age" [*NYT* December 8, 1993]. This 'it' is not the web however, but the new Mosaic browser, which is "so popular that its use is causing data traffic jams on the Internet". Traffic metaphors are now complimentary. Conflating the browser with the network privileges the front-end software. A sub-headline announces that Mosaic—the first 'killer app' of network computing—offers "A Better Way to Browse" [*sic*]. The web itself meanwhile is relegated to:

[…] an international string of computer databases that uses an information-retrieval architecture developed in 1989 by Tim Berners-Lee, a British computer specialist at the CERN physics laboratory in Geneva

While at least crediting its founder, the article pitches the physicist's older European architecture against Mosaic, "created by a small group of software developers and students at the supercomputer center in Champaign, who set out 18 months ago to create a system for browsing through the World-Wide Web". This discourse promotes youth, efficiency and goal-oriented processes over grand open visions. Before Mosaic, according to the article, finding information meant "knowing—and accurately typing—arcane addresses and commands like Telnet […]" Unlike the *Guardian*, the *NYT* would not offer such instructions to readers.

The article quotes Berners-Lee on his moment of realisation about the web's value, which he describes as "the difference between the brain and the mind [...] Explore the Internet and you find cables and computers. Explore the Web and you find information." Thus, the *story* offers a 'eureka' moment of invention, popular in technology narratives though not necessarily representative of how innovation actually happens (Flichy, 2007; Winston, 1998). But the *argument* is that the older web 'architecture' needs a new 'system' to improve it. Berners-Lee later reflected that the media "didn't take the time to investigate deeper [and] started to portray Mosaic as if it were equivalent to the Web" (1999, p. 78), clearly a source of frustration to him. Although an intertextual analysis cannot reveal how discourse is constructed, it does suggest the possibility that his involvement in the article was part of an attempt to join the discourse and set the record straight.

The article amplifies its argument by quoting 'passionate proponents' of Mosaic: a computing researcher says it gives "a sense of limitless opportunity"; Mitch Kapor, founder of Lotus and "evangelist for Mosaic" describes it as "a turning point"; it is "the first window into cyberspace" according to the director of the NCSA, while a telecoms industry representative claims "very quickly we'll have a new Madison Avenue kind of industry". Another sub-headline states the 'sudden and dramatic' success of Mosaic is "Helping Shape a Debate" around the national information infrastructure. Only Tim O'Reilly (of O'Reilly publishing) provides a contrary voice, applauding attempts to bring the "exciting end of the internet" (the web) to "the average user", but protesting that Mosaic is "currently for the haves [...]" Browsers are worthless unless the 'average user' can actually get online. O'Reilly, however, is not disinterested either, having coincidentally just launched his $100 'Internet-in-a-box' software package to bring users online. Clearly, the discourse communities represented in coverage are no more neutral than the texts.

Finally, the article explains Mosaic's 'point and click' system for exploring treasures of the web: 'click' to view a selection of cultural artefacts in France, or NASA satellite movies, or President Clinton's speeches, or digital music samples from MTV or to see if "a certain coffee pot in a computer science laboratory at Cambridge University in England is empty or full."[4] There is undoubtedly some cultural stereotyping in these examples—France is synonymous with art and culture, the US with global and state affairs and the UK with quirky academic humour. The realisation has yet to dawn that music sharing, the real 'killer app' of the internet, would deprive MTV of such future cultural relevance.

April 1994: The arrival of the web

Coverage of the web begins quietly in 1994. By March, just four articles refer to the web (from the US, Canada, Australia and UK), mostly reviews of 'how to' books for internet 'beginners' and some commentary on web user growth. Suddenly however, coverage ramps up with 11 articles appearing in April and increasing each month thereafter to 108 in November alone. The year total (401) shows a 40-fold increase in coverage over 1993—the web had arrived.

Certain events in the preceding months undoubtedly played a role in pushing the web onto the news agenda: the launch of Netscape (by ex-NCSA researchers) to produce commercial web browsers, America Online's new 'mainstream service' for home users, (triggering complaints about a potential 'flood'[5]) and major news organisations launching 'experimental' websites of their own—a vote of confidence in the project.[6] Each had a particular impact on consolidating this new demographic of 'average user'. Meanwhile, world news events in April included South Africa's first free democratic elections, where Nelson Mandela was sworn in as president, and the death of Kurt Cobain. An extended feature published in the UK *Observer* (April 30, 1994) and syndicated in Canada's *Gazette* (May 7, 1994) uses both stories to illustrate the power of the web:

> Moments after Kurt Cobain's corpse had been found, Nirvana fans were able to console one another instantly and across continents. Only last week, even while newspaper plants were just starting to churn into action, an infonaut in a London bedroom was flicking through the first returns from the South African elections, relayed by a new voter in Johannesburg, the ink still stained on his fingers.

While perhaps no different to news at any other time, events have taken on a new significance due to the web. The speed of communication is suddenly a competitor to the 'churn' of newspapers, giving 'infonauts' the ability to explore, communicate and console each other in ways that paper and ink cannot. This empowering aspect of the web's interactivity would continue to have a strong discursive force in later years (see Barry & Doherty, 2016).

April 1994 also saw the start of the Rwandan genocide, a catastrophic event arising in coverage throughout the year due in part to awareness and fundraising activities on the web, showcasing alternative uses in attracting new users, for example:

> ReliefRock is on EarthWeb's World Wide Web server at the URL (Uniform Resource Locator or address) of: http://www.earthweb.com:2800/reliefrock.html Users can also Gopher there via earthweb.com 2801, or by telnetting to telnet earthweb.com 280 [...].
> (*Guardian*, October 10, 1994)

Readers today might find this a convoluted approach to advertising a fundraising concert, but it illustrates how then, a 'website' was still an unfamiliar concept. Web content was described in terms of 'access' to it rather than by its 'address', rather like showing someone how to receive a letter without a standardised postal system. Many users still had only text browsers, hence naming both the server (hosting the site) and the URL (its address).[7] Although the web was growing, 'Gopher' and 'Telnet' instructions were required for many still accessing the internet via alternative protocols, at least in the UK.[8] Indeed computer science researchers were only beginning to examine what people were even doing on the web, with the first studies emerging on such activities as 'general' and 'serendipitous' browsing (e.g. Catledge & Pitkow, 1995).

Average users—Infonauts in search of URLs

By mid–1994, a new style of news report was shaping discourse around the web, where dedicated 'tech' journalists showed readers how to access it and what could be found. Newspapers had dedicated web sections, for example 'Netwatch' in the *Guardian*, 'Cyberspace' in the *Observer* and the *New York Times* and 'Computimes' in the *Irish Times*. Most coverage still remained in the financial and business pages however, revealing how editors characterised their readership for web coverage.[9] These 'how to' reports (see Table 4.3) directly address a new demographic, who may not have had institutional access or support, thus meeting the needs of 'home' users who needed information on accessing the web.

Table 4.3: A selection of the 'How to' articles appearing with increasing frequency in 1994.

Article	Source
How to access the vast data of Internet Hardware/Software	*Globe and Mail*, (Canada), May 15, 1994
GETTING CONNECTED; Wendy Grossman weighs up the ways on to the Net	*The Guardian* (UK), May 26, 1994
INTERNET: UNTANGLING THE THREADS; Just having a connection to the Internet is not enough, you need the software to make the best use of it.	*The Guardian* (UK), June 2, 1994
Caught in a Web: Point-and-click methods promise to make the Internet more accessible than ever	*Irish Times* (Ireland), September 9, 1994
AN BEGINNER'S GUIDE TO Going Online	*Newsweek* (USA), November 1994
The Executive Computer; Getting On-Line—the Microsoft Way	*New York Times* (USA), November 20, 1994
Are you connected to the Net?	*Straits Times* (Hong Kong), December 12, 1994

Then, a rare cosmic event in 1994 triggered bigger questions on the impact of this new medium:

> The Web came into its own this year when the comet Shoemaker Levy-9 dive-bombed into Jupiter, with the latest images surfacing on the Internet hours before they were broadcast through the more conventional media. (*Independent*, December 12, 1994)

Astronomer and science communication researcher Steve Miller expressed concern about the web and its "public dissemination of scientific information":[10]

> […] messages were arriving faster than they could be read […].Observers and theoreticians alike were under great pressure to announce or interpret the latest hot discovery. Science had to be carried out on the hoof. (*Guardian*, December 15, 1994)

Somewhat ironically, the 'average user' was becoming interested in physics after all. Meanwhile the web was displaying its capacity to dismantle traditional information distribution structures. Miller's concern however, is with simplistic connections being made between the availability of scientific information on the web and a "return to the happy days of the 18th and early 19th century when the present cultural divide between scientists and the rest did not exist". His interjection is one of the first social science commentaries to enter public discourse on the web, a sign of wider recognition of its significance and potential.

Bringing it all back home

At the first world wide web conference held at CERN in 1994, Berners-Lee recalls being struck by meeting people using the web in all sorts of unforeseen ways. In particular, one user "had a home server that allowed people to visit his house, look at a cutaway model of it, see where the computers were in it and browse his bookshelves" (1999, p. 93). This concept of bringing the web into the home was also taking root in public discourse, especially following the launch of the White House website by the Clinton administration in October 1994, which received extensive coverage worldwide. Although the site mostly focused on official presidential information, it was the "cutesy pictures of the president's family" with 'cheery welcomes', 'guest book' and 'virtual tour' that drew most attention in Australia (*The Age*, November 15, 1994). Pictures of the first family and their pets seemed to bind the 'website' with the concept of 'home' in public discourse and also established the culturally critical role of cats on the web.[11] Indeed, 'home' arises as both a structural and structuring element of the web:

> When you find a Web site, its home page will appear like a welcome mat, indicating what's available on that server and suggesting other places that might be interesting. (*Sydney Morning Herald*, November 8, 1994)

The 'home' page helps domesticate users to the culture of the web. Articles explain how browsers even have a built-in a 'homing' device—"preconfigured to connect to its 'home' WWW server on startup" [*Guardian*, June 2, 1994]. Users are being encouraged to join a 'homesteading' movement on the web—"build an interactive 'Home Page,' post your wedding photos, and invite the world to help you name your first child" [*Washington Post*, November 7, 1994]—and potentially increase their social capital, where "the audience for any home page is the whole world" [*Washington Post*, December 4, 1994]. After all, "everyone seems to want their own home page […] a URL on your business card says more about you than e-mail ever can" [*Guardian*, October 20, 1994]. The 'home page' has a valuable social cachet, privileging the web over other internet services. By the end of 1994, even Santa Claus has joined in, giving "easy access to the North Pole from home computers" (*Gazette*, December 21, 1994).

These discourses reflect the domestication of the web where, like Socks the cat,[12] a technology becomes house-trained. It adapts to people by becoming easier to access and use, while the home environment itself becomes increasingly mediated by the web (see also Berker, Hartmann, Punie, & Ward, 2006). Throughout 1994, everyday domestic events are happening on the web: "Students can order pizza via Internet" (*Gazette Canada*, August 24, 1994), "Flowers by Internet courtesy of Mosaic" (*Globe and Mail*, June 15, 1994) along with reports on localised cultural 'homepages' for hockey (Canada) or football (UK) coverage. This diffusion targets readers of markedly different cultural interests, illustrating that there is (or soon will be) a website for everyone and everything.

Concerns with the effects of domestication however, also arise in a syndicated article published in two locations with two very different headlines. The original article titled "A Network Heaven in Your Own Front Room" in the UK (*Guardian* April 30) is re-titled "Anarchy on the information superhighway: from science and communications to evil and the bizarre" (*Gazette* May 7) in Canada. The author addresses the technological invasion of the homestead in light of the lack of regulation and the reality that "no one owns the internet":

> […] a world where governments have next to no power, and where children are equal, if not superior, to adults. It is a world of philosophers and bandits, of big business and science. It is a place where pornographers and Nazis walk freely, where criminals roam unchecked and where anarchy reigns […]

Conflicting discourses around the heavenly/evil web reflect technological determinist perspectives on new media entering the home (see Haddon, 2006; Kraut & Brynin, 2006; Silverstone 2006). But moral panic (for Canada at least) subsides into a discussion of information freedom, education and opportunities for the less-abled, while also addressing the threat of 'disenfranchisement', as the web becomes "as necessary a part of your life as having a telephone today". Lastly, the article describes how all these possibilities and networks "are connected to each other in the form of a world-wide web […]" and thus for the first time, we see the web in print news in lower-case lettering, no longer a subset of the internet, but a familiar and everyday phenomenon.

WEAVING FURTHER DISCOURSES ON THE WEB

North American discourses on 'home' in the sample align with Flichy's (2007) discourses of the *imaginaire*, joining similar socio-cultural themes of 'frontier' 'community' and 'individualism'. UK discourses however, tend to focus more on the political rather than 'moral' economy of the home (see Silverstone, 2006), noting that the web offers opportunities to those in marginalised locations via their homes (*Herald* [*Glasgow*] October 27, 1994) but also linking the web with the potential for low quality 'teleworking', even leading to a "decline in home ownership" (*Guardian*, December 8 1994). These conflicting discourses are important for understanding the heterogeneous domestication of the web, culturally, economically even ethically. Collectively, they illustrate how the web changed the meaning of home from a physical place to a temporal/cultural online space sometime around 1994. Later discourses from 1995 onwards could reveal how the concept of home would be reconfigured into something we ultimately take with us (see Morley, 2006) embodied in today's mobile, ubiquitous and pervasive web. They might even offer insights into the decoupling of *home* from the concept of *privacy*, with its implications for the 'contextual integrity' of data (see Nissenbaum, 2009) and legal and ethical frameworks of web use.

Meanwhile the first article to reference the web in 1992 touched on how it could connect people, but its social significance was not yet recognised, as content was still the 'new new thing' (Lewis, 1999). Two years later we see the domestication of the web turning it into an active space for producing as well as accessing content. This domestic web weaves a new fabric of abstractions, by facilitating the construction of identities and communities around content where the killer applications commercialising the web would eventually emerge (see Dean, 2000). Further analysis could investigate these themes of community and social connection, which though rare in the early years, slowly gain ground in public discourse. This also bears upon the role of women, similarly scarce in early public discourses on the web. Later discourses are likely to reflect more gendered structures, values and uses of the web as well as a widening gender gap in the new web industries after 1994 (see Kantor, 2014) along with the compelling and enduring web metaphors of female 'weaving' and male 'surfing' (Paasonen, 2005).

As we move inexorably towards web-only sources as 'archives for contemporary life' (Brügger and Finnemann, 2013) and thus as sources for public discourse, conducting similar historical analyses will become more challenging, as we do not know what proportion of discourse any selection of web material represents (Brügger, 2012). Volume increases, time is compressed and sources are not fixed, suggesting that contextual integrity may not be stable enough for similar analyses 25 years from now. However, web history has much yet to gain from historical public discourses, of which this chapter offers just an introductory glimpse.

Birth narratives

Birth—whether of people or technologies—is a highly narrative process and frequently subjected to the competing storylines of different narrators, offering prospective predictions, concurrent reports on progress and retrospective commentaries on birth strategies, unforeseen circumstances and luck, along with the occasional questioning of parenthood. All these narratives are reflected in the public discourse: first capitalised, titled and defined in business pages exploring its grand potential; then differing perspectives on the structure and scaling of an 'experimental' project, pitching commercial potential against utopian ideals; claim and counterclaim over origins and finally going beyond theoretical potential to recognition of a diverse, domesticated and *accessible* web.

While the public discourse acknowledges familiar personalities around the web's birth, it is arguable that Kurt Cobain, Santa Claus, Shoemaker Levy-9 and Socks the White House cat did more to embed its potential in the public mind. Rather than focusing on birth, perhaps Arendt's (1958) concept of *natality* is more appropriate, placing emphasis on the capacity of this new entity for acting and producing the unexpected. The potential of the web is revealed through its birth *rate*, from arrival to acceleration in public discourse, where narratives take time to develop. A curious parallax effect for historiography is that some of these discourses are in fact closer to us than they appear. Access, cultural diversity, pressure to react and the ever-shifting notion of home remain fundamental to the continuing project of the web.

APPENDIX A

The LexisNexis 'Major World publications (English)' source contains 193 international titles. For the complete list see: https://www.nexis.com/results/shared/sourceInfo.do?sourceId=F_GB01NBSimplSrch.CS00900491

The following table outlines the number of articles for each paper returning search results from 1992 to 1994:

Table A1: Number of articles returned for each newspaper.

Newspaper	Articles referencing 'world wide web' from 1992 to 1994
The Guardian	92
The Age (Melbourne, Australia)	61
The New York Times	39
USA Today	28
The Sydney Morning Herald (Australia)	26

Newspaper	Articles referencing 'world wide web' from 1992 to 1994
The Washington Post	22
Ottawa Citizen	17
The Independent (London)	15
South China Morning Post	14
The Sunday Times (London)	11
The Observer	9
The Times (London)	9
The Globe and Mail (Canada)	7
Tampa Bay Times	7
The Advertiser/Sunday Mail (Australia)	6
Australian Financial Review	5
The Irish Times	5
The Straits Times (Singapore)	5
Daily Variety	4
The Gazette	4
The Herald (Glasgow)	4
The Philadelphia Inquirer	3
Information Bank Abstracts	2
National Post	2
Nikkei Asian Review	1
The Wall Street Journal	1

APPENDIX B

List of articles cited in this analysis:

Table B1: Articles cited in the analysis.

Article headline	Publication, Location	Date
"Computer-Friendly Homes Increasing; Electronic Bulletin Boards Provide Many Residents With Comfort, Communication"	*Washington Post*, USA	December 27, 1992

Article headline	Publication, Location	Date
"The Executive Computer; A Web of Networks, an Abundance of Services"	*New York Times*, USA	February 28, 1993
"Krol's tools dispel web of Internet chaos"	*The Age*, Australia	March 23, 1993
"Microfile"	*The Guardian*, UK	September 30, 1993
"Jams Already on Data Highway"	*New York Times*, USA	November 3, 1993
"The world in a web",	*The Guardian*, UK	November 11, 1993
"A Free and Simple Computer Link",	*New York Times*, USA	December 8, 1993
"Promises, promises; The innovations of 1993 could take years to reach users"	*The Guardian*, UK	December 30, 1993
"A network heaven in your own frontroom"	*The Observer*, UK	April 30, 1994
"Anarchy on the information superhighway: from science and communications to evil and the bizarre"	*Gazette*, Canada	May 7, 1994
"Microfile"	*The Guardian*, UK	June 2, 1994
"COMPUTERS AND YOU"	*Globe and Mail*, Canada	June 15, 1994
"Hungry in cyberspace;"	*Gazette*, Canada	August 24, 1994
"Big Bang"	*Newsweek*, USA	September 26, 1994
"Setting up home"	*The Guardian* UK	October 20, 1994
"Silicon Glen urged to get on Superhighway"	*Herald*, Scotland	October 27, 1994
"Future of Improved Graphics Rests With Children Today"	*Washington Post*, USA	November 7, 1994
"Web browsers help ease route into the world"	*Sydney Morning Herald*, Australia	November 8, 1994
"White House's all-singing, all-dancing affair"	*The Age*, Australia	November 15, 1994

Article headline	Publication, Location	Date
"Future Schlock; The High-Tech Highway Has Become Littered With Lowbrow Culture"	*Washington Post*, USA	December 4, 1994
"Internet a political climate change"	*The Guardian*, UK	December 8, 1994
"Cyber Santa is coming to town"	*Irish Times*, Ireland	December 12, 1994
"Internet. Stop spreading the news?",	*The Guardian*, UK	December 15, 1994
"Santa Claus and his reindeer learn to fly in cyberspace	*Gazette*, Canada	December 22, 1994
"Not just for nerds who bathe in jello: 1994: moments that made the year"	*TheIndependent*, UK	December 26, 1994

REFERENCES

Arendt, H. (1958). *The human condition*. Chicago, IL: University of Chicago Press.

Barlow, J. P. (1996). *A declaration of the independence of cyberspace*.Retrieved from https://www.eff.org/cyberspace-independence

Barry, A. (2001). *Political machines: Governing a technological society*, London. Athlone Press

Barry, M. (2012). *The age of interactivity: An historical analysis of discourses around interactivity in Ireland 1995–2009* (PhD thesis). Dublin City University.

Barry, M., & Doherty, G. (2016). What we talk about when we talk about interactivity: empowerment in public discourse. *New Media & Society*. Retrieved from http://nms.sagepub.com.elib.tcd.ie/content/early/recent

Beaudoin-Lafon, M., & Mackay, W. (2009). Prototyping tools and techniques. In A. Sears, J. A. Jacko (Eds.), *Human-Computer interaction: Development process* (pp. 121–144). Boca Raton, FL: CRC Press Taylor & Francis.

Berker, T., Hartmann, M., Punie, Y., & Ward, K. J. (2006). Introduction. In T. Berker, M. Hartmann, Y. Punie, & K. J. Ward (Eds.), *Domestication of media and technology* (pp. 1–18) Maidenhead, UK: Open University Press.

Berners-Lee, T. (1993). *List of www servers, 1993*. Retrieved from https://groups.google.com/forum/?hl=en#!msg/comp.infosystems.www/9zYfH-QEBrM/u7zGsRUDrj4J]

Berners-Lee, T., & Fischetti, M. (1999). *Weaving the web*. London: Orion Business Books.

Braman, S. (2011). The framing years: Policy fundamentals in the internet design process, 1969–1979. *The Information Society, 27*(5), 295–310.

Braman, S. (2012). Privacy by design: Networked computing, 1969–1979. *New Media & Society, 14*(5), 798–814.

Brügger, N. (2012). Web historiography and internet studies: Challenges and perspectives. *New Media & Society, 15*(5), 752–764.

Brügger, N., & Finnemann, N. O. (2013). The web and digital humanities: Theoretical and methodological concerns. *Journal of Broadcasting & Electronic Media, 57*(1), 66–80.

Catledge, L. D., & Pitkow, J. E. (1995). Characterizing browsing strategies in the World-Wide Web. *Computer Networks and ISDN Systems, 27*, 1065–1073.

Dean, J. (2000). Community. In T. Swiss (Ed.), *Unspun: Key concepts for understanding the World Wide Web*. New York, NY: New York University Press.

Denardis, L. (2009). *Protocol politics: The globalization of Internet governance*. Cambridge, MA: MIT Press.

Flichy, P. (2007). *The internet imaginaire*. Cambridge, MA: MIT Press.

Fuller, M., & Matos, S. (2011). Feral computing: From ubiquitous calculation to wild interactions. *The Fibreculture Journal, 19*. Retrieved from http://nineteen.fibreculturejournal.org/fcj-135-feral-computing-from-ubiquitous-calculation-to-wild-interactions/

Gee, J. P. (2014). *An introduction to discourse analysis: Theory and method* (4th ed.). Abingdon: Routledge.

Gillies, J., & Cailliau, R. (2000). *How the web was born*. Oxford: Oxford University Press.

Gregory, J. & Miller, S. (2000) *Science in Public: Communication, Culture and Credibility*. Cambridge, MA: Basic Books

Haddon, L. (2006). Empirical studies using the domestication framework. In T. Berker, M. Hartmann, Y. Punie, & K. J. Ward (Eds.), *Domestication of media and technology* (pp. 103–122). Maidenhead, UK: Open University Press.

How John Perry Barlow views his internet manifesto on its 20th anniversary. (2016, February 8). *The Economist*. Retrieved from http://www.economist.com/news/international/21690200-internet-idealism-versus-worlds-realism-how-john-perry-barlow-views-his-manifesto

Jorgensen, M., & Phillips, L. J. (2002). *Discourse analysis as theory and method*. London: Sage.

Kantor, J. (2014, December 23). A brand new world in which men ruled. *New York Times*. Retrieved from http://www.nytimes.com/interactive/2014/12/23/us/gender-gaps-stanford-94.html?_r=0

Kraut, R., & Brynin, M. (2006). Social studies of domestic information and communication technologies. In R. Kraut, M. Brynin, & S. Kiesler (Eds.), *Computers homes and the internet: Domesticating information technology*. Oxford: Oxford University Press.

Lacy, S., Riffe, D., Stoddard, S., Martin, S., & Chang, K.-K. (2001). Sample size for newspaper content analysis in multi-year studies. *Journalism Quarterly, 78*(4), 836–845.

Lewis, M. (1999). *The new new thing: A Silicon Valley story*. New York, NY: WW Norton.

Mansell, R. (2012). *Imagining the internet*. Oxford: Oxford University Press.

Morley, D. (2006). What's home got to do with it? In T. Berker, M. Hartmann, Y. Punie, & K. J. Ward (Eds.), *Domestication of media and technology* (pp. 21–39).Maidenhead: Open University Press.

Nissenbaum, H. (2009). *Privacy in context: Technology, policy and the integrity of social life*. Stanford, CA: Stanford University Press.

Paasonen, S. (2005). *Figures of fantasy: Internet, women and cyberdiscourse*. New York, NY: Peter Lang Publishing.

Poynter Institute. (2004). *New Media Timeline*. Retrieved from http://www.poynter.org/2004/new-media-timeline-1990/28754/

Raggett, D., Lam, J., & Alexander, I. (1996). *HTML 3: Electronic publishing on the World Wide Web*. Reading, MA: Addison-Wesley.

Silverstone, R. (2006). Domesticating domestication: Reflections on the life of a concept. In T. Berker, M. Hartmann, Y. Punie, & K. J. Ward (Eds.), *Domestication of media and technology* (pp. 229–48). Maidenhead: Open University Press

Van Leeuwen, T. (2008). News genres. In R. Wodak, & V. Koller (Eds.), *The handbook of communication in the public sphere* (pp. 343–63). Berlin: Walter de Gruyter.

Winston, B. (1998). *Media, technology and society*. Abingdon: Routledge.

Wodak, R., & Meyer, M. (2009). Critical discourse analysis: History, agenda, theory and methodology. In Wodak, R., & Meyer, M. (Eds.) *Methods of critical discourse analysis* (pp. 1–33) London: Sage.

NOTES

1. Retrieved from https://www.w3.org/People/Berners-Lee/1991/08/art-6484.txt
2. For example, 'How the web went world wide' as reported by the BBC in 2006, available at http://news.bbc.co.uk/2/hi/technology/5242252.stm
3. As noted by LexisNexis. For more details on sources and sample see Appendices.
4. A reference to what is regarded as the first webcam image—the 'Trojan Room' coffee pot at Cambridge university (see http://www.cl.cam.ac.uk/coffee/qsf/coffee.html)
5. Veteran 'net' users report being frustrated with delays online caused by 'newbies', as reported by *Time* magazine in July 1994 [available at http://time.com/vault/issue/1994-07-25/page/57/]
6. Many websites were still described as 'experimental' in articles throughout the sample, but by December 1994 major news institutions such as *The Daily Telegraph, NPR, BBC, The New York Times, Wired Magazine, Financial Times* and *The Irish Times* had invested in their own graphical websites (Poynter Institute, 2004).
7. Tim Berners-Lee (1993) had recently circulated a list of the one hundred servers then known, and in 1994 they still numbered only in the hundreds (see Raggett, Lam, & Alexander, 1996).
8. A search for internet 'Gopher' in the same news sources on LexisNexis returns 23 articles for 1993 compared to 10 for 'world wide web'.
9. This relationship between technology and finance in news reporting reflects a shift in how newspapers conceptualised its readers—first as 'audience' or 'users' of content, then as 'consumers' of ICT products and services, then as 'shareholders' and investors in applications and devices, where the news outlet increasingly plays the role of market analyst (Barry, 2012).
10. Miller would later co-author with Jane Gregory *Science in Public: Communication, Culture and Credibility* (2000), which helped establish the field of science communication research.
11. 'Socks' was the White House cat whose photograph and 'voice' (an audio 'Miaow!' on click) made it one of the most popular sites on the web that year (*New York Times*, November 1994).
12. See note 11

The web OF culture AND media

CHAPTER FIVE

Inside THE great firewall

The web in China

MICHEL HOCKX

INTRODUCTION

The People's Republic of China was fully connected to the internet in 1994 (Yang, 2009, p. 29). Soon after this the first WWW sites started to appear, first at universities, later with commercial content providers. By the late 1990s access to computers and to the WWW started to become more common, mainly in the big cities. Following the widespread adoption of Unicode (UTF-8) and improvements in Chinese character input methods, the Chinese WWW space began to grow exponentially. According to statistics from the China Internet Network Information Center (CNNIC) there were 3.57 million websites registered with China-based registrants in June 2015, roughly half of them in the .cn domain. The nationwide internet penetration rate was nearly 50%. Mobile phones were by far the most popular means of accessing the internet, with a utilization rate of 90%, as opposed to 68% for desktops, 42% for laptops, 33% for tablets, and 16% for TVs (China Internet Network Information Center, 2015).

STATE CONTROL AND SCHOLARLY BIAS

As is well known, online space in China is subject to strict state regulation. The physical infrastructure of the internet in China is all state-owned or state-controlled. The Chinese government "starts from a position of control over and ownership of Chinese cyberspace" (Herold, 2011, p. 1). On that basis it grants WWW users a certain amount of freedom, which it can curtail if necessary (Herold, 2011, p. 2). The vast majority of Chinese WWW users, like their counterparts in Western countries, use the WWW mainly for entertainment and social interaction, yet Western scholarship of the Chinese internet has shown a strong bias towards analyzing what these users are not allowed to do. This tendency of Western scholars to make Eurocentric assumptions about what Chinese netizens should want, rather than study what they actually do, has been called "digital orientalism" (Herold, 2013, p. 11). Along similar lines, Tsui has pointed out the misleading nature of the oft-used phrase 'Great Firewall of China', a metaphor stemming from outdated, Cold War-era assumptions about the significance of 'sending' Western messages into China, which underestimates the complexity of networked communication across national borders and also underestimates the high levels of online communication and discussion taking place between netizens inside China (Tsui, 2007).

It is certainly true that sophisticated firewall technology prevents computers inside China from connecting to certain blacklisted IP addresses outside the country, unless a VPN connection is used. In addition a certain amount of content filtering takes place at the national access level. However, much more censorship effort is put into controlling communications between netizens inside the country. This is much harder to do, as it relies on keyword filters and other mechanisms that generally require human involvement. Research has shown that keyword censorship on popular platforms such as the microblogging site Weibo is a complex affair, with only very few words completely blocked and most other acts of censorship dependent on human censors' interpretation of how certain sensitive words are used and whether or not virtual communications attempt to instigate real-life activism. Criticism of the government is most definitely allowed and in fact widespread, but calls for offline activism are quickly removed and censorship activity is increased around the anniversaries of political events, especially the annual anniversary of the 1989 massacre on June 4th (King, Pan, & Roberts, 2013). The government also employs unknown numbers of netizens who are paid to join online debates and express pro-government sentiments. These individuals are popularly referred to as the 'Fifty Cents Party', as it is rumored that they are paid fifty cents for each word they post online.

Despite the at times heavy-handed state interference, WWW culture is thriving in China and the rich cultural world inside the 'Great Firewall' is definitely worth noting and studying. The next section offers an overview of some of the main phenomena and trends on the WWW in the People's Republic of China (PRC) during the past fifteen years. After that follows a short case study of the remarkable popularity of online novels and online literature in China, and its repercussions for the country's publishing industry as a whole.

THEORETICAL BACKGROUND AND APPROACH

My research on Chinese WWW culture in general, and online literature in particular, is grounded in theoretical paradigms belonging to the discipline of the sociology of literature, and especially the work of Pierre Bourdieu (Hockx, 2012). Cultural production in China is characterized by intricate relationships between symbolic capital (critical acclaim), economic capital (market success), and political capital (state intervention). In previous research I have looked at the way in which the introduction of new printing technologies, specifically low-cost magazine publication, altered the structure of the Chinese literary field in the early twentieth century (Hockx, 2003). The arrival of the WWW and related technologies appears to have brought about equally significant changes in the balance of power between the literary community, the publishing industry, and the state. From the start of the current century onwards, reading online literature has consistently been among the top ten reasons for Chinese netizens to go online, unlike the situation in any other countries that I am aware of. It therefore makes sense to use online literature, and especially online fiction, which has emerged as the greatest challenger to the existing print publishing system, as a concrete angle to study the history of the WWW in China in its cultural specificity.

The research generally used a hermeneutic approach, following the development of a small number of literary websites over time, closely reading online works as well as online documents related to literature and literary production, paying attention especially to ways in which online literary production affects aesthetic paradigms, and the ways in which it puts pressure on traditional publishing mechanisms, including publishing control mechanisms. To provide further qualitative support for conclusions drawn about the relationship between online literature and publishing reform, some interviews were carried out with online authors, editors of literary websites, and state officials responsible for the regulation of online publishing. Archival material, especially material preserved by the Internet Archive Wayback Machine, was used to deepen understanding about the historical development of the Chinese WWW.

PRC WEB CULTURE

In today's China the WWW is generally a highly commercialized space, dominated by a small number of large companies such as Alibaba, Baidu, Sina, and Tencent, all of which also have significant business interests outside China. WWW sites based in China also find extensive audiences among Chinese people living overseas. Worldwide, Chinese is the second-most often used language on the WWW.

Most WWW activity in the PRC revolves around commercial web portals and online services providers. In the past few years, online shopping through portals like Taobao and Tmall, both owned by the Alibaba company, has experienced tremendous growth, with some notable innovations taking place in the process, especially Alibaba's successful transformation of a relatively unknown festival ('Singles Day' on November 11) into the world's biggest-grossing online shopping phenomenon (Berke, 2015). China also has a very big market for online gaming and is one of the world's main centers for 'gold farming'. 'Gold farming' refers to the practice whereby highly proficient gamers living in low-wage countries are paid to spend money playing certain online games in order to accumulate in-game currency, which is then transferred to less proficient gamers residing in the developed world (Arnason, 2015).

Personal homepages have played a relatively small role in the development of the web in China, especially after thousands of such pages were closed down when the government changed the registration rules for websites in 2005. Specifically, all websites engaged in any form of 'information services' (including news services) were instructed to register with state offices in their localities and any unregistered sites were removed from the WWW (Lau, 2005, p. 4). This move by the authorities effectively prevented the development of the WWW as a sphere for independent journalism and public opinion, unless in the context of large, commercially operated and therefore generally state-friendly internet portals.

Chinese-language WWW portals tend to present themselves as very crowded spaces, with huge amounts of text and links, often in small font, crammed onto a single screen. Most sites also feature almost constant pop-up advertisements, some of which move across the screen. Whereas this style can come across as disorientating for Western users (including Western users who can read Chinese), it seems to pose no particular problem to Chinese users who navigate their way quickly and efficiently through the masses of information provided on a single page. More research is needed to find out if the format is really experienced as user-friendly or if it has been imposed by corporate practices. There is some evidence, for instance in the popularity of online literature (see below), that Chinese users are generally more tolerant of using the WWW for reading traditional, linear texts.

Forums

Web-based discussion forums, sometimes referred to as BBSes, were and continue to be the backbone of online activity in China. Most websites run forums and there are also very many portals that specialize in hosting forums on all kinds of topics. Chinese netizens seem to enjoy the communicative aspect of forums. Forum-related terms such as 'post' and 'thread' have become part of everyday parlance, especially among younger people. Forums also provide a more informal space for debate that is perhaps more difficult to find in the more tightly controlled world of print. Already in the early days of the WWW, forums would at times produce significant cultural phenomena that would also be discussed in the mainstream media. A good example is the online diary of the terminal cancer patient Lu Youqing, published on a forum at http://www.rongshuxia.com in the year 2000, which gave rise to extensive debates about the Chinese healthcare system and related ethical issues not only on the internet but also in print media and on television (Hockx, 2015, pp. 43–55).

Blogs

Blogs started to become popular in China after the establishment of the Sina blogging portal in 2005. Although the distinction between a blog and a forum is not always clear cut, since blogs can potentially also be run by communities devoted to discussing specific topics of interest, it is more usually the case that blogs feature writings by a single individual. Moreover, the blog format privileges the constant publication of new content by its owner, to which readers can respond, but unlike with forums the number of responses has no impact on the order in which the blog posts are presented. A blog, therefore, is more like an individual chronicle or journal.

China has had a number of celebrity bloggers over the years. The earliest blogger to achieve fame was a young woman using the pseudonym Muzimei, whose controversial 'sex diaries' published on http://www.wenxue.com shocked some and delighted others as early as 2003 (Cf. Farrer, 2007). However, China's most famous blogger by far has been Han Han, a hugely popular novelist and racing celebrity, who started a blog on the Sina site in October 2005 and quickly attracted millions of followers. On his blog he developed a unique style of satirical writing, often commenting on current political and social affairs, his sharp wit and social critique often balancing on the borderline between what is and is not permissible in China, resulting in occasional censorship of some of his posts. Whenever one of his blog posts was censored, he would leave only the title listed on the main page of his blog, and replace the content with a single full stop. Once his readers understood this gesture, they would often post comments of support or outrage when they came across another censored post. This led to the extraordinary phenomenon of blog posts consisting of only a short title and a full stop receiving tens of thousands of readers' comments. So important a cultural figure was Han Han that in 2010 he was included in *Time* magazine's annual list of most influential people in the world (Elegant, 2010). A selection of his blog posts was translated into English and published in book form (Han Han, 2012).

In recent years Han Han has been less active on the WWW, instead focusing his attention on a new project, a daily magazine called *One*, distributed directed into mobile devices via its own application (Hockx, 2015, pp. 106–107). He has also been actively fighting against online violations of authors' copyright. In 2012 he successfully sued Baidu for allowing electronic copies of his printed novels to be shared on its online text-sharing site (Deng Jingyin, 2012). Baidu and other sites have since been more careful not to allow uploads of copyrighted material published in China. However, illegal upload and download of electronic copies of English-language books continues to take place in China on a massive scale, apparently without any significant attempts by the government to intervene.

Weibo

China is often referred to in the Western media as "the country that blocks Facebook, YouTube, and Twitter." Of these three, arguably YouTube is the one that users in the PRC most dislike not having access to. The local equivalent Youku.com ranks as low as 23rd on the country ranking for China on http://www.alexa.com, which is quite low for a video sharing site. However, China has for many years had a perfectly viable alternative for Facebook and Twitter in the form of Weibo, the microblogging site operated by the Sina company. Weibo is like Twitter in that it only allows posts containing 140 characters or less. In the Chinese language a single character represents at least a syllable, in some cases even a whole word, therefore much more content can go into 140 Chinese characters than into 140 English characters. In addition, Weibo has for some time been offering an option to submit longer posts as images, allowing users of Sina's blogsite to automatically reproduce their blog posts onto their Weibo pages. Recently Weibo decided to abolish the 140-character limit altogether. Compared to Twitter, Weibo was also much earlier in developing ways of uploading images together with text and for quite some time it was this function that attracted Chinese users to Weibo even if they did have access to Twitter. Weibo also runs countless groups and communities, as well as a private messaging function and the ability to label people as 'friends'. It offers a number of the social media functions that users outside China get from Facebook.

The popularity of Weibo reaches well beyond the PRC. The fact that it was developed specifically to suit the needs of Chinese language users means that many Chinese speakers outside the PRC also prefer it to Twitter. In Alexa's global ranking, representing the world's most popular websites, Weibo currently (January 2016) ranks 16th while Twitter ranks 10th. It is worth mentioning here in passing that Baidu.com, China's alternative to Google, ranks 4th in the world (Google is 1st) and that Taobao.com, China's highly successful online shopping portal, ranks 12th in the world (Amazon is 6th). This forcefully underscores the point made above about the complexities of internet communication. Not only does the world inside the great firewall get by without the core websites associated with the 'free' world, but it even exports websites and applications that are preferred by Chinese users outside China over the 'free world' alternatives, despite the fact that these sites and applications are based in China and subject to censorship and control. Conventional views of what Chinese users need and what 'Western' users expect when it comes to media access seem no longer to be valid.

WeChat

In recent years, the popularity of first blogging and later microblogging in China has given way to a new type of social media: WeChat. WeChat is in essence a messaging application, similar to WhatsApp. In addition to one-to-one text and voice messaging, the application also allows users to share texts (without length restrictions) and images among their friends or within closed groups. The WeChat software was designed to run on mobile phones and membership is linked to the mobile number, although it will run on tablets and desktops as well. The voice message feature, which was enabled early on, is extremely popular as it helps users to get around the need to type or write Chinese characters on a touch screen, which can be time consuming. The group sharing features are also very popular, since they allow users to speak their minds much more openly, knowing they are only addressing a closed group of friends and no public record of the conversation appears anywhere on the web. As a result, many discussions about 'sensitive' topics that might be removed from web-based applications such as Weibo are continuously ongoing on WeChat and are almost impossible for the authorities to control. WeChat groups are limited to 100 users, unless a subscriber links their payment card to their WeChat account, in which case they can form larger groups. At the same time, they can use their WeChat account to carry out a whole range of purchases and utility bill payments, using the application's built-in QR scanner. Given the very high proportion of Chinese users accessing the internet through mobile devices, it is not surprising that social media are moving away from WWW sites on public servers and featuring more direct communication methods. By now, WeChat has become an indispensable tool for anyone wishing to carry out successful communication, including business communication, with counterparts in China.

ONLINE LITERATURE

The annual reports on the Chinese internet provided by CNNIC always contain a table listing the most popular reasons for netizens to go online. These tables clearly show the development of trends over time, for instance the rise and fall in popularity of blogs and, more recently, the beginning decline in popularity of microblogs. What is most remarkable about these tables, however, is that they consistently indicate that around 30% of Chinese netizens go online to read literature and that reading literature is consistently among the Top 10 activities engaged in online by Chinese users of the internet. I am not aware of any other country in the world where online reading of literary work is so popular, or indeed where this is an independent category for which statistics are calculated. The popularity of such websites in China requires some explanation.

The websites officially categorized as providers of online literature all focus on the production and consumption of popular genre fiction, i.e. romance fiction, martial arts fiction, historical fiction, science fiction, fan fiction, erotic fiction, and so on. Although such fiction certainly also exists in print in China, its markets have never been as big as in other countries. Worldwide business conglomerates selling popular fiction such as Harlequin/Mills & Boon have never been able to crack the Chinese market. This is due in part to the control over the print publishing market by state-owned publishers, and in part by the Communist Party's insistence that literature for mass audiences should be 'healthy' and elevating, rather than merely entertaining. Although ideological control on literary production has been relatively relaxed since the 1990s and publishing has become much more commercial, including a steady stream of bestsellers (Cf. Kong, 2005), prior to the arrival of internet literature there were not really any Chinese publishers successfully specializing in the production of pulp fiction on a large, commercial scale.

In 2003, a website calling itself 'Qidian' (Starting Point, http://www.qidian.com) discovered this niche in the market and established a highly successful business model, so successful that by 2004 the website was ranked in Alexa's Top 100 of most popular websites in the world. Although nowadays it is ranked much lower than that (around 1,000), it still attracts millions of unique visitors on a daily basis. Moreover, there are also many other websites in China that have copied their business model and helped the market for online genre fiction to grow.

The 'Starting Point' business model is simple. The core of the website is made up of a number of discussion forums, each devoted to a different genre. Visitors to the site are encouraged to upload their own creative writing to one of the forums, preferably in the form of serialized novels, uploading new chapters with some regularity. Readers are encouraged to comment on the submissions and to 'like' them or rate them. When a certain novel starts to attract a relatively large and loyal readership visiting each new instalment, the website enters into negotiation with the author and offers them a contract. After both parties have signed the contract, the site moves the novel behind a paywall. Readers who, having read the first one hundred chapters or so, have become hooked on the novel are encouraged to take out subscriptions to that particular serialization, so that they can continue reading. The cost of a subscription to an ongoing novel is very low, but with numbers of subscribers potentially reaching into the millions, the amount of money earned can still be considerable. The website pays 70% of earnings out to the author as their fee, and pockets 30% itself as income for the site. Once certain authors have established themselves they can also be offered longer-term contracts, not limited to just one novel. Moreover, the website also acts as an agent for its most successful authors and tries to help them to get their novels published in print.

The success of 'Starting Point' is based in part on its clever adaptation of the popular discussion forum format. Prior to 2003, this format was used by some websites to promote literary writing and discussion about literature, but none of them had found a viable and sustainable business model. 'Starting Point' also introduced many different types of rankings and statistics as part of the site, encouraging friendly competition among writers and giving readers and fans a sense of ownership as their responses directly impact on the success and status of their favorite novels. To some extent, sites like 'Starting Point' are grass root communities where readers can become writers and amateur writers can become celebrities, all through more or less democratic processes and without the intervention of literary critics or other representatives of the establishment. Shih-chen Chao refers to this situation where community members can be both writers and readers as 'prosumption' of literature (Chao, 2012). Such communities of course can be found all over the WWW outside China as well, especially for the various genres of fan fiction, but crucially outside China such sites would never charge their readers. Examples of online fiction achieving commercial success in other countries are rare, the main exception being the massive sales figures of the novel *Fifty Shades of Grey* by E. L. James, which originated in a work of online *Twilight* fan fiction. Again, though, the online version, although massively popular as well, was always available for free (and was removed as soon as the print version became available).

The remarkable success of online genre fiction has also had a wider and more significant impact on the Chinese publishing system as a whole, making it a good example of how the WWW is bringing about changes in Chinese society despite the state's attempts to keep it under control. In order to understand this it is important to know that Chinese publishing laws stipulate that no book publication can be legal unless it carries an ISBN number, usually referred to as the 'book number' (*shuhao*). This is different from the situation in most Western countries, where it is certainly the norm for books to carry ISBN numbers, but not having such a number does not make the publication illegal. In China, the publishing system was reformed in such a way in the 1990s that most of the actual publishing activity (sourcing and editing manuscripts, graphic design, printing, distribution, marketing) could be done by private commercial companies, but that the official act of making the publication legal, by assigning a book number, could only be carried out by state-owned publishing houses. This system ensures that the state maintains a level of control over what gets published, with state-owned publishers acting as *de facto* censors, while at the same time it allows those same publishers to operate more commercially, by outsourcing most of the work to private enterprises and charging them for the service of assigning a book number.

This system has for the past decade been confronted with the increasing popularity of online genre fiction. Websites such as 'Starting Point' have by now published hundreds of thousands of full-length novels online and sold the right to read them to millions of readers. For all practical purposes, the novels they publish should count as 'books', even if they are not in print. However none of them carry book numbers. In short: what these websites have achieved is that they have created a massive publishing market that completely circumvents the traditional system of control and has forced the authorities to come up with different regulation measures, bringing about a major change in what had been a long-standing state monopoly. This change will undoubtedly make its impact felt beyond the relatively small field of literary publishing and affect other areas of publishing as well.

I have discussed the Chinese government response to the boom in online fiction in detail elsewhere (Hockx, 2015, pp. 113–130), basing my conclusions in part on interviews with officials and website editors. In short, the situation is that the official state regulator acknowledges that it is impossible to deal with the massive amount of online publications in the same way as print publications. It would simply be too much work to handle all the applications for 'book numbers'. Instead, the regulator encourages online publishers to self-register and as part of this process they need to provide evidence of their awareness of the relevant laws, and their editors must provide evidence of having received the relevant training (including training in how to censor potentially sensitive publications). Websites that comply with the self-registration requirement are exempted from regular checks on their content and only need to submit updated documentation when they re-register each year. Since the most commercial sites have all complied (so as not to lose their business), this has enabled the regulators to gain a general overview of this particular branch of business. This is also why official statistics on internet use in China can feature 'online literature' as a separate category, because the websites in question are seen and registered as a separate type of content provider.

There are, however, many smaller websites that make less money and see less need to self-register and that are willing to publish work that is a bit less mainstream and a bit more risqué, especially various types of erotic and pornographic fiction. This poses an additional problem for the regulators because, for ideological reasons, the Chinese state does not wish to impose age-related restrictions on pornographic material. The official position adopted by the Communist Party ideology is that pornography is not 'healthy' and should have no place in Chinese society, and therefore there can be no legal age (over 18 in most Western countries) for viewing or reading such material. In addition to the various forms of political censorship, which are perhaps less relevant to the study of online literature, most of which is apolitical in nature, it is moral censorship that plays an important role in internet regulation in China. Over the years different methods have been adopted, ranging from banning specific online novels for their pornographic content, to 'naming and shaming' websites publishing pornographic material (which generally only served to make those websites more popular), to putting pressure on the editors of such websites to clean up their act and keep their authors within certain limits. In recent years, this latter policy appears to have been relatively successful, as websites previously featuring quite explicit texts and equally explicit illustrations and advertising have now generally adopted a somewhat more circumspect approach, removing most of the visual material and publishing fiction that is still erotic in nature but rarely explicit in its use of language or its descriptions.

In January 2015, the Chinese regulators issued new guidelines for online literature, which many interpreted as restrictive, especially in their insistence on 'healthy' content, but which also called for more collaboration between (private) online publishers and (state-owned) print publishers. This can also be seen as a sign of recognition of the innovations brought about in publishing in the WWW context and a step towards finally abolishing the outdated 'book number' system for print publications as well. Meanwhile, online literature of a more elitist and less popular nature has also made its mark and in recent years several authors of novels that first appeared on the WWW have been nominated for some of China's most prestigious literary prizes.

CONCLUSION

Perceptions of the World Wide Web in China as characterized by nothing but censorship and repression, or as a barren place cut off from global trends by an all-controlling firewall do not do justice to the rich social and cultural significance that the WWW has in China today. Not only do Chinese content and services providers participate fully in the global competition for WWW success, operating with ease across the borders that are supposed to surround China's web space, but even inside the so-called Great Firewall the WWW in China is showing many examples of creativity and innovation. Moreover, some of the unique social and cultural practices that have been developed on the WWW inside China, such as the practices surrounding online fiction, have forced the state to loosen its control in some areas. This shows the unique ability of the WWW to provide creative individuals or businesses with spaces where they can do new things. At the same time, the case of Chinese online fiction also shows that WWW culture is not by definition a uniform, globalizing force, but that it can have surprising local characteristics.

REFERENCES

Arnason, S. L. (2015). *Regulating online games in China: Policy, practice, innovation, and change* (PhD dissertation). University of Edinburgh, Edinburgh.

Berke, J. (2015, November 14). *How Alibaba turned an obscure, made-up Chinese holiday into a $14.3 billion shopping extravaganza that's bigger than Black Friday.* Retrieved February 5, 2016 from http://www.techinsider.io/how-alibaba-made-143-billion-on-singles-day-2015-11

Chao, S. (2012). *Desire and fantasy on-line: A sociological and psychoanalytical approach to the prosumption of Chinese internet fiction* (PhD dissertation). University of Manchester, Manchester.

China Internet Network Information Center. (2015). *The 36th statistical report on internet development in China.* Retrieved from http://www1.cnnic.cn/IDR/ReportDownloads/201601/P020160106496544403584.pdf

Deng Jingyin. (2012, September 18). *Han Han wins cash in Baidu copyright suit.* Retrieved February 5, 2016 from http://www.globaltimes.cn/content/733717.shtml

Elegant, S. (2010, April 29). The 2010 TIME 100—Artists—Han Han. *Time.* Retrieved from http://content.time.com/time/specials/packages/article/0,28804,1984685_1984940_1985515,00.html

Farrer, J. (2007). China's women sex bloggers and dialogic sexual politics on the Chinese internet. *China Aktuell: Journal of Current Chinese Affairs, 4,* 1–36.

Han Han. (2012). *This generation: Dispatches from China's most popular blogger.* (A. H. Barr, Ed. & Trans.). London: Simon and Shuster.

Herold, D. K. (2011). Introduction: Noise, spectacle, politics: Carnival in Chinese cyberspace. In D. K. Herold & P. Marolt (Eds.), *Online society in China: Creating, celebrating, and instrumentalising the online carnival* (pp. 1–19). Abingdon: Routledge.

Herold, D. K. (2013). Through the looking class: Twenty years of research into the Chinese internet. Retrieved from http://repository.lib.polyu.edu.hk/jspui/bitstream/10397/5789/1/Herold_Through_Looking_Glass.pdf

Hockx, M. (2003). *Questions of style: Literary societies and literary journals in modern China, 1911–1937.* Leiden: Brill.

Hockx, M. (2012). The literary field and the field of power: The case of modern China. *Paragraph, 35*(1), 49–65.

Hockx, M. (2015). *Internet literature in China.* New York, NY: Columbia University Press.

King, G., Pan, J., & Roberts, M. E. (2013). *A randomized experimental study of censorship in China.* Presented at the American Political Science Association, Chicago. Retrieved from http://people.fas.harvard.edu/~jjpan/experiment.pdf

Kong, S. (2005). *Consuming literature: Best sellers and the commercialization of literary production in contemporary China.* Stanford, CA: Stanford University Press.

Lau, M. W. (2005). *Internet development and information control in the people's Republic of China* (CRS Report for Congress). Washington, DC: Congressional Research Service, The Library of Congress.

Tsui, L. (2007). An inadequate metaphor: The great firewall and Chinese internet censorship. *Global Dialogue, 9*(102). Retrieved from http://www.worlddialogue.org/content.php?id=400

Yang, G. (2009). *The power of the internet in China: Citizen activism online.* New York, NY: Columbia University Press.

CHAPTER SIX

Blogs AS cultural products

A multidimensional approach to their diffusion in Italy (2001–2008)

ELISABETTA LOCATELLI

The chapter investigates the early years of blogs diffusion[1] in Italy (2001–2008)[2] considering them as cultural products (Colombo, 2003; Griswold, 1994). It will investigate the phenomenon applying an original approach aimed at examining how blogs' technological, cultural, economic, and institutional dimension changed over time. It will show both the continuity between the origins of blogging in the USA and the peculiarities of Italian blogosphere, which are to be observed from their very inception, such as the adoption of blogging like an online diary or the creation of online and offline micro-communities.

THEORETICAL FRAMEWORK: THE CULTURAL PRODUCT

Following Hine (2000), the internet can be intended both as culture and as a cultural artefact. Considering the internet as a culture means to conceive it as a "place, cyberspace, where culture is formed and reformed" (Hine, 2000, p. 9), whereas, considering it as a cultural artefact means seeing it as a "product of culture"—a technology that is used by different social groups, "with contextually situated goals and priorities. It is also a technology which is shaped by the ways in which it is marketed, taught and used" (Hine, 2000, p. 9).

The same dynamics can be applied to blogs. On the one hand, they have developed a new culture and altered the present one; on the other hand, they were (and are) socially and culturally shaped by the context their part of.

An especially powerful theoretical framework for understanding this duality is to interpret blogs as a cultural product that is "a shared significance embodied in a form" (Griswold, 1986, 1994). The relationship between culture and society is conceived as governed by four dimensions (social world, receiver, cultural object, creator) arranged like a baseball diamond (Griswold, 1994, p. 15).

Colombo (2001, 2003) expands semantically these dimensions into socio-cultural environment, consumption, cultural product, and production. Moreover, defining a medium per se Colombo introduces four dimensions—namely the technological, economic, institutional and cultural (Colombo, 2006, p. 30), that in the research here described were used to analyse the socio-cultural environment and the production of blogs.

In the frame of cultural products like blogs, technology enables the existence of the objects but, at the same time, it is also shaped by user's habits and practices (Siles, 2012a). The economic dimension refers to the resources needed to access a service or buy a cultural product, as well as to the business and marketing strategies apt to promoting it. The institutional dimension includes all the entities that influence the cultural products: the law, rules, economic subjects, and regulatory bodies. Last but not least, is the cultural dimension. According to Hannerz culture is composed of "overt forms" interpreted by human minds through "externalized meanings" (Hannerz, 1992, p. 4). Blogs, then, are parts of a culture but they also are externalised means that reflect and produce culture.

METHODOLOGY

The data analysed in our exploration come from a multi-sited research project (Marcus, 1995) where the main reference to sociology was integrated with other perspectives (Alasuutari, 1999) with a continuous comparison between objectives and techniques, as recommended by Grounded Theory (Charmaz, 2000; Glaser & Strauss, 1967; Strauss & Corbin, 1990).

The qualitative methodology comprised three steps. First, an explorative analysis of the Italian blogosphere and of the early development of blogging in the US was done examining blogs,[3] journal articles, and academic and non-academic publications. Also, some of the early US bloggers were contacted via e-mail. Afterwards, a participant observation of three bloggers' meetings in Italy was done with short individual interviews.[4] We, then, chose to concentrate on personal blogs. Three phases in the development of personal blogs were identified: early bloggers (1999/2000–2001); the age of Splinder (2003–2006); mainstreaming (2006–2008).

The second methodological step comprised 25 semi-structured interviews (done in 2007) aimed at investigating the individual repertoire of routines and practices involved in maintaining the blog.

The third phase consisted in the semiotic analysis (Cosenza, 2008) of 50 blogs (the interviewees' plus 25 other blogs sampled following the same criteria) doing an in-depth analysis of blog's structure and of a selected number of posts.

The sample of interviewees and blogs was selected through theoretical (Mason, 1996; Silverman, 2000) and snowball sampling (Bailey, 1987). The following criteria were considered: blogs' opening date; city of residence (Milan, Rome and Turin, chosen for the significance of their blogospheres); gender (14 males and 11 females); and the kind of content posted (text, photo, and video).

RESULTS

The technological dimension: the evolution of the platforms

A brief digression into the US context is important to understand how the phenomenon started and settled.

According to the historical investigation (Blood, 2002; Locatelli, 2014), between 1992 and 1995, the 'What's New' pages started by Mosaic and Tim Berners-Lee (see also Winer, 2000) were the 'forefather' of blogs. They were webpages composed of texts and hyperlinks aimed at updating early internet users about their projects and trending internet news (Blood, 2002). Furthermore, Mosaic was organised in reverse chronological order: the latest posts were read first. Between 1995 and 1997 in the US, a small group of 'enthusiastic surfers' created a 'particular type of website' (Blood, 2002, p. 2) comprising various links with a brief description in reverse chronological order.

At first, weblogs were regularly updated personal websites that replaced email and newsletters as a way to recommend interesting webpages to friends (Blood, 2002)—a practice termed 'social resource discovery' (Ammann, 2013, p. 203). They were dynamic and rich in content, whereas other kinds of websites were static and seldom updated. Later on, Cameron Barrett's (2002) weblog rules (Ammann, 2013; Blood, 2002) gave the blog a new meaning, making it more similar to a web zine, that is to say to a series of essays (Ammann, 2013, p. 204). On this basis Derek Powazek could define blogs as a tool for "identity production" (Ammann, 2013, p. 204). The final step of this process is the introduction of permalinks that recognized "the view of the blog post as 'content' in its own right, as having intrinsic value rather than merely referential value" (Ammann, 2013, p. 204).[5]

In this process, technological restrictions (primarily internet connection speed and cost) and technical opportunities (the birth of World Wide Web and the possibility to create new forms of content management systems) were enabling factors that led internet users to create new tools of communication. Blogs also introduced important technological innovations for the development of the web, such as the reverse chronological order of content and the RSS format. The former is not just a technicality, in that it gave bloggers the chance to develop a precise narrative structure.

Between 1999 and 2003, the creation of ready-to-use web-based software—like LiveJournal, Blogger, Frontier and Pitas (Blood, 2002)—marked a new phase in blogging's development because an internet connection and a browser were the only requirements to open a blog, and therefore non-internet users also approached the idea of opening a blog, which could by now include different kinds of content ranging from photos to videos.

When first blogs were opened in Italy in 1999/2000, blog's meaning was already established as an online space useful for self-publishing and customizable following blogger's needs.

Many of the early Italian bloggers, like those in the US, were professional programmers or web designers, and they looked to the US as a technical and cultural guide. Blogs existence was known in heterogeneous ways. One of the first Italian bloggers, Antonio Cavedoni,[6] said in his interview that he opened his blog on Blogger during a web design conference where he met Derek Powazek and decided to immediately follow his example (Locatelli, 2014). Others decided to start blogging after discovering the early US blogs while surfing the web (Locatelli, 2014). Flexibility and ease of use were two important factors in blogs' success. The knowledge exchange was important in consolidating the blogging community: new features were improved by sharing scripts and plugins and imitating what others were doing. Thus, blog's functions were in continuous evolution according to technical developments. Examples of this are the introduction of the comments area and the blogroll (a list of friends' blogs). These new features were gradually implemented, advising readers of blog's changes: "In the column on the left, under 'Friend Blog', I put the list of blogs that link to mine. So let me know if you link to me" (Interview with M, Milan, 2001, text).[7]

The growth of Splinder, the first Italian web-based blogging platform, in 2003 was crucial for creating the Italian bloggers community, because it marked the start of a new era.[8] Actually, it removed the linguistic barrier inherent in English-language platforms and offered some features (e.g. chat, private messaging, and directories for navigating blogs) that favoured the creation of micro-communities. Thus, the functions of self-publishing and of creating and maintaining social relationships became linked, marking another important shift in blog's definition. This period (2003–2006) was also marked by experimentation of various blogging platforms, many of them linked to online portals, such as Virgilio or Excite. Bloggers who started blogging during these years were more aware of blogs' technical and communicative potential. They were no longer internet enthusiasts or communication professionals, on the contrary, they had various jobs and skills. They were motivated by curiosity and passion, for example some of them liked to work on

HTML coding to make the blog their online 'home' (Locatelli, 2014): "You teach yourself […], so I started to work on the template, because I like graphics" (interview with F, Rome, 2003, text).

Of the various platforms that have blossomed since 2006 (some dedicated to specific formats like photos or videos), two of them emerged as Italy's favourites—WordPress and Blogger—marking blogging's move into the global mainstream. Since then, blogs became established self-publishing tools, while their social function was slowly migrating to social network sites (Facebook opened in 2004 and exploded in popularity in Italy in August 2008.) Bloggers still liked to personalise their blogs with widgets and plugins (like antipixels, feed subscribers, animated GIFs, tagboards), and the blog network was still a primary source of information about new features. Some bloggers also made their way by publishing posts with tips and tricks: "There was the case of a blogger who created free template for others and gained a lot of feedbacks in this way" (interview to F, Milano, 2006, text).

The cultural dimension: a new web culture

The cultural dimension includes several aspects of blogging, ranging from the features they introduced into web culture, to their functions, or the spread of blogs culture.

New features

Blogging culture is deeply rooted in that of the web. On the one hand, the technological evolution described above shows how much of 1990s web culture merged into blogging culture. On the other hand, blogging culture clearly influenced web culture, by introducing new habits.

The first convention that blogs introduced was the emphasis on the newness featuring the proposed content, which was first of all indicated by the reverse chronological order of publication ('last in, first out'). In this way, the syntactic arrangement of the published contents acquires a semantic relevance. This format remained stable from 'What's New' pages, to weblogs intended as lists of interesting links, to weblogs as diaries (about the consolidation of the weblog format see also Siles, 2012a). This standard soon led to the practice of live-blogging, in which a post is updated over time as an event unfolds. Journalism soon adopted that habit too, producing articles following the real-time development of an event. The same structure was also used as a standard way to organise content in the early years of social network sites timelines, although it has now been replaced by organizing contents by relevance.

A second habit that blogs helped to establish is that of linking to a quoted source. We refer here particularly to 'endorsement' (link in the body of the post) and 'attribution' link, that is to say to links that are "a credit for a 'borrowed' link" (Ammann, 2011, p. 30). The hypertext link acquires several meanings—underlining, for example, that the source is worthy of note (or deplorable, in extreme cases)—but the practice also has ethical and deontological implications, because it is comparable to academic quotations, which are important for acknowledging the origins of a certain idea. Reciprocal linking was important also because it helped to expand the social network around the blogs giving it more visibility: "If someone linked you because he/she liked your post [...] this opened you another blogosphere" (interview to M, Milano, 2003, text+photo).

The functions of blogging

A key-step towards the understanding of blogs' social metamorphosis is to observe how their functions have changed over time.

When in 1997, Jorn Barger (1997) coined the term 'blog' to denote his own website, "a daily running log of the best webpages I visit", he also implicitly allowed the specific group of internet users and the culture associated with blogging to be identified (Siles, 2012b). It is around this format (Ammann, 2009, 2011; Siles, 2011) that the very first blogging community aimed at the "social resource discovery" (Ammann, 2013) grew; it was fed by the diffusion of "link attribution [practices] as a form of direct reciprocity, a shared norm that precipitated the routinisation of the network's social relations" (Ammann, 2011, p. 33).

The second turn occurred when the meaning of the blog shifted to a personal website containing writings and acquiring specific features. As described above, the blog became a self-publishing space featuring tools for readers to interact with it.

From that moment on, other functions emerged over time: blogs became diaries, themed journals, and places to be creative.

The study evidenced that the bloggers belonging to the three identified phases shared most of the functions, however, some of them still seem to be peculiar of each particular phase. As the study focused on personal blogs, their main function was to work as personal diaries. In particular, early bloggers kept their blogs as online spaces for expressing their thoughts and feelings, and giving an account of their everyday lives. Similarly, blogs were also places to reflect on life: "For me, it is a tool for writing, for expressing myself through writing" (interview with M, Milan, 2003, text). They became spaces where blogger's creativity could be expressed, also by experimenting different kind of contents, such as photos and videos: "I hope that [through photos] I express how I feel during the day" (interview with F, Turin, 2006, photo). For some bloggers, writing had also a therapeutic function, pouring out feelings and emotions and sometimes complementing a poor social life: "I'm a single mother with two children [...] and when I encounter difficulties, when I'm sad or down, I think that in any case I can write on my blog and it helps me to give vent to my feelings" (interview with F, Turin, 2006, text + photo).

Beside this creative/expressive function, blogs had also a cognitive function—they worked as alternative sources of information to replace or complement traditional media, often about specific themes, like IT or web communication: "I discovered […] a new channel of information" (interview with M, Milan, 2001, text).

A later function that emerged over time and was more evident in the third group was the use of blogs as a personal-branding tool, with the specific purpose of building an online presence and establishing a professional identity.

Furthermore, blogs also have a social function, in that they can work as tools able to bring people together both online and offline. We shall develop this topic in the next section.

Spreading the word: online/offline social relations

From its very beginning, as described above, blogs created online and offline connections among bloggers, thus workings as self-publishing tools as well as means to establish social relationships.

The shared enthusiasm for the new publishing and communication tool led early bloggers (in both the USA and Italy) to create micro-communities around blogs, reading each other regularly and meeting offline (Blood, 2002; Di Rocco, 2003). Di Rocco (2003) compares the early Italian bloggers to a 'club' with a familiar way of 'chatting' together. An important defining element of the Italian early community was the web design newsletter *Nartlist* led by Antonio Cavedoni and Frederic Argazzi, two of the first Italian bloggers. The glue that kept this group together was a common interest in the internet and the web: they were tech fans with a shared passion for blogging—their brand new tool: "It seems that we really were the first bloggers [in Italy]. […] When blogging became a craze, that group of people produced an explosion of creativity" (interview with F, Milan, 2000, text). The analysis of their blogs showed some very intense activity in that period, with posts, links and comments (when enabled). Initially, social relations were not visible on blogs, as there was no area for commenting, and people commented via instant messaging (ICQ) or email instead. Later on, the public comment area was introduced, and therefore the discussions became public.

The early bloggers also arranged offline meet-ups, mainly between 2002 and 2005: "We met at conferences [on web design], because there weren't so many of us in Italy working on the web (interview with M, Modena, 2000, text)".

The type of blog-centred social interactions evolved over time: on the one hand, there were peer-to-peer exchanges, while on the other, some bloggers became more famous and better known than others (also see the phenomenon of A-list bloggers described by Maratea, 2007).

By 2003, blogging was no longer a niche: blogs increased their visibility (also thanks to the attention received by newspapers and journalists) and some of the early bloggers felt uncomfortable with such developments of the blogosphere, to the extent that they closed their blogs: "Suddenly the blog wasn't a toy any more […]. It is not your private room any more, the Junior Woodchucks book that you and your friends used to find useful" (Di Rocco, 2003, p. 74).

If the first blogging community slowly disappeared, new kind of communities appeared, either aggregating around specific platforms or on a geography base. The role of Splinder, an Italian blogging platform, is particularly relevant in what we identified as the second phase of the development of the Italian blogosphere (2003–2006). It offered a variety of tools for connecting publicly or in private with others bloggers and had various options for promoting a blog that helped to connect bloggers and generate micro-communities based on common interests or reciprocal appreciation. In this period, the importance of links driving traffic to blogs grew, as described above. Hence, being mentioned by a famous blogger or in magazine articles about blogging could be an important step towards public acknowledgment of a blogger as such. Still, social relationships were deep, and blogs have loyal readers: "I have an attached circle of readers" (interview with F, Turin, 2003, text).

During this second phase the presence of the comments area became an established feature, thus consolidating the use of blogs for both self-publishing and social relations purposes. If comments were scarcely used by the early bloggers, who mainly conceived the blog as a space for self-expression ("I never wanted, nor I had comments" (interview with F, Milan, 2000, text)), for the bloggers of the second period, the presence of comments helped instead to build closer relations with their readers. Sometimes they even became like forum threads with very long discussions, whereas, in other cases, they hosted trolls that bothered other readers.

Meeting offline was still important for the bloggers of this second group, although they met mostly locally and after spending more time reading and commenting on blogs than the early bloggers.

The third group knew that they had readers, regular or casual, and actively engaged in activities to further enlarge their followers. Bloggers used tactics (De Certeau, 2010) to encourage people to visit their blog, such as organising little competitions, asking for readers' opinions, linking to other posts or blogs, and adding widgets to display the blog subscribers, Facebook friends or the latest comments.

Offline meetings happened either at major events or locally (if the bloggers lived in the same city, for example). Big events about the blogosphere, for web enthusiasts or professionals generally were organised, like BarCamps and the BlogFest. BarCamps were organised locally or around a specific topic as informal opportunities for bloggers to meet and share knowledge.[9] The tight connection of BarCamps with local territories is a peculiarity of the Italian blogosphere and is rooted in Italian culture. In some cities (like Turin) also networks of urban blogs (it is to say blogs entirely dedicated to a city) grew (Locatelli, 2014).

BlogFest (now Festa della Rete) was a major event organised by Gianluca Neri (one of Italy's first and foremost bloggers) as a gather to meet up and reflect on the state of the Italian blogosphere with the support of business sponsors. All these events helped to spread blogging culture.

The economic dimension: new forms of profit

The economic dimension is highly relevant to the development of blogging. From this point of view, blogging contributed to establish the free web, which has also ushered in new business models.

The first blogging platforms were free (Stone, 2002). In this framework, we must not forget blogging's role in spreading Creative Commons licences as an alternative to copyright for protecting knowledge and creativity.[10] Opening a blog is still free while a fee is generally required for the activation of advanced options; social network sites work in the same fashion. Lurkin (2006) and Anderson (2009) would later call this business model 'Freemium'—basic services are provided free of charge, while advanced/professional ones require payment.

In their early years, internet connection speed was very slow (28KB/s) and the possibility that blogs gave to quickly share links allowed users to save money and time if compared with sharing links via e-mail.

When the first blogs started in Italy, this free culture was already established and it attracted several users, because it did not imply a high-risk economic invest-ment: "With this, I don't spend a cent, and I don't earn a cent; [it is] really a hobby, a game" (interview with F, Turin, 2005, text+photo+video).

The free model was also adopted by Splinder, which sold advertising space for its economic upkeep, selecting advertisers according to their relevance for the community.

A key milestone in blogging history was the integration of blogs into the business strategies of multinationals like Google, which acquired Blogger in 2003. This transition marked the spread of the blogging phenomenon and sparked global interest in its profitability. In the same years, several companies added blogs to their commercial offering for consumers, e.g. Microsoft with Windows Live Spaces.[11] Italian web companies such as Excite or Virgilio repli-cated a similar strategy. From this point of view, an important aspect in shaping the development of blogs was how these platforms marketed blogs as an 'online diary', contributing in shaping the meaning and function of blogs around writing and self-telling.

Another aspect to consider is that a blog can be a personal-branding tool for professionals who wish to position themselves among other experts, thus using the blog as a mean for identity formation and presentation. The sample of interviewees we addressed to include Diego Bianchi, who used his blog and video-blog as a new tool for self-expression and gradually became very well known. His skills at video storytelling grew to the extent that he now presents a TV programme for the Italian public-service broadcast company aired on Rai3.

The study shows different examples of knowledge exchanges among bloggers, for example to solve problems or add new features. In addition, interviewees reported various forms of economic support:

> Once, I had no more money; I really didn't have any money. I had to update the domain, but the 35 euros required to the domain were just vital to me—I just couldn't afford it. So, very simply, I wrote that I couldn't renew the domain, that I was sorry, and I backed it all up for better times when I'd have the possibilities to pay for the domain again. And, you know, money came in. (Interview with M, Milan, 2001, text)

Lastly, a blog can bring in revenue if it hosts advertising or if it becomes part of an information network.

In the mentioned cases, the blog's economic sustainability is strictly connected with the quality of its content and the existence of a benefit for readers.

The institutional dimension

Finally, there is the institutional dimension.

On privacy issues, the interviewees reported that they were gradually becoming more careful about sensitive data, mainly about their families and children. For example, one of Splinder's strengths was the chance to easily chat with other bloggers while retaining the desired level of anonymity.

Three relationship models regarding identity and privacy protection were found across the three bloggers of the three phases: conformity, filtering and concealment. With conformity, there is a substantial correspondence between author and blogger.[12] The blog shows the blogger's full name and a personal description including job, age, interests, photos and contacts. Little discretion is exercised about other people mentioned in the blog, like family members.

The second model, filtering, consists in putting only some non-sensitive elements in the blog and preserving the importance of others by keeping them reserved, for example by publishing a fictionalised biography.

The concealment model was used by bloggers with a nickname who hid all the sensitive data that could make them identifiable. The facts, stories and thoughts are real, but the person behind the blog is not recognisable. The first model is preferred by male bloggers; the latter two, by females.

As for the prevention of defamation, the Italian blogosphere is far from being near to finding a solution. Even though the first blogs appeared in Italy in 2000,

Italian legislators are still debating about the blogs' status and how to regulate them. Proposed laws continue to vacillate between equating blogs to newspapers and websites.[13]

The debate revolves around various factors: the nature of the blog (should a blog be considered a publishing product?); the blogging space (is it public or private?); responsibility for the content (should it rest with the author or the hosting service?); responsibility for comments (do they belong to the blogger or to the commenters?); and intellectual property (does the traditional copyright model still apply?).

The correct starting point should not be to consider all blogs together but to evaluate blogs relating them to a sort typology based on information such as who is the author, on which platform it is hosted, and what is the nature of the posted content.

CONCLUSIONS: BLOGS AS A MULTI-FACETED PHENOMENON

The use of the theoretical framework of the cultural product enabled a deep analysis of the Italian blogosphere's historical development through a complex, multifaceted perspective useful to show the crucial steps determining the process of blogs' shaping.

Three phases were identified: 1999/2000–2003 early bloggers (the opening of the first blogs); 2003–2006 (the success of Splinder, the first Italian blogging platform); 2006–2008 (when Google redesigned Blogger, and the blogosphere went mainstream).

The study evidenced that blogs were culturally appropriate for their time (Colombo, 2001, 2003): they were a tool that could identify internet surfers' needs, e.g. to try out new forms of web publishing and to create personal online spaces. Data showed a continuous shaping and shifting of blog's meaning and function: from online diary, to a tool for self-publishing and building social relations, to a place where to build an online identity with fewer online interactions (that often moved to social network sites). The results, thus, confirm that also in Italy the process of adoption of blogging was non-linear, but rather went through many stages and was continuously shaped by several factors; this set the Italian situation in line with to the early stages of blogging in the US, as evidenced by other research using different approaches (Ammann, 2009, 2011, 2013; Siles, 2011, 2012a, 2012b). The same approach could be profitably applied to see how blogs were incorporated in other cultural contexts or to other objects like social network sites.

The research evidenced that there was and still is a mutual shaping between technology, culture, society, economy, and institutions as it happened in the US (Siles, 2012a). It also showed that in Italy, despite the early and broad diffusion of blogging, the institutional element has been struggling to find the right way to interpret and regulate the new phenomenon.

Among the several factors that contributed to the shaping of the phenomenon, the research showed that the social and technological context had a strong influence in differentiating blogging 'appropriation' (Silverstone & Hirsch, 1992) among the three highlighted phases. On the contrary, the individual process of adoption (time, space, and privacy management)—were similar across the three phases.

The study revealed that social relations within the Italian blogosphere changed shifting through various stages: in the first group they were similar to a 'community of interest' (Rheingold, 1993) whereas in the second and third group mainly 'weak ties' (Granovetter, 1973) were developed. A persistent common element across the blogosphere is the existence of supportive ties, a feature of online communities highlighted by Baym (2006).

Data evidenced also that blogging culture transformed the broader culture of the web introducing new features and habits. It is the case of the reverse chronological order used to organise contents that changed the traditional order imposed by print, which used to arrange the content to be read from right to left (Ong, 1982).

Considering the economic dimension, the study demonstrated that blogs reinforced the logic of the free development of the internet, in contrast to the capitalist economy in relation to which the latter has always had a double-edged relationship (Castells, 2001). The choice to offering free blogging services reveals traces of the hacker culture—one of the internet's main cultural components (Castells, 2001) in calling for the free propagation of services, data and culture.

Furthermore, it is worth noting that blogging activity can have also economic returns in non-pecuniary form, as showed by the wide net of exchanges and supportive ties evidenced in the frame of the research. It can be said that in the blogosphere there is a 'gift economy' based on interpersonal relationships build upon scarce resources like time, attention and trust (De Biase, 2007). They are components of the "happiness economy", in which values and trust are nurtured and preserved by social relationships (De Biase, 2007, p. 147).

The study has some limitations. It is restricted to the early days of blogging in Italy, so it would be useful to extend it to more recent years, including the relations with social network sites, and applying it to other types of blogs (like journalistic, corporate, professional ones). It would also be very interesting to investigate the mainstreaming of blogging after 2008 and the connections between blogging and mass media or the phenomenon of influencers.

A major limitation of the cultural-product approach is that, when applied to blogs, it is difficult to include the development of social relationships; here, they were included in the cultural dimension. A further limitation is that, with just a small sample of bloggers, the economic and institutional dimensions barely emerged during interviews and blog analyses. For a deeper insight, platform owners, professionals and lawmakers should also be interviewed.

REFERENCES

Alasuutari, P. (1999). Cultural images of the media. In P. Alasuutari (Ed.), *Rethinking the media audience: The new agenda* (pp. 95–104). London: Sage.

Ammann, R. (2009). Jorn barger, the newspage network and the emergence of the weblog community. In *Proceedings of the 20th ACM conference on Hypertext and hypermedia* (HT '09). ACM, New York, NY, USA, pp. 279–288.

Ammann, R. (2011). Reciprocity, social curation and the emergence of blogging: A study in community formation. *Procedia—Social and Behavioral Sciences, 22,* 26–36.

Ammann, R. (2013). *Weblogs 1994–2000: A genealogy* (PhD dissertation). University College London, London.

Anderson, C. (2009). *Free: The future of a radical price.* New York, NY: Free Press

Apogeoonline (2011, January 10). *A che punto sono le leggi di internet?.* Retrieved January 18, 2016, from www.apogeonline.com/filirossi/leggi-internet

Bailey, K. (1987). *Methods of social research.* New York, NY: Free Press.

Barger, J. (1997). *MISC: "Weblogs" are the best formats for hotlists.* Retrieved April 20, 2016 from https://groups.google.com/forum/#!msg/comp.infosystems.www.announce/fel3t0fDTT4/_XTZ2ies9koJ

Barrett, C. (2002). Anatomy of a weblog. In J. Rodzvilla (Ed.), *We've got blog: How weblogs are changing our culture* (pp. 25–27). Cambridge, MA: Perseus Pub.

Baym, N. K. (2006). Interpersonal life online. In L. A. Lievrouw & S. Livingstone (Eds.), *Handbook of new media: Social shaping and social consequences of ICTs. Updated student edition* (pp. 35–54). London: Sage.

Blood, R. (2002). *The weblog handbook: Practical advice on creating and maintaining your blog.* Cambridge, MA: Perseus Pub.

Castells, M. (2001). *The internet galaxy: Reflections on the internet, business and society.* Oxford: Oxford University Press.

Charmaz, K. (2000). Grounded theory. Objectivist and constructivist methods. In N. K. Denzin & Y. S. Lincoln (Eds.), *Handbook of qualitative research* (2nd ed., pp. 509–535). London: Sage.

Colombo, F. (2001). L'industria culturale e i suoi margini. In F. Colombo, L. Farinotti, & F. Pasquali (Eds.), *I margini della cultura. Media e innovazione* (pp. 43–68). Milano: Franco Angeli.

Colombo, F. (2003). *Introduzione allo studio dei media.* Roma: Carocci.

Colombo, F. (2006). Technological innovation and media complexity. DTT in the light of a new theoretical prospect. In F. Colombo & N. Vittadini (Eds.), *Digitizing TV: Theoretical issues and comparative studies across Europe* (pp. 21–35). Milano: Vita & Pensiero.

Cosenza, G. (2008). *Semiotica dei nuovi media* (2nd ed.). Roma-Bari: Laterza.

De Biase, L. (2007). *Economia della felicità: dalla blogosfera al valore del dono e oltre,* Milano: Feltrinelli.

De Certeau, M. (2010). *L'invenzione del quotidiano.* Roma: Lavoro.

Di Rocco, E. (2003). *Mondo blog. Storie vere di gente in rete.* Milano: Hops Libri.

Glaser, B. G., & Strauss, A. L. (1967). *The discovery of grounded theory: Strategies for qualitative research.* Chicago, IL: Aldine.

Granovetter, M. S. (1973). The strengths of weak ties. *American Journal of Sociology, 7*(6), 1360–1380.

Griswold, W. (1986). *Renaissance rivals: City comedy and revenge tragedy in the London theatre 1576–1980.* Chicago, IL: University of Chicago Press.

Griswold, W. (1994). *Cultures and societies in a changing world.* Thousand Oaks, CA: Pine Forge Press.

Hannerz, U. (1992). *Cultural complexity: Studies in the social organization of meanings.* New York, NY: Columbia University Press.

Hine, C. (2000). *Virtual ethnography.* London: Sage Publications.

Locatelli, E. (2014). *The blog up: Storia sociale del blog in Italia.* Milan: Franco Angeli.

Lurkin, J. (2006 March 23). *My Favorite Business Model.* Retrieved January 18, 2016 from http://avc.blogs.com/a_vc/2006/03/my_favorite_bus.html.

Maratea, R. (2007). The e-rise and fall of social problems: The blogosphere as a public arena. *Social Problems, 55*(1), 139–160.

Marcus, G. E. (1995). Ethnography in/of the world system: The emergence of multisided ethnography. *Annual Review of Anthropology, 24,* 95–117.

Mason, J. (1996). *Qualitative researching.* London: Sage.

Ong, W. J. (1982). *Orality and literacy: The technologizing of the word.* London: Methuen.

Rheingold, H. (1993). *The virtual community: Homesteading in the electronic frontier.* Reading, MA: Addison-Wesley.

Rogers, E. (1962). *Diffusion of innovation.* New York, NY: The Free Press.

Siles, I. (2011). From online filter to web format: Articulating materiality and meaning in the early history of blogs. *Social Studies of Science, 41*(5), 737–758.

Siles, I. (2012a). The rise of blogging: Articulation as a dynamic of technological stabilization. *New Media & Society, 14*(5), 781–797.

Siles, I. (2012b). Web technologies of the self: The arising of the "Blogger" identity. *Journal of Computer-Mediated Communication, 17*(4), 408–421.

Silverman, D. (2000). *Doing qualitative research: A practical handbook.* London: Sage.

Silverstone, R., & Hirsch, E. (1992). *Consuming technologies: Media and information in domestic spaces.* Abingdon: Routledge.

Stone, B. (2002 January 01). *The amazingly true story of blogger!* Retrieved January 18, 2016 from https://groups.google.com/forum/#!msg/comp.infosystems.www.announce/fel3t0fDTT4/_XTZ2ies9koJ

Strauss, A. L., & Corbin J. M. (1990). *Basics of qualitative research: Grounded theory procedures and techniques.* Newbury Park, CA: Sage.

Winer, D. (2000 October 14). *Saturday, October 14, 2000.* Retrieved January 18, 2016 from http://scripting.com/2000/10/14.html

NOTES

1. The term 'diffusion' clearly echoes Rogers (1962).
2. The research was part of the PhD thesis of the author, discussed on May 22, 2008 at the Università Cattolica del Sacro Cuore (Italy) and later published in Locatelli (2014).
3. Older or not available archives were retrieved through Archive.org.
4. The video-blogging event "Vlogeurope 2006" (Milan, November 18, 2006); the conference 'Piùblog' held at the Fiera della Media Editoria (Rome, December 8–10, 2006); 'RomeCamp', Barcamp in Rome (January 21, 2007).
5. About the stabilization of the blog format from filter to a web format see also Siles (2011, 2012a).

6. To provide a record of that period, the interviewed bloggers agreed to be cited with their full name.
7. Each interviewee is identified with gender, city of residence, the year in which his/her blog was opened, and the main format of published posts.
8. Created in 2001, it closed in early 2012.
9. The BarCamp is a very informal meeting format where each participant can make a presentation or actively participate in the organisation. For more information, see http://barcamp.org/w/page/402984/FrontPage.
10. https://creativecommons.org.
11. Launched in 2004 as MSN Spaces and closed in March 2011.
12. The author coincides here with the real named person behind the blog; the blogger is the image of them created via the blog.
13. For a brief history of the proposed laws, see Apogeoonline (2011).

CHAPTER SEVEN

Born outside THE newsroom

The creation of the Age Online

SYBIL NOLAN

INTRODUCTION

Twenty-five years after the birth of the web, the newspaper industry in the West appears moribund, at least as an industry that produces newspapers. In the USA, the Pew Research Center has documented how, in the space of just two decades, the financial value of once-robust newspaper groups like the Boston Globe and the Philadelphia Inquirer declined by up to 95% (Mitchell, Jurkowitz, & Guskin, 2013), thanks to falling advertising revenues and declines in circulation. In May 2016, the *Tampa Tribune*, once the 36th largest daily newspaper in the country, was bought by its rival and closed (Gillin, 2016). A decade earlier, it had been selling almost 240,000 copies daily and more than 300,000 on Sunday (BurrellesLuce, 2007). In Britain, the *Independent*, after massive falls in sales was transformed into a web-only publication in March 2016 (Duke, 2016; "Independent becomes the first national newspaper", 2016). In Australia, Fairfax Media, the nation's second largest newspaper group, excised key digital assets from its newspaper business, and announced a A$989 million write-down of the legacy assets (Fairfax, 2016). It also confirmed that its major mastheads would ultimately cease to be printed on weekdays (Hywood, 2016).

As Keith Herndon noted in his study of the decline of American newspapers, many critics argue that newspapers took too long to change their business model and adapt to the internet environment: "[B]y the time the industry understood that its model had to change, readers, advertisers, and investors no longer cared"

(2012, p. 171). One of the tasks of journalism studies now is to understand journalism's part in this failure. From the beginning of online news, circa 1994, the mainstream press demonstrated its nervousness about the quality and indeed the legitimacy of user-generated content in online editions (Deuze, 2003; Matheson, 2004, pp. 445–446; Nolan, 2003). As late as 2000, Mark Deuze noted, few mainstream news sites offered extensive external links, partly because of concerns over copyright and the ethics of deep-linking (2003, p. 212). This half-hearted embrace of the web's hypertextuality reflected ethical and legal debates about copyright and intellectual property, as well as journalists' understandings of their professional role. Pablo Boczkowski (2004, p. 82) documented the way some online journalists working for the *New York Times* resisted linking to the websites of the companies they reported about. "Is that like doing PR for the company?" one asked. To such reporters, ignoring or breaching deeply inscribed rules of traditional news reporting felt transgressive.

As Donald Matheson has argued, to step outside journalism's conventions seemed to threaten journalism's institutional claim to authority (2004, p. 446). It took years for many newspaper people to understand that using the web's specific affordances could actually *increase* journalism's kudos, as brilliantly demonstrated in the #PanamaLeaks investigation of 2016. Now journalism studies must ask to what extent the failure of newspapers is the result of journalists' inability to adapt to the opportunities offered by hypertexuality and interactivity. Alternatively, to what extent is it the responsibility of other actors in this complex industry, for example proprietors who have shown a tendency to enter the online realm hastily, establishing poorly-funded and inadequately-staffed 'place holders' to protect their brands and market positions (Nguyen and Garcia, 2012, p. 4; van Heekeren, 2010, pp. 25–26).

With these questions in mind, this chapter explores the creation of the Age Online, the first major newspaper website in Australia, and among the first in the world. Owned by the *Age* newspaper in Melbourne and its parent, the Fairfax organization, the site began life on February 7, 1995 ("Let's meet on the internet," 1995a; Cowie, 2015), a year before the *New York Times* created its own website ("Who we are", 2016), and when only about 60 newspapers in the United States maintained an online presence (Shedden, 2007, p. 140). The *Age* beat other Australian entrants into cyberspace by a matter of months: not only its sister paper, the *Sydney Morning Herald*, but also the national broadcaster, the Australian Broadcasting Corporation (ABC). Yet, while the history of ABC Online has been well documented (Burns, 2000, 2008; Inglis, 2006; Martin, 1999, 2004), the *Age*'s pioneering efforts have gone relatively unnoticed. Even the newspaper itself covered the site's early history sparingly (Cowie, 2015; van Niekerk, 2005).

If little attention is paid to digital media history as it unfolds, then the speed and scope of the changes experienced during the first years of the web make it difficult to analyse accurately *ex post facto* (Boczkowski, 2004, p. 12). Thus in 2012, the British media scholar George Brock (2012) wrote on his website that "the flagship Fairfax papers in Sydney and Melbourne came to digital late", an observation I recognized as incorrect, because I happened to have been working at *The Age* when the Age Online started. Similarly, two recent business studies of Fairfax Media and its commercial decline in the digital era barely mention the Age Online, even though these accounts are written by former Fairfax journalists (Ryan, 2013; Williams, 2013). One of them (Williams, 2013, p. 33) depicts a founder of Seek. com.au, a start-up that eventually lured away much of Fairfax's classified job advertising, asking in 1997: "why would newspapers not go online?". But by then, both Fairfax and its opponent, News Ltd, had established online advertising operations (Outing, 1997a, 1997b). These instances seemed to suggest 'lateness' as a quality of Australian newspaper web history, yet further investigation reveals a different or more complex reality.

Siles and Boczkowski (2012, pp. 1386–1387) argue compellingly that historical research is one of the best tools for understanding the current state of newspapers. Given the inherent complexity of the newspaper industry, many conditions and practices usually combine to fashion newspapers' responses to changing circumstances. Uncovering how these factors are imbricated can illuminate media success stories or failures in surprising ways. As the journalism scholar Barbie Zelizer (2004, p. 81) writes, "the most valuable historical inquiries are those that redress the givens of old".

The starting point for this research was the newspaper's own archive and Fairfax's annual corporate reports. However, given the sketchiness of the historiography, the most significant aspect of the project was interviews with five key actors in the creation of the *Age*'s website. The subjects of these semi-structured interviews were selected by referral, by which method I eventually identified most of the small team involved. Not all were able to be interviewed in the time available, but those who participated ranged from senior management to a university student employed casually on the site. I also drew on my own experience working as a journalist on the newspaper (not the website) during the years 1989–1996, and my knowledge of the conditions that then prevailed. The validity of the approach used here is well recognized (Prins, 2001, pp. 140–141). The researcher's experience constitutes a 'second record' against which to test the documentary and oral accounts.

LIBRARIANS DOING IT FOR THEMSELVES

Some time late in 1994, the *Age*'s managing director, Stuart Simson, went down to the newspaper's library at the suggestion of chief librarian, Sibylle Noras. She wanted to demonstrate to Simson the world wide web and its application to newspapers, and her computer was one of the few terminals in the building with an internet connection. Simson (2015) remembered that he was immediately "fascinated—there was no other way of putting it". A journalist by background, and a former CEO of a business magazine called *BRW*, he saw the web's potential for engaging and building audiences. "At *BRW* I'd learned the importance of extending the publication's reach. The penny dropped that this was going to be something that could have significant implications for publishers."

Simson was one of the new brooms brought in during a tumultuous period of ownership change at the *Age* and its parent company, Fairfax. After five generations, the Fairfax family had lost control of its publishing empire in 1990 (Prisk, 2014, p. 452). The Canadian media magnate Conrad Black, chief owner of the *Daily Telegraph* in London, subsequently gained a 15% stake in Fairfax, enough to take over the daily management of its papers (Ryan, 2013, p. 92). Simson was appointed to lead the *Age* subsidiary in Melbourne which had been associated with Fairfax since 1972. "The *Age* business was strong but it needed some change, and that was the direction I was given," Simson recalled (2015). The newspaper's Monday–Friday circulation (about 211,000 copies daily) was already beginning to come under pressure, due to media fragmentation and consumers' reduced reading time. Simson backed Noras's plans to take *Age* content online. He also appointed her manager of new media, and a member of his executive team.

To journalists, the library seemed an unlikely place to start a newspaper site. Yet around the world, it was knowledge workers best equipped to imagine the web's application who often initiated such projects (Brügger, 2012a, p. 95; Burns, 2000, p. 95; Falkenberg, 2010, p. 248). Librarians who used information technology for indexing and archiving quickly saw the point: the first web server built outside CERN was created at Stanford University by a librarian who wanted to use it to help scientists working on the Stanford Linear Accelerator to share their documents with colleagues in other countries (Berners-Lee & Fischetti, 1999, pp. 45–46). In Australia, librarians' familiarity with information technology, and their awareness of its benefits, made them early adopters of the web (Goggin, 2004, p. 61; Rayward, 2002, p. 13).

The *Age* library subscribed to online databases such as Lexis-Nexis and Reuters. Noras, with a graduate degree in library and media studies, understood the global movement to creation of commercial digital newspaper archives (Herndon, 2012, pp. 153–154). When she realized that Reuters was making available some of the world's best newspaper archives and that Australia was a gap in their holdings, she visited the news agency's head office in London, and negotiated a deal for the *Age* to supply the company with an electronic daily package of the paper's core news and business coverage, to be made available 48 hours after its publication in Melbourne (Noras, 2015). Fairfax also began experimenting with CD technology, which in the early 1990s seemed the future trajectory of digital content development (Burns, 2000, p. 92; Noras, 2015). Noras and her team helped produce a commercial series of CDs of indexed *Age* content. She recalled 'huge changes' at Fairfax at this time: "somewhere between the land of opportunity and the land of total confusion" (Noras, 2015).

As at many other newspapers (Herndon, 2012, p. 154), digital archiving and the advent of a website was a 'co-mingled process' at the *Age*. Noras personally was fascinated by the potential of the world wide web. She had an internet connection installed at home and spent many spare hours 'surfing' the web. Between 1990, when the first web protocol, server and browser/editor were created, and 1993, when the software was made publicly available (Clarke, 2013, p. 98), Noras had begun attending annual conferences of the American newspaper librarians' association, where people were already discussing the potential for newspapers on the web. She also made contact with Steve Outing, an editor and reporter who had worked for the *San Francisco Chronicle*, *San Jose Mercury News,* and *Boulder Daily Camera* before becoming an activist promoting the development of news online. In June 1995, he launched a website for *Editor & Publisher* which provided a hyperlinked list of newspaper web pages (Outing, 1995a, p. 68). In August that year, he began writing a daily column online. New media was "the most exciting and promising sector of the newspaper business in the mid–90s," Outing wrote, but added the rider that "unfortunately, information about how to turn newspaper new media projects into profit centers is hard to find" ("Letters section," 1995b).

Noras corresponded with Outing via email, and credited his advice and her contacts with American newspaper librarians in helping her understand developments in online newspapers in the US. She was not an IT person herself, and *The Age* was still run from dedicated terminals connected to a mainframe computer. The limited knowhow in Australia about the web at that point is difficult to remember or imagine today. Clarke (2013, p. 99), a principal historian of the web's development in Australia, writes that by 1992, there was "a fairly small but well-established and highly capable community of people in academe, with the technical capacity to use and develop Internet facilities". The first website in Australia went live in mid-1992 at life.anu.edu.au. By mid–1994, the 'pioneer' phase of the web was over and 'early adopters' in Australian industry, government and community organisations began to look for opportunities to enter web publishing (Clarke, 2013, p. 101).

Using her library contacts, Noras negotiated for the Age site to be served on Vicnet, the web service launched by the State Library of Victoria in 1995. The Age Online's first URL was http://www.vicnet.net.au/vicnet/theage.html. (Later, it became http://theage.com.au.) The *Age*'s HTML files were uploaded to Vicnet using FTP, by a senior Age librarian, Frank Prain, who also created some of the site's first pages. It is clear from the inaugural page itself and an associated item in the newspaper (Cowie, 2015) that Noras and Prain set out to create a 'homepage' for the *Age* rather than an online newspaper. Indeed, this was how the site was described in the pages of the Computer Age section ("Let's meet on the internet," 1995a). The site contained only a small selection of articles, which followed the form of abstracts, partly because this was a system the librarians understood, but also because of concerns about staff journalists' copyright. Newspapers had understood that they owned most of the publication rights in stories written by staff journalists, until a case brought by two journalists in 1990 raised significant doubts (Davies, 1994, p. 3; Gettens, 1998, p. 21; Gibson, 1998, p. 67). When the *Age* website started, the journalists' union and management were still trying to negotiate an agreement that would acknowledge staff reporters' residual rights in their work (Davies, 1994, p. 4; Noras, 2015).

Each item published on the early Age Online essentially consisted of a headline, reporter's byline, date, and a short abstract of a news article from the paper. These abstracts were written by an experienced sub-editor specially employed for the function, Mary Riekert, who had previously worked overseas and for the *Sunday Age*. Her ability to write short news paragraphs which captured the gist of what was going on in Melbourne meant the *Age* site soon attracted an audience of expatriates overseas, even though items were not uploaded until 24 hours after publication in the newspaper. Riekert not only compiled the content but composed it in HTML and uploaded it to Vicnet. A conference paper delivered by Gary Hardy of Vicnet noted the site's popularity:

> we currently host the first tentative experiment in web publishing by The Age, Melbourne's major daily newspaper. The arrival of The Age has more than doubled the amount of traffic on our server. The Age pages dominate the VICNET top twenty pages retrieved each week. (Hardy, 1995)

In terms of visual impact, the early Age Online pages were sparsely populated and cartoonishly illustrated. These arcane media objects, winkled out of a mysterious combination of 1s and 0s, appeared crudely fashioned especially when compared with the sophisticated design of the daily newspaper.

Great Moments in Sport 1996
THE AGE
MELBOURNE, AUSTRALIA, Friday December 20 1996

NEWS | SPORT | BUSINESS | ENTERTAINMENT | COMPUTERS | EDUCATION

Book *of the* Year
And the winner is ...

Racism row threatens universities' Malaysian plans

Jim Schembri interviews Geoffrey Rush

EG's *Christmas Comedy Guide*

THE AGE
The fight for Fairfax
Murdoch: I'm out but Packer in

VICTORIA'S $3 BILLION CAR INDUSTRY UNDER A CLOUD

The Martin Bryant story   The Telstra sale   Victoria 2010: A special report

GOOD WEEKEND: 52 Weekends Away

Figure 7.1: Earliest image of The Age Online still extant on the Wayback Machine. By this time, the copyright dispute had been resolved, and reporters' stories ran in full on the site. Screenshot: June 2, 2016.

Nevertheless, Riekert remembers receiving emails from readers outside Australia who were excited by the Age Online coverage. She witnessed the powerful impact of the web firsthand after the site covered renewed French nuclear tests in the Pacific in late 1995 (Riekert, 2015). For the first time, Riekert combined her own summaries of *Age* reporters' copy with content from other sources, compiling the copy in much the same way that a senior sub-editor would edit breaking news from the wire services. The site also gave readers access to photographic coverage of the story. This was the breakthrough moment when it became clear that the Age Online should be covering news, not just providing an online archive. The response by email was 'huge', according to Riekert. Readers in Europe wanted to know more than they were learning about the tests in their home media.

Evaluating what 'huge' meant in those early days is difficult. Noras (2015) remembered that she collated and counted all emails and drew down as much information as she could from the system, reporting this data to her superiors in Melbourne and Sydney. But content management systems and databases were not yet standard web tools, and A. C. Nielsen had not begun compiling its list of the most popular websites (Mayrhofer, 1996, p. 157). There are clues here and there in company documents. In its 1996 annual report, the *Sydney Morning Herald* site was said to receive 100,000 'hits' a day (Fairfax, 1996, p. 51). In any case, it is clear that at the Age Online, as at many other early media sites, staff embraced read-ers' response by email. At the ABC Online, members of staff were also "besieged with emails from listeners," Martin wrote (2004, p. 28). Boczkowski (2004, p. 92) reported that journalists he interviewed in 1998 who contributed copy to the *New York Times*' online computer section valued the email feedback they received—sometimes as many as 100 emails per story, which not only praised or criticized, but suggested follow-ups and different angles. Interactivity assisted newspaper journalists pioneering online news.

Yet if the Age Online drew excited approval from readers, inside the *Age* build-ing it was a distinctly different story. Fairfax journalists took industrial action in late 1995 over the company's commercial exploitation of their work in online formats, especially the creation of the CD-ROM archives series (Turner, 1996, p. 309). This led to an agreement in which staff ceded their secondary electronic copyright in return for an annual payment by the company (Turner, 1996, p. 309). While this issue was working itself out, Riekert found herself the target of criticism from other journalists, including former colleagues from the *Sunday Age*. "People were really hostile," she recalled. Staff journalists were reluctant to join the online team, she said. This aligns with my memory: some reporters expressed puzzlement about why a journalist with Riekert's skills and professional experience wanted to be associated with an online operation that originated in the library and operated near, but not in, the newsroom. There was a longstanding tradition among Australian journalists that theirs was an occupation *sui generis*, and if not a closed shop, then something approaching it (Lloyd, 1985, p. 121).

Mary Riekert (2015) recalled a meeting in which the *Age*'s then editor, Alan Kohler, rebuffed requests for editorial assistance for the website. Kohler had no recall of such a meeting. But he remembered the website as 'marginal', noting that "We as an editorial group didn't get involved in the website" (2016). Consequently, the site in its first year or more had a catch-as-catch-can quality, as people sym-pathetic to the experiment contributed their expertise, whether skills in writing

HTML, designing buttons or creating gifs. Noras also hired as a casual employee a student named Caroline Casey, who would go on to become Yahoo7's Director of Product and Audience in Sydney (2014-2017). Casey remembered that many staff journalists did not have email accounts or a means of connecting to the internet in the early days, which meant that they did not read what the Age Online published, and did not have much insight into the website andgeneral developments in webcoverage (Casey, 2015). The *Age* letters to the editor page did not advertise an email address until late January 1995 ("Letters section," 1995b). The novelty of email, even for journalists, is revealed in an announcement in the *Age*'s arts and entertainment section in February 1995, relating that the section, "as ever at the cutting edge of the multi-media-driven cultural revolution" ("Arts and entertainment internet link," 1995c), now had an internet connection: people from the arts world could make contact by 'buzzing' arts@theage.com.au.

THE AGE ONLINE AND ADVERTISING

Caroline Casey had completed a Business degree majoring in media, and was studying television, and working as a temp, when she landed her role at the Age Online. She was brought in to input data—specifically, classified advertisements. Perhaps the most remarkable part of the early history of the website was its involvement in advertising. Both Simson and Noras recalled that putting advertising online was one of Simson's earliest priorities. Advertising for the paper was already composed electronically, using Atex software (John Fairfax Holdings, 1994, p. 14). But attempts to transfer the files into an HTML context failed, so "we started by putting up IT jobs from the Saturday *Age*, re-keying them from the paper", Simson remembered (2015). "I suggested we get the IT recruitment consultants in for a drink in the boardroom one Friday night and we showed them what was happening. I reckon we were the first newspaper in Australia to put classified up online."

At that early stage the website did not possess an HTML text editor: Casey, like Riekert handling the editorial content, composed the ads in Notepad, using copy which had already been set for the paper. She then uploaded the ads to the site using FTP. Classified advertising first appeared in the Age Online during the 1995/1996 financial year, and as a result of this work the Fairfax@Market website was set up, officially launched on the Melbourne and Sydney websites sites on 15 July 1996 (John Fairfax Holdings, 1996, p. 10). Steve Outing (1997a, p. 22) in an article about the growth of digital advertising in Australia, reported that the Fairfax@Market ads were in bitmap format.

Figure 7.2: Fairfax advertising site running on the Age Online, May 1996. Screenshot from the Wayback Machine, November 3, 2015.

At first these online advertisements were described on the website as a free service to readers. The Internet Archive shows that by December 1997, Fairfax@Market included a simple web form that enabled readers to contact the company about placing a classified ad. The process was not direct, however. Filling out the form resulted in an advertising representative contacting the sender by phone or email to confirm the placement of an ad, and its price. Fairfax's competitor, News Ltd, used the same approach for selling classifieds. However, by then News's ad copy was composed in HTML, and its job ads carried active links containing employers' email addresses. Fairfax@Market recorded 3000 user sessions a day, with traffic growing at 10% per month (Fairfax, 1997, p. 28).

THE END OF THE BEGINNING

By the middle of the 1990s, Fairfax's new management was repositioning the company, broadening its base as an information publisher to become "a major provider of news, information, entertainment and education" (Street, 1995, p. 6). The 1995 annual report contained the announcement of "a platform for the development of related multi-media and electronic publishing operations" (Mullholland, 1995, p. 9) with the creation of two new divisions, Fairfax Productions and Fairfax Digital Media. However, the same report noted that the company's main activity in the forthcoming year would be the commissioning of its new printing plant at Chullora in Sydney, created at a cost of A$315 million. In Melbourne, A$83 million had been spent on a colour press and other upgrades (Fairfax, 1995, pp. 9–10). This typified leading newspapers' approach in this era. Newspapers continued to evolve their old media formats while also entering the new media sphere (Falkenberg, 2010, p. 239).

Despite Fairfax's rhetoric and its increasing involvement in the online sphere, the company remained newspaper-minded, Alan Kohler's account suggests. Hired before the *Age*'s CEO Stuart Simson, Kohler reported primarily to the Fairfax group's editorial director in Sydney, with a 'dotted line' to Simson on profit and loss (Kohler, 2016). He recalled that his brief was to be a 'change agent'; developing the paper's online presence was not part of that brief, despite Simson's enthusiasm for the web. To Kohler, the internet was a 'distraction and a threat': in the long term potentially a challenge to the newspaper's dominance in the Melbourne classified advertising market, but in the short term largely irrelevant to his principal task of reversing circulation decline. (He was unable to do this, and left the position in October 1995.)

Kohler's account reflects the competing agendas and contradictory directions that afflict organizations undergoing major transformation. The development of the *Age* and *SMH* websites needs to be seen in their full corporate context, the thorough-going reform agenda that engulfed the company in the years 1992–1996. The company's *Telegraph* bosses wanted to update and rationalize the company's press operations; reform industrial relations, especially in printing and auxiliary areas; and in Victoria, improve relationships with the incoming Premier, Jeff Kennett, a politician of whom the *Age* had long been critical (Nolan, 2014, p. 13). Their ultimate aim was to boost circulation and profitability, and they succeeded. In 1995–1996, the company earned A$216.5 million before tax, an annual increase in profit of 28% (Turner, 1996, p. 293). Yet for staff across the paper it was a difficult, deeply uncertain period.

In addition to a redundancy program among non-editorial staff, some high-profile well-respected journalists departed the organization or were redeployed. At the coalface of newspaper production, journalists and staff in the pressroom faced considerable stress getting the paper 'to bed' on deadline as the publishing systems were updated and pressroom rationalisation rolled out. Meanwhile, the company's share register was besieged by Kerry Packer, an Australian media magnate who had long expressed interest in acquiring all or part of Fairfax's newspaper operations (Mayrhofer, 1995, pp. 121–122).

Ownership instability contributed in a major way to the fortunes of Fairfax's digital innovators. Mulholland stepped down as CEO in late 1995, to return to his home country of South Africa. Conrad Black sold out of Fairfax in late 1996, because the Australian government would not give him permission to own a majority shareholding in the company. Brierley Investments bought Black's share. As the name suggests, BIL was an investment, not a media, company. "They were entrepreneurs, opportunists, everything was for sale at a price," Colleen Ryan wrote in her book *Fairfax: The Rise and Fall* (2013, p. 101).

Stuart Simson was one of five senior executives who resigned shortly after the arrival of Mulholland's successor, Bob Mansfield (Mychasuk, 1996, p. 32). Simson had resolved to focus on digital media. He started an internet portal at Telstra, Australia's national telecoms company, and eventually became chair of emitch, the largest digital advertising company in Australia. Noras was disheartened by the change of leadership, and left Fairfax in 1997 for another executive position in digital. Riekert went freelance at the end of 1995, writing IT stories and doing website development. She worked again for the Age Online after it was brought under the editorship of a veteran sections editor, Alan Morison. Casey remained at Fairfax until 2001, when she left to work in Europe. By then, she had written for the newspaper for several years, and had also worked on Fairfax innovation plays including a trading site. On her return to Australia in 2014, after stints at CNN, Turner Broadcasting, and A&E Networks, she was puzzled to hear people in her field say that Fairfax had been late to digital (Casey, 2015).

CONCLUSION

In terms of overturning 'old givens', this chapter has shown that the *Age* not only played a pioneering role in the creation of online news in Australia, but also, from the outset, directed its attention to online advertising. This latter revelation is a significant aspect of the website's history that had been lost. It shows that in 1995, forward-looking newspaper executives could already see the threat that internet advertising posed to the press.

The online originators at the *Age* were mainly from the editorial library and from management: the website was born outside the newsroom, and this created difficulties from the start. The first website team was understaffed and under-resourced, initially straitjacketed by copyright restrictions, resisted by many staff journalists, and unable to overcome the indifference of editorial leadership in the first year or more of its life. Many *Age* journalists reacted defensively to the web, consistent with patterns observed by Deuze, Boczkowski, Matheson and others.

However, the Age Online's early history also reveals a more complex patterning specific to the *Age* and its parent company. The Age Online and its sister site in Sydney were created during an extraordinary period of corporate change and challenge, one that was unmatched in the Fairfax group's 20th-century history. Multiple changes of management, and conflicting messages even within management teams, contributed to the uneven development of the Age Online and associated sites. Meanwhile, management's emphasis on reforming work practices and upgrading press systems made it clear that the company placed the highest value on its newspaper activity. The company's chief executive, Stephen Mulholland, boldly predicted to shareholders that newspapers would remain "the single most important source of in-depth information into the next century" (1996, p. 9). No doubt this newspaper-mindedness contributed to conditioning many staff journalists' resistance to Fairfax's websites.

At the national Australian broadcaster, the ABC, the website grew from inside the organisation, from the bottom up. From early in its life, "staff came to see the website as a *part* of the ABC" (Burns, 2000, p. 98). Despite pressure from some ABC board members and from business to separate off the website activity, perhaps to commercialize it, the corporation's then managing director, Brian Johns, soon made clear through the One ABC policy that ABC Online was "indivisible from radio and television, drawing resources and content from ABC program makers across all networks and around the country" (Martin, 1999, p. 106). In contrast, it was not until 2007 that Fairfax finally integrated its traditional and online newsrooms completely, so that editors of the online and print editions sat opposite each other (Simons, 2007, p. 150). And it was only in 2012 that Fairfax introduced a 'Digital First' policy (Lannin & Hobday, 2012) that put its websites front and centre of its editorial mission.

As previously noted, the continuing 'newspaper-mindedness' of the *Age* was typical of established papers moving towards the internet. Yet the greatest challenge that this particular newspaper faced was not stasis, but an excess of change. The opportunities offered by the web often appeared irrelevant or even as threats to an editorial group struggling to come to terms with radical ownership instability and repeated changes of management and management agendas. Such factors, which are outside the agency of journalists and their immediate managers, should not be overlooked in the history of newspapers and the web. As a final footnote to this case study, speculation mounted in 2017 over the future of the Fairfax newspapers, as the board of Fairfax Media Ltd confirmed the company was being courted by two prospective buyers (Fairfax Media Ltd, 2017).

ACKNOWLEDGEMENTS

The author wishes to thank the five former *Age* staff who participated in interviews for this paper, as well as Michelle Stillman, the head of the *Age* editorial library, who gave valuable archival assistance.

REFERENCES

Arts and entertainment internet link. (1995c, February 6). *The Age*, p. 15.

Berners-Lee, T., & Fischetti, M. (1999). *Weaving the web: The original design and ultimate destiny of the world wide web by its inventor.* San Francisco, CA: HarperSanFrancisco.

Boczkowski, P. (2004). *Digitizing the news: Innovation in online newspapers.* Cambridge, MA: MIT Press.

Brock, G. (2012). *Murdoch, MailOnline and other accelerating disruptions.* Retrieved March 9, 2016 from http://georgebrock.net/murdoch-mailonline-and-the-rapidly-evolving-bigger-picture/

Brügger, N. (2012a). The idea of public service in the early history of DR online. In M. Burns & N. Brügger (Eds.), *Histories of public service broadcasters on the web* (pp. 91–104). New York, NY: Peter Lang.

Brügger, N. (2012b). Australian internet histories, past, present and future: An afterword. *Media International Australia, 143,* 159–165.

Burns, M. (2000). ABC online: A prehistory. *Media International Australia, 97,* 91–103.

Burns, M. (2008). *ABC online: Becoming the ABC.* Saarbrücken: VDM Verlag Dr. Muller.

BurrellesLuce (2007). *2007: Top blogs, newspapers, consumer magazines.* Retrieved May 30, 2016 from http://www.burrellesluce.com/top100/2007_Top_100List.pdf

Casey, C. (2015). Interview with the author.

Clarke, R. (2013). Morning dew on the web in Australia, 1992–1995. *Journal of Information Technology, 28,* 93–110.

Cowie, T. (2015). *Happy 20th birthday to theage.com.au.* Retrieved March 6, 2016 from http://www.theage.com.au/victoria/happy-20th-birthday-to-theagecomau-20150205-136rp0.html

Davies, A. (1994). Electronic newspapers—Who owns the copyright? *Communications Law Bulletin, 14*(1), 2–4.

Deuze, M. (2003). The web and its journalisms: Considering the consequences of different types of newsmedia online. *New Media & Society, 5*(2), 203–224.

Duke, S. (2016, February 15). London's *Independent* to stop printing. *The Australian Business Review.* Retrieved July 30, 2016 from http://www.theaustralian.com.au/business/media/londons-independent-to-stop-print-edition-go-digital/news-story/aa85501c2d6d815c35852f0ea1659acf

Fairfax Media Ltd. (2016). *Domain Group segment creation and significant items to be reflected in the 2016 full year results.* Retrieved August 1, 2016 from http://www.fairfaxmedia.com.au/pressroom/au--nz-press-room/au---nz-press-room/domain-group-segment-creation-and-significant-items-to-be-reflected-in-2016-full-year-results

Falkenberg, V. (2010). (R)evolution under construction: The dual history of online newspapers and newspapers online. In N. Brügger (Ed.), *Web history* (pp. 232–254). New York, NY: Peter Lang.

Gettens, K. (1998). New copyright laws. *Communications Law Bulletin, 17*(3), 21–23.

Gibson, G. (1998). *The journalist's companion to Australian law.* Melbourne: MUP.

Gillin, P. (2016). R.I.P. Tampa Tribune. *Newspaper Death Watch* [blog]. Retrieved May 30, 2016 from http://newspaperdeathwatch.com/

Goggin, G. (2004). Net acceleration: The advent of everyday internet. In G. Goggin (Ed.), *Virtual nation: The internet in Australia* (pp. 55–70). Sydney: UNSW Press.

Hardy, G. (1995, May 1). *VICNET and the web in the wider Victorian community.* Ausweb95 Conference, Southern Cross University, Ballina, NSW. Retrieved March 11, 2016 from http://ausweb.scu.edu.au/aw95/libraries/hardy/index.html

Hywood, G. (2016, May 6). Macquarie Australia conference presentation commentary. Retrieved June 1, 2016 from http://www.fairfaxmedia.com.au/ArticleDocuments/193/FAIRFAX%20Macquarie%20Australia%20Conference%20060516.pdf.aspx?Embed=Y

The Independent becomes the first national newspaper to embrace a global, digital-only future. (2016, February 13). *The Independent.* Retrieved June 2, 2016 from http://www.independent.co.uk/news/media/press/the-independent-becomes-the-first-national-newspaper-to-embrace-a-global-digital-only-future-a6869736.html

Inglis, K. (2006). *Whose ABC? The Australian Broadcasting Corporation, 1983–2006.* Melbourne: Black Inc.

John Fairfax Holdings Ltd. (1993). *Annual report.* Sydney: John Fairfax.

John Fairfax Holdings Ltd. (1994). *Annual report.* Sydney: John Fairfax.

John Fairfax Holdings Ltd. (1995). *Annual report.* Sydney: John Fairfax.

John Fairfax Holdings Ltd. (1996). *Annual report.* Sydney: John Fairfax.

Kohler, A. (2016). Interview with author.

Lannin, S., & Hobday, L. (2012). Fairfax puts digital first in newsroom overhaul. *ABC News.* Retrieved March 16, 2016 from http://www.abc.net.au/news/2012-06-27/fairfax-unveils-details-of-newsroom-overhaul/4096276

Letters section. (1995b, January 28). *The Age*, p. 10.

Let's meet on the internet. (1995a, February 7). *The Age*, p. 34.

Lloyd, C. (1985). *Profession: Journalist.* Sydney: Hale & Iremonger.

Martin, F. (1999). Pulling together the ABC: The role of the ABC Online. *Media International Australia, 93*, 103–117.

Martin, F. (2004). Net worth: The unlikely rise of ABC Online. In G. Goggin (Ed.), *Virtual nation: The internet in Australia.* Sydney: University of NSW Press.

Matheson, D. (2004). Weblogs and the epistemology of the news: Some trends in online journalism. *New Media & Society, 6*(4), 443–468.

Mayrhofer, D. (1995). Media notes. *Media International Australia, 76*, 110–132.

Mayrhofer, D. (1996). Media notes. *Media International Australia, 80*, 141–166.

Mitchell, A., Jurkowitz, M., & Guskin, E. (2013). Historic deals of major U.S. newspaper companies. Pew Research Center, August 7, 2013. Retrieved July 6, 2016 from http://www.journalism.org/2013/08/07/historic-deals-of-major-u-s-newspaper-companies/

Mullholland, S. (1995). *Fairfax annual report.* Sydney: John Fairfax Holdings Ltd.

Mychasuk, E. (1996, January 16). Syme boss goes. *Sydney Morning Herald*, p. 32.

Nguyen, A., & García, A. (2012). When public service is the name of the game: The evolution of British and Spanish public service broadcasters in online journalism. In M. Burns & N. Brügger (Eds.), *Histories of public service broadcasters on the web* (pp. 1–16). New York, NY: Peter Lang.

Nolan, S. (2003). *Online journalism: The search for narrative form in a multilinear world.* Proceedings from the 2003 Digital Arts and Culture Conference, Melbourne, Australia. Retrieved June 2, 2016 from http://citeseerx.ist.psu.edu/viewdoc/download?doi=10.1.1.525.2857&rep=rep1&type=pdf

Nolan, S. (2014). Age. In B. Griffen-Foley (Ed.), *A companion to the Australian media* (pp. 12–14). Melbourne: Australian Scholarly Press.

Noras, S. (2015). Interview with the author.

Outing, S. (1995a). Editor & Publisher launches page on the world wide web. *Editor & Publisher, 128*(25), 68.

Outing, S. (1995b, August 18). Welcome to my first "Stop the Presses!". *Editor & Publisher.* Retrieved March 9, 2016 from http://www.editorandpublisher.com/news/welcome-to-my-first-stop-the-presses-column/

Outing, S. (1997a, January 29). State of the art classifieds, Australian style. *Editor & Publisher.* Retrieved March 9, 2016 from http://www.editorandpublisher.com/columns/state-of-the-art-classifieds-australian-style/

Outing, S. (1997b). Digital ads down under. *Editor & Publisher, 130*(12), 21.

Prins, G. (2001). Oral history. In P. Burke (Ed.), *New perspectives on historical writing* (2nd ed., pp. 120–156), University Park, PA: Pennsylvania State University Press.

Prisk, M. (2014). Sydney Morning Herald. In B. Griffen-Foley (Ed.), *A companion to the Australian media* (pp. 12–14). Melbourne: Australian Scholarly Press.

Rayward, W. B. (2002). A history of computer applications in libraries. *IEEE Annals of the History of Computing, April–June,* 4–14.

Riekert, M. (2015). Interview with the author.

Ryan, C. (2013). *Fairfax: The rise and fall.* Melbourne: Melbourne University Press.

Shedden, D. (2007). New media timeline. *Poynter Online.* Qtd in Herndon, K. L. (2012) *The decline of the daily newspaper: How an American institution lost the online revolution.* New York, NY: Peter Lang.

Siles, I., & Boczkowski, P. (2012). Making sense of the newspaper crisis: A critical assessment of existing research and an agenda for future work. *New Media & Society, 14*(8), 1375–1394.

Simons, M. (2007). *The content makers: Understanding the media in Australia.* Melbourne: Penguin.

Simson, S. (2015). Interview with the author.

Street, L. (1995). *Fairfax annual report.* Sydney: John Fairfax Holdings Ltd.

Turner, G. (1996). News media chronicle, July 1995 to June 1996. *Australian Studies in Journalism, 5,* 265–311.

van Heekeren, M. (2010). News in "new media": An historical comparison between the arrival of television and online news in Australia. *Media International Australia, 134,* 20–30.

van Niekerk, M. (2005). *Online to the future.* Retrieved April 20, 2016 from http://www.theage.com.au/news/National/Online-to-the-future/2005/01/27/1106415726255.html

Who we are. (2016) *New York Times.* Retrieved March 15, 2016 from http://www.nytco.com/who-we-are/culture/our-history/

Williams, P. (2013). *Killing Fairfax: Packer, Murdoch and the ultimate revenge.* Sydney: HarperCollins.

Zelizer, B. (2004). *Taking journalism serious: News and the academy.* Thousand Oaks, CA: Sage.

Methodological reflections

CHAPTER EIGHT

THE challenges OF 25 years OF data

An agenda for web-based research

MATTHEW S. WEBER

THE PROMISE OF THE WEB AS A FRONTIER FOR RESEARCH

Even during the early days of the web, scholars recognized that the uncontrolled growth of the web was producing a complex and vast information ecosystem (De Kunder, 2012). The web today is an amalgamation of interconnected hubs and spokes of information, and increasingly, an integrated mix of media, including text, photos, audio, movies and live-streaming video. Moreover, new genres and technologies, including social media and mobile standards, further complicate the web-based information landscape. In 2016, estimates indicate that there were at least 4.7 billion indexed World Wide Web pages across the globe (Albert, Jeong, & Barabasi, 1999). Thus, the World Wide Web (the web, for short) has transformed into a complex and central medium for global communication.

The web is a unique record of human interaction and an unparalled record of social development. On the other hand, the web does not exist in a single place, and much of the data contained on the web—present and past—is either inaccessible or has been lost due to a lack of appropriate techniques for preservation (Ankerson, 2012). There are, in addition, many technical challenges associated with researching web data—whether scholars are working with Big Data at scale, or focusing on specific histories of particular phenomena or periods in the web's development (Brügger & Finnemann, 2013; Milligan, 2016).

Despite the numerous challenges that exist, recent years have seen a substantial growth in rigorous and important web-based research. For instance, research tracing the development of the Yahoo! GeoCities provides an important snapshot of social organizing in the 1990s (Milligan, 2016). Websites from political campaigns provide critical records for historians and political scientists who wish to examine the discourse and narrative of political events (Davis, 1998; Margolis, Resnick, & Tu, 1997). Moreover, as a source for research, the web provides for more than historical scholarship. A 2012 study demonstrated that the aggregation of users on Facebook. com could provide social scientists with fertile ground for experiments; Facebook researchers used experimental conditions to test whether or not social influence could impact the likelihood that connected peers would participate in elections (Bond et al., 2012). Arguably, a list of potential research using the web could parallel the number of web pages that are currently in operation.[1] And yet, in many regards research utilizing web data is still limited in a number of ways.

This chapter takes a forward-looking perspective to consider key research problems that have challenged researchers in the past, and will likely continue to challenge researchers in the future. I approach this work from the perspective of a computational social scientist; my work is centered at the intersection of computer science and the social sciences, but my worldview skews towards the social. My worldview on the challenges of web-based research comes from this perspective, but my hope is that the agenda set forth here will inspire others to consider some of these critical issues in their own research. The focus herein is on the use web data as an object of study, although some consideration is given to the use of tools to collect web data. With that perspective in mind, this chapter highlights three specifics research challenges that face researchers working with web data today. First, the scope of the web poses questions with regards to the size and time dimensions of research. Second, the nature of web data points to questions regarding the reliability and validity of web data. Third, the type of data on the web poses significant questions with regards to the ethics research using web data.

QUESTIONS OF SIZE AND TIME

Scholars who sets out to conduct research using data from the web—regardless of field or domain—should address questions regarding size and time dimensions pertaining to their data. Whether these issues are addressed at the outset, or later in data collection and analysis, they will rear their ugly heads inevitably. Questions regarding the data size have implications for all phases of research, as has clearly been demonstrated in prior research. At the most basic level, researchers must address how much data is needed. For instance, 1 million records may sound like a significant amount data, but it is not quite as much if the records are simply lists of uniform resource locators (URLs). On the other hand, 1 million archived web pages would require a significant amount of sources in order to store, access and analyze. Thus, it is important to ascertain the type of data that is needed, and the fields (e.g. URLs, images, text, video) that are required.

Consider the following examples, drawn from diverse domains such as library science, history, and political science, which have tackled critical questions addressing issues of and leveraging the scale of big data.

Computationally based historical studieshave allowed historians to explore historical records in order to better understand patterns that existed in past generations. Much of this type of analysis utilizes web data but focuses on small-scale analyses. For instance, researchers have used archived web data for everything from exploring labor movements in Australia prior to World War I (Mark, 2015) to examining the nature of web memorials in the wake of the September 11, 2001 terrorist attacks in New York City (Foot, Warnick, & Schneider, 2005) to an examination of Danish public broadcasting (Brügger, 2012). Mark drew upon a small web archive of digitized songs written by a notable member of the Industrial Workers of the World movement in Australia at the beginning of the 20th century. It is important to remember that not all web data originated online; some of the most valuable resources are repositories of material be preserved for future generations.

In the second example, Foot, Warnick and Schneider sought to examine the social practice of memorialization as realized through digital objects. The authors focused their research on the 9/11 attacks in New York City, but in order to select an appropriate sample they first began with a set of 60 websites, which were then reduced to a subset of 8 based on key variables relevant to the research. In this case, Foot and colleagues wanted websites that were coproduced by a number of individuals, and were sites that focused specifically on memorialization. Thus, although the focus was on native digital content, and there was a relatively large pool of data to draw upon, the authors had specific filters to narrow the scope. Brügger used an archive of a single website, that of Danish public service broadcaster DR, to study the historical representation of the broadcaster in an online context.

Humanities research is not restricted to small-scale analyses. For instance, historical databases, such as those built by the British Library's BUDDAH Project, provide resources for future explorations in this area. BUDDAH aims to provide researchers with access to records of the British web domain, including audio and visual elements. One case study utilizing the BUDDAH project sought to examine public responses to Beat culture (e.g. the work of notable figures such as William Burroughs, Allen Ginsberg and Jack Kerouac) via content available on modern web pages (Cran, 2015). Navigating through 65 terabytes of archived web data, the author was able to find a wealth of resources documenting varied aspects of public dialogue on the topic. At the same time, however, the scale of the data created a 'needle in the haystack' problem for the researcher; it was difficult to locate the necessary records to recreate the desired history, as it is often difficult to search longitudinally in time when the specific URLs are unknown.

The time dimension is often difficult to disentangle from the size issue; for instance, Brügger's examination was restricted to a single website, but focused on an 11 year period. On the other hand, Foot, Warnick and Schneider looked at eight websites, but focused on a narrow timeframe in 2001. When traversing time, one key variable that should be considered is the frequency of sampling. A more granular sampling window will generate large datasets. If a fine level of granularity is not required, one can capture a wide swath of time with a relatively small dataset (e.g. weekly snapshots vs. hourly snapshots).

Many readers will be more familiar with the Big Data aspect of web-based research. As the examples from humanities and social science research illustrate, when dealing with web-based data it is certainly not a requirement to manage millions of data points. On the other hand, large-scale datasets offer a unique opportunity to examine social phenomena at a scale that previously was not possible. Data traces have enabled political scientists to examine ecosystems of political interactions, as well as large-scale patterns of political action. In one noteworthy study, researchers sought to examine broad patterns of social influence as it occurs in individuals' social networks. The researchers felt that observation studies were narrow, and moreover, they had access to a unique pool of research subjects. Thus, the research team conducted a large-scale social experiment via Facebook on 61 million potential voters. The study tested contagion and social influence, and found that strong ties are highly important with regards to motivating political action (Bond et al., 2012). In this case, large-scale data were used as the size of the data afforded the statistical power needed to effectively argue for a certain perspective; similar effects have been shown in small-scale studies of contagion, but this research provided an opportunity to utilize the scale of web data to test the nature of these phenomena in practice. Moreover, although this case focused on a very small window in time, the required scale of data points increased the size of the dataset.

Similar to the example of contagion and Facebook, Twitter data have been used to understand and predict voting trends in political elections (McKelvey, DiGrazia, & Rojas, 2014), and to predict key topics of discussion in politics (Rill, Reinel, Scheidt, & Zicari, 2014). In these examples, the scale was necessary to enhance the predictive power and validity of the data. From a discourse perspective, political big data has been used to understand how individuals talk about politics, and how different political spheres develop (Colleoni, Rozza, & Arvidsson, 2014). Historical data sources further enabled researchers to examine shifts in political discourse over longer periods of time (Zeng & Greenfield, 2015). In each of these examples, the size of the dataset was notably large, but the decision to utilize data at such a scale was made as a result of the research questions that were asked. These examples underscore the need to let the research question guide the choice of data selection.

In addition, the size of the web, and its continuing evolution (e.g. the time dimension), present unique opportunities for computer scientists. For instance, recent research uses the scale of Facebook to test and examine the lifecycle of mobile apps (Kloumann, Adamic, Kleinberg, & Wu, 2015). Kloumann and her colleagues were able to analyze the application usage data for 83,000 apps in a one-year period, and user behavior for 1.4 billion users in a five-year period to examine the intricate relationship that exists between the popularity and sociality of a mobile application in determining the success of that application. These types of data mining challenges test the limits of current computer modeling capabilities, and provide countless opportunities for computer scientists to test newer, more efficient and more reliable methods for mining and predicting behavior based on web-data traces. Again, the decision to use large-scale data was guided by a need to test particular algorithms.

Clearly, significant advances in computing technology have provided researchers with improved access to large-scale data sources. Pair these advances with the decreasing cost of high-performance computing, and there is great potential in the future for continued advancements with regards to large-scale research using web data sources. On the other hand, when thinking about the size and scale of web-based data, the above discussion underscores the importance of considering the nature of the research questions being asked, as well as the type of analyses being conducted. Moreover, one research question can often be answered in multiple ways; although there is much to be said for the appeal of large datasets, there is often much to be gained from exploring the nuance of smaller datasets. Finally, the aggregate of various scales of research provides a future opportunity for the triangulation of findings to further enhance of understanding of the social world.

QUESTIONS OF RELIABILITY AND VALIDITY

To some degree, any good research study inevitably addresses questions of reliability and validity. When working with web based data, however, these questions are amplified due to the nature of the data. In some cases, the challenges aren't as complicated. For instance, The New York Times made its entire archive from 1851 to present available and searchable via its web portal (http://query.nytimes.com/search/sitesearch/#//). Similarly, the Digital Preservation unit of the Library of Congress maintains a robust directory of curated digital archive content (http://www.digitalpreservation.gov/collections/); the majority of the content includes specific information about the nature of the data and how it was collected.

In the cases above, there are clearly defined parameters that provide information regarding the nature of the aggregated data. In general, however, web data is plagued by questions of reliability and validity in part because the data vary so widely. In general, reliability of a study refers to the degree to which that study can be replicated in repeated trials (Wheaton, Muthen, Alwin, & Summers, 1977). On the other hand, validity refers to the degree to which a study measures a selected phenomenon (Golafshani, 2003). These general concepts can similarly be applied to the context of web data. Reliability, when dealing with web data, implies that a collection of web data consistently captures the same data. On the other hand, validity implies that web data consistently captures data related to the same topic. The underlying concepts are the same, but the ambiguity of the web domain and the constant flux of both content and technology, creates unique challenges. Thus, reliability and validity questions can emerge in a number of different aspects when working with web data. In particular, it is often difficult to know how complete web data are; thus, it is hard to accurately assess the validity of a given dataset. Moreover, the fact that web data are often in flux means that a study conducted at one point in time may not be reliably replicated in the future.

First off, consider contexts where a researcher is working with historical or archived web data. The average life span of a web page has been calculated at around 3 years (Agata, Miyata, Ishita, Ikeuchi, & Ueda, 2014). Thus, it is often difficult to know what percent of a given topic is actually captured in archival resources. For example, one analysis of archived Twitter data tracking six major social events between 2009 and 2012 found that after 1 year approximately 11% of Tweets related to the topic were no longer recoverable, and after 2 years 27% of Tweets were no longer recoverable. After just 2 years, only 41% of the original content had actually been archived for future use (SalahEldeen & Nelson, 2012). A researcher working with this data would be faced with the challenging fact that more than half of the related content was *not* saved. This raises questions regarding potential biases that may exist (e.g. is there a systematic pattern to the missing data, such as geographic coverage).

A number of research strategies have been suggested in order to address issues of degradation and missing data, but overall this is an ongoing challenge facing web researchers. Some efforts have focused on developing more effective strategies for archiving web content. One proposal suggests focusing archival efforts on capturing data that changes the most frequently, in order to capture the majority of new content (Spaniol, Denev, Mazeika, Weikum, & Senellart, 2009). Elsewhere, researchers have suggested crawling strategies should prioritize archival efforts based on the size and relative position of websites within their larger ecosystems (Song, Liu, Wen, & Ma, 2004).

A number of recent studies have taken existing sets of archived web data and examined the content in order to address the pervasiveness of issues related to reliability and validity. For instance, a sample of web archive data found significant difference in the national origins of archived data (Thelwall & Vaughan, 2004); for instance, the researchers found in their analysis that websites in the United States were overrepresented, which websites in China were underrepresented. Knowing such issues exist is a first step, but any large-scale analysis of such a domain would ultimately have to correct for such biases.

Brügger and Finnemann (2013) examined the nature of archived web content, and identified a number of key concerns regarding archived web content. For one, archived web content is often not a mirror of the live web; content is not archived in full, images are often omitted, and only a portion of a given domain may be saved. Archiving is also reactive; it is challenging to keep up with changing code standards and new web phenomena. It is near impossible to predict major events that spur the launch of new websites and web domains. The result is that archived web content is often inconsistent and unreliable; the provenance of the data becomes a key concern, but is often unknown.

Notably, challenges of data reliability and validity are not restricted to the techniques used to collect and archive data. In an example, from communication research, Foot and colleagues (Foot, Schneider, Dougherty, Xenos, & Larsen, 2003) examined the meaning and context behind linking relationships that exist in political websites. The authors found that much of the extant literature on hyperlinking chose one of two approaches—large-scale network analysis or rhetorical analysis of the content of the link. And yet, an analysis of the findings of these studies revealed that gaps often existed. Rhetorical analyses were often too narrow, whereas large-scale networks studies captured too broad a range of interactions. Instead, the authors made a methodological choice to focus on a small subset of 535 websites in their sample, and to employ human coders to analyze the nature of the relationships in their hyperlink data. In short, there is a need to triangulate and validate web data wherever possible in order to insure the accuracy of research results.

As Milligan (2016) notes, the first step is for researchers simply to be aware of the limitations that exist in the data they are utilizing. Notably, most web sources are fragments. The best known sources of archived data is arguably the Internet Archive (archive.org), a non-profit organization founded with the mission of archiving web content and establishing a new library of digital information. The Internet Archive does not, however, contain social media data. Moreover, there are many gaps, especially when one moves beyond .com commercial domains. National libraries around the world have also created country repositories; the British Library contains a notable example, and the Danish government has established a strong web archiving program. The end result is a mass of data, but also a fragmented set of disconnected collections.

Challenges of reliability and validity are likely to persist moving forward, and accelerate as the web becomes increasingly mobile and social. One study of Twitter data sources found that there were significant differences in the results of statistical analyses depending on the source of Twitter data (Driscoll & Walker, 2014). One estimate found that approximately 65% of requested archived pages from user searches on the 'live web' pointed to web content that no longer exist on the live web

(AlNoamany, AlSum, Weigle, & Nelson, 2014). From a research perspective, this type of trend means that researchers examining web data will increasingly need to rely on some form of archived web database, but researchers will need to be more aware of the limitations of such datasets.

QUESTIONS OF ETHICS

Questions regarding the size, scale, reliability and validity of data are numerous, but they are not insurmountable. In fact, many of the aforementioned research points to a path forward, be it through statistical correction, enhanced specification of data collection techniques or mapping of datasets, among other approaches, potential solutions exist and present an opportunity for future research. Significant ethical questions lay lurking below the surface of many of the studies this chapter has touched on, as well as for many of the data sources.

Web archiving efforts generally work to respect requests for privacy while balancing the need for preservation; for instance, the Internet Archive crawls all available web content, but does not make content publicly available where there is a clear request to exclude a page from crawls (e.g. robots.txt files). In another example, the national Danish web archive similarly does not observe robots.txt exclusions; moreover, the Danish effort will also crawl content that is password protected when it is possible to purchase or obtain a password (e.g. to crawl password-protected newspaper archives). In this way, data are not collected if they are protected in a way that is designed to prevent public access (e.g. corporate intranets are not crawled). Twitter data is another ethical grey area; social media data often contains records of social interaction, including personal comments. But Twitter data that is scraped and collected by researchers is often aggregated without permission. Returning to the example of Bond et al.'s (2012) social experiment via Facebook on 61 million votes, what is notable is that participants were never made aware that they were engaging in a scientific research study. The research team manipulated participants by showing an 'I Voted' button in some cases, but not in others. In that case, there was no clear potential that research participants could face any harm, but nevertheless most research oversight boards would recommend making participants aware of their role in research.[2]

Indeed, a central challenge with regards to ethics of web based research is that many of the existing mechanisms for oversight are working to catch up with technology. In the United States, for instance, Institutional Review Boards vary dramatically from state-to-state and from university-to-university, and have been slow to develop clear guidelines for dealing with web-based data sources. In the midst of ongoing policymaking about data use, governments are instituting legal regulations to address the issues of big data (for example, legislation stipulating a 'right to be forgotten' now exists in the European Union) (Greenleaf, 2014). In the case of 'right to be forgotten' legislation, current regulation focuses specifically on search results and the right to be excluded from search engines such as Google. Archives are a murkier area of study; it is less clear what right publics have to be forgotten in archived web content.

Reinforcing the aforementioned challenges, boyd and Crawford (2012) outline numerous ethical challenges associated with conducting social science research in a large-scale data space. While lauding the potential of big data to help to advance science in a number of ways, the authors warn that big data may be a "troubling manifestation of Big Brother, enabling invasions of privacy, decreased civil freedoms, and increased state and corporate control" (p. 664). For example, as noted, consent is rarely gathered from individuals whose information is tracked. It is impractical, in many cases, to gather permission from each and every individual when dealing with millions of users. Further, when using archival data, it is often impossible to obtain individual permission, or to determine the provenance of the data. As the aforementioned archiving efforts underscore, the prevailing approach today is to collect data that are in the public sphere and to make such data available as part of archives.

In another notable and well known illustration of the issues of privacy and data collection, Harvard researchers released a data set tracking undergraduate students in at unidentified university (Lewis, Kaufman, Gonzalez, Wimmer, & Christakis, 2008). Others quickly realized that the composition of the data that was released allowed researchers to trace the origins of the dataset, identifying both the university and the students, who were unaware that the data had been collected. To this end, Andrejevic (2014) utilizes the term 'big data divide' to characterize the distinction between those who mine and collect big data, and those who are the subject of this data collection. The subjects of data collection often feel powerless, and experience a loss of control over their personal information. As more work examines big datasets, Bowker (2005) also warns that "data should be cooked with care" (p. 184). In other words, the interpretation of Big Data should be undertaken with care, and ethical issues must be considered as a component of study construction and analysis.

On the opposite side of the debate, scholars have asked how aggregated data can be used by journalists without explicit permission from subjects (Fairfield & Shtein, 2014). There is a focus on the aggregation of data without explicit permission, and moreover, the aggregation of data used to predictively assess trends such as relationships between individual behavior and health outcomes. The authors give an example of aggregated data to reveal patterns of behavior; for instance, certain patterns in social media use could unintentionally reveal sexual orientations of individuals who have not chosen to make such behavior public. Thus, results of aggregate analyses can be used to a variety of ends, all enacted without individual permission. Similarly, many questions persist regards the aggregation and use of content that is contributed in journalism spaces by members of the public; such content—in the form of comments and social media activity—is increasingly considered public domain (Lewis, 2012). Such challenges of privacy and ethics will need to be addressed as this space continues to expand, and an ongoing dialogue between researchers and administrators is key to this process (Brown & Marsden, 2013).

For scholars today, there is an opportunity to engage in research that sets an agenda for discussion of ethics and data privacy. For example, studies such as Lewis's work at Harvard underscore the identifying nature of social media data. Researchers working with web-based data can contribute to this discussion by helping scholars to better understanding *what* data can contribute to identification and *how* researchers can better deidentify existing datasets. Moreover, the policy researchers should have a voice in helping scholars to better understand fair use and privacy rights.

UNANSWERED QUESTIONS AND FUTURE CHALLENGES

The balance of this chapter points to numerous challenges that surround web-based research. Although web-based research presents a number of challenges it is a wide-open landscape for research across disciplines, from the humanities to the social sciences to computer science.

Indeed, beyond the scope of this chapter, Chen and Zhang (2014) point to new opportunities including challenges pertaining data capture, storage, curation, analysis and visualization. In short, the challenges—particularly for larger datasets—range from the sourcing of data through to analysis and the presentation of results. A trend in big data is to translate large-scale datasets into aggregate variables for use in statistical analyses such as multivariate regressions and time series analysis. Recent commentary further notes that there are statistical challenges associated with large-scale data sources. Such datasets are frequently used to calculate correlations between different variables, and yet analysis of such correlations often generates misleading findings, and lacks causal power (Marcus & Davis, 2014).

The future of web-based research also points to the need for new methods of analysis and inquiry. Existing methodological techniques, such as standard linear regressions, are often quite limited in power when used for large data. In addition, these techniques often overestimate the significance of variables. Nevertheless, there are a number of options for research in this space; for example, some have pointed to penalized linear regression models as a key method for theory building using big data (Hindman, 2015). Analytically speaking, statistical packages such as STATA and R are able to handle large-scale data; in addition, communities of scholars willing to assist with research challenges often support these tools. That said, there is a learning curve that must be overcome by researchers in order to access and engage with data. Sampling issues must be accounted for, as well as temporal biases resulting from when data were collected (Howison, Wiggins, & Crowston, 2011). These issues may further limit the predictive capacity of big data (Dhar, 2013), and must be accounted for regardless of discipline.

Looking beyond purely methodological issues, the type of data available to researchers continues to change. In part, librarians and scholars have focused increasing attention on web archiving as a critical record of societal interaction and recent modern history. The result has been a redoubled effort on improving web data collection techniques. Moreover, resources and technology for archiving have increased substantially in the past decade. For instance, in 2016 the Archive-IT web archiving platform had been utilized by more than 350 institutions to archive more than 9 billion documents in more than 2700 archives. A 2013 survey by the National Digital Stewardship Alliance suggests that, "web archiving programs nationally are both maturing and converging on common sets of practices". The challenges of modern web research point to 25 years of new opportunities for research and analysis.

REFERENCES

Agata, T., Miyata, Y., Ishita, E., Ikeuchi, A., & Ueda, S. (2014, September 8–12). *Life span of web pages: A survey of 10 million pages collected in 2001*. Paper presented at the 2014 IEEE/ACM Joint Conference on Digital Libraries (JCDL).

Albert, R., Jeong, H., & Barabasi, A.-L. (1999). Internet: Diameter of the World-Wide Web. *Nature, 401*(6749), 130–131.

AlNoamany, Y., AlSum, A., Weigle, M. C., & Nelson, M. L. (2014). Who and what links to the internet archive. *International Journal on Digital Libraries, 14*(3–4), 101–115.

Andrejevic, M. (2014). The big data divide. *International Journal of Communication, 8*, 1673–1689.

Ankerson, M. S. (2012). Writing web histories with an eye on the analog past. *New Media & Society, 14*(3), 384–400. doi:10.1177/1461444811414834

Bond, R. M., Fariss, C. J., Jones, J. J., Kramer, A. D., Marlow, C., Settle, J. E., & Fowler, J. H. (2012). A 61-million-person experiment in social influence and political mobilization. *Nature, 489*(7415), 295–298.

Bowker, G. C. (2005). *Memory practices in the sciences*. Cambridge, MA: MIT Press.

boyd, d., & Crawford, K. (2012). Critical questions for big data. *Information, Communication & Society, 15*(5), 662–679. doi:10.1080/1369118X.2012.678878

Brown, I., & Marsden, C. T. (2013). *Regulating code: Good governance and better regulation in the information age*. Cambridge, MA: MIT Press.

Brügger, N. (2012). The idea of public service in the early history of DR online. In M. Burns & N. Brügger (Eds.), *Histories of public service broadcasters on the Web* (pp. 91–104). New York, NY: Peter Lang.

Brügger, N., & Finnemann, N. O. (2013). The web and digital humanities: Theoretical and methodological concerns. *Journal of Broadcasting & Electronic Media, 57*(1), 66–80. doi:10.1080/08838 151.2012.761699

Chen, C. L. P., & Zhang, C.-Y. (2014). Data-intensive applications, challenges, techniques and technologies: A survey on Big Data. *Information Sciences, 275*, 314–347. doi:10.1016/j.ins.2014.01.015

Colleoni, E., Rozza, A., & Arvidsson, A. (2014). Echo chamber or public sphere? Predicting political orientation and measuring political homophily in twitter using big data. *Journal of Communication, 64*(2), 317–332. doi:10.1111/jcom.12084

Cran, R. (2015). *'All writing is in fact cut ups': The UK Web archive and beat literature*. Retrieved from Institute of Historical Research: http://sas-space.sas.ac.uk/id/eprint/6101

Davis, R. (1998). *The web of politics: The Internet's impact on the American political system*. Oxford: Oxford University Press.

De Kunder, M. (2012). *The size of the world wide web*. Retrieved from http://www.WorldWideWebSize.com

Dhar, V. (2013). Data science and prediction. *Communications of the ACM, 56*(12), 64–73. doi: 10.1145/2500499

Driscoll, K., & Walker, S. (2014). Big data, big questions/working within a black box: Transparency in the collection and production of big twitter data. *International Journal of Communication, 8*, 20.

Fairfield, J., & Shtein, H. (2014). Big data, big problems: Emerging issues in the ethics of data science and journalism. *Journal of Mass Media Ethics, 29*(1), 38–51. doi:10.1080/08900523.2014.863126

Foot, K., Schneider, S. M., Dougherty, M., Xenos, M., & Larsen, E. (2003). Analyzing linking practices: Candidate sites in the 2002 US electoral web sphere. *Journal of Computer-Mediated Communication, 8*(4). doi:10.1111/j.1083–6101.2003.tb00220.x

Foot, K., Warnick, B., & Schneider, S. M. (2005). Web-based memorializing after September 11: Toward a conceptual framework. *Journal of Computer-Mediated Communication, 11*(1), 72–96. doi:10.1111/j.1083–6101.2006.tb00304.x

Golafshani, N. (2003). Understanding reliability and validity in qualitative research. *The Qualitative Report, 8*(4), 597–606.

Greenleaf, G. (2014). Sheherezade and the 101 data privacy laws: Origins, significance and global trajectories. *Journal of Law, Information and Science, 23*(1), 4–49.

Hindman, M. (2015). Building better models: Prediction, replication, and machine learning in the social sciences. *The ANNALS of the American Academy of Political and Social Science, 659*(1), 48–62. doi:10.1177/0002716215570279

Howison, J., Wiggins, A., & Crowston, K. (2011). Validity issues in the use of social network analysis with digital trace data. *Journal of the Association for Information Systems, 12*(12), 767–797.

Kloumann, I., Adamic, L., Kleinberg, J., & Wu, S. (2015). *The lifecycles of apps in a social ecosystem*. Paper presented at the Proceedings of the 24th International Conference on World Wide Web, Florence, Italy.

Lewis, K., Kaufman, J., Gonzalez, M., Wimmer, A., & Christakis, N. (2008). Tastes, ties and time: A new social network dataset using Facebook.com. *Social Networks, 30*(4), 330–342.

Lewis, S. C. (2012). The tension between professional control and open participation. *Information, Communication & Society, 15*(6), 836–866. doi:10.1080/1369118X.2012.674150

Marcus, G., & Davis, E. (2014, April 7). Eight (no, nine!) problems with big data. *The New York Times*, p. A23.

Margolis, M., Resnick, D., & Tu, C.-c. (1997). Campaigning on the internet parties and candidates on the World Wide Web in the 1996 primary season. *The Harvard International Journal of Press/Politics, 2*(1), 59–78.

Mark, G. (2015). Joe Hill centenary and IWW songs in Australia. *Labour History, 109*, 169–174. doi:10.5263/labourhistory.109.0169

McKelvey, K., DiGrazia, J., & Rojas, F. (2014). Twitter publics: How online political communities signaled electoral outcomes in the 2010 US house election. *Information Communication & Society*, *17*(4), 436–450. doi:10.1080/1369118x.2014.892149

Milligan, I. (2016). Lost in the infinite archive: The promise and pitfalls of web archives. *International Journal of Humanities and Arts Computing*, *10*(1), 78–94.

O'Reilly, T. (2007). What is Web 2.0: Design patterns and business models for the next generation of software. *Communications & Strategies*, *1*, 17.

Rill, S., Reinel, D., Scheidt, J., & Zicari, R. V. (2014). PoliTwi: Early detection of emerging political topics on twitter and the impact on concept-level sentiment analysis. *Knowledge-Based Systems*, *69*, 24–33. doi:10.1016/j.knosys.2014.05.008

Salah Eldeen, H. M., & Nelson, M. L. (2012). Losing my revolution: How many resources shared on social media have been lost? In Zaphiris P., Buchanan G., Rasmussen E., Loizides F. (Eds.), *Theory and Practice of Digital Libraries. TPDL 2012. Lecture Notes in Computer Science* (pp. 125–137). Berlin, Germany: Springer.

Song, R., Liu, H., Wen, J.-R., & Ma, W.-Y. (2004). *Learning block importance models for web pages*. Proceedings of the 13th international conference on World Wide Web. http://dx.doi.org/10.1145/988672.988700.

Spaniol, M., Denev, D., Mazeika, A., Weikum, G., & Senellart, P. (2009). *Data quality in web archiving*. Proceedings of the 3rd Workshop on Information credibility on the Web. http://dx.doi.org/10.1145/1526993.1526999.

Thelwall, M., & Vaughan, L. (2004). A fair history of the web? Examining country balance in the internet archive. *Library & Information Science Research*, *26*(2), 162–176.

Wheaton, B., Muthen, B., Alwin, D. F., & Summers, G. F. (1977). Assessing reliability and stability in panel models. In D. R. Heise (Ed.), *Sociological Methodology* (pp. 84–136). San Francisco, CA: Jossey-Bass.

Zeng, R., & Greenfield, P. M. (2015). Cultural evolution over the last 40 years in China: Using the Google Ngram viewer to study implications of social and political change for cultural values. *International Journal of Psychology*, *50*(1), 47–55. doi:10.1002/ijop.12125

NOTES

1. This chapter focuses broadly on data drawn from the World Wide Web. Increasingly, this type of data increasingly intersects with internet data (see O'Reilly 2017 for a relevant discussion of the differences between the two domains).

2. See Schroeder (2014) for a more complete accounting of the ethical issues surrounding this study, as well as details regarding the response in both the academic and popular presses.

CHAPTER NINE

Historical website ecology

Analyzing past states of the web using archived source code

ANNE HELMOND

In this chapter I offer a historical perspective on the changing composition of a website over time. I propose to see the website as an ecosystem through which we can analyze the larger techno-commercial configurations that websites are embedded in. In doing so, I reconceptualize the study of websites as historical website ecology. The website's ecosystem can be detected by examining the source code in which a website's connections with third parties have become inscribed. If archived, this provides a way to examine changes in a website's ecosystem and transformations in the techno-commercial configurations of the web through the changing composition of a website. Moving the site of analysis from the content of websites to the context of websites opens up new areas for web historical research. Focusing on the archived source code of websites does not only enable analyzing web technologies used to construct them, which can tell us something about the web's underlying infrastructure, providing insights into how the web is built and how websites are connected, but can also serve as a means to investigate the web's economic underpinnings, to understand the business models of websites and third parties and trace the economically valuable data flowing between them. In this chapter I take a contextual approach to historical website analysis by viewing the website as an environment that is inhabited and shaped by third parties such as social media platforms, advertisers, analytics companies and content-delivery networks, embedding the website in various technological and commercial relations with these actors. This shift from website content to website context is what I refer to as the website's ecosystem as a way to study changes in the techno-commercial environment of the web.

I position the historical study of a website's ecosystem as a contribution to web historiography, which is concerned with writing histories of the web (Ankerson, 2012; Brügger, 2009, 2013; Foot & Schneider, 2010). To operationalize my contribution, I turn to web archives as important tools for web historians to uncover previous states of the web. I argue that while the web archive of the Internet Archive Wayback Machine focuses on snapshots of single websites (Brügger, 2009; Ben-David & Huurdeman, 2014; Rogers, 2013) the source code of these snapshots contains valuable information about a website's relations with third parties that we can employ for the reconstruction of historical website ecosystems. That is, I propose treating the source code as a demarcation object that determines the dynamic interrelations between websites and external actors, by focusing on the code snippets of third-party objects that enable these connections. Whilst archived source code may be used to analyze different aspects over time, such as a website's relations with social media platforms through sharing features and login systems, the web technologies used, as well as insights into the business practices of websites through their use of online advertising and analytics, in this chapter I focus on one particular technological type of third-party connection that is established through tracking mechanisms embedded in websites. Trackers are of particular relevance because of the increasing interest and use of (big) data collected on people visiting websites and the changes in techniques from third parties to collect data on external websites (Turow, 2011). In a case study on trackers on the New York Times (NYT) website I examine how we can employ archived source code to reconstruct the historical tracking ecologies the NYT website has been embedded in between 1996 and 2011.

WEBSITE ECOLOGY

Mayer and Mitchell claim that websites are increasingly being shaped by third-party content and functionality (2012). For example, webmasters can use social media platforms to embed sharing functionality with social buttons, and advertising servers to display dynamically-generated personalized ads to generate income. In these scenarios, the website is no longer a self-contained unit but has become informed and molded by these other actors on the web.

Thus, I would like to introduce the notion of *website ecology*, that is the study of the complex socio-technical relations between websites, users, social media platforms, tracking companies, and other actors in the website's environment. In doing so, I draw parallels with media ecology, defined by Neil Postman as "the study of media as environments [...] their structure, content, and impact on people" (1970). Shifting media ecology's focus away from studying the effects of media on people towards the materiality of these media environments, Matthew Fuller argues for understanding media ecology as "the massive and dynamic interrelation of processes and objects, beings and things, patterns and matter" (2005). Here, I am particularly interested in the 'softwarization' of media (Berry, 2012; Manovich, 2013, p. 5), a term used to reconceptualize media ecology after our 'media becomes software' (Manovich, 2013, p. 156). David Berry employs the term ecology as "as a broad concept related to the environmental habitus of both human and non-human actors" (2012) to describe our current media system as a 'computational ecology' which is comprised of distinct 'software ecologies' (2012).

Following these authors, I draw from ecology in a similar manner to analyze changes in the composition of the web by studying the relations between a website and its environment. Website ecology looks at the dynamic and shifting relations between websites and third parties, which do not only become interconnected through users' web activities such as linking pages, but also through software features such as social buttons and data connections created by trackers on websites. An ecological approach to understanding websites allows for the analysis of websites as dynamic spaces where these complex relations between users, websites and third parties such as tracking companies and advertisers get encoded.

STUDYING WEBSITES AND THEIR ENVIRONMENTS THROUGH THE SOURCE CODE

Previous approaches to studying the website in its networked environment have focused on how websites establish relations with other websites through linking, therewith embedding the website in a hyperlink network (Park, 2003; Rogers, 2002). Greg Elmer and Ganaele Langlois describe these approaches as "Web 1.0 methods focused on mapping hyperlink networks" (2013, p. 43) to analyze the connections between websites and the networks they form. Previously, Elmer has called for detecting new indicators of networking and to develop

> a broader vision for the analysis of web code, expanding beyond the mapping of HREF tags (hyperlink code) toward an understanding of the larger structure and deployment of all web code and content (including text, images, met tags, robot.txt commands and so on). (2006, p. 9)

In this chapter I contribute a new approach that examines the source code for scripts that create connections with third parties. Web 2.0, or now commonly referred to as the social web, is characterized by new forms of networked connectivity, Elmer and Langlois argue, which move beyond the hyperlink and which require new methods to map these new types of connections (2013, p. 44). They outline the 'building blocks' of what they refer to as Web 2.0 "cross platform based methods" in which they trace objects across platforms to detect their channels of circulation and analyze the different types of relationships that they form (2013, p. 45). Here, I build on Elmer and Langlois' idea of cross platform analysis with a novel method that traces cross connections from within a website by employing the embedded third-party objects.

A cross platform approach shifts the attention away from the hyperlink as the prime connection mechanism towards other web objects that create interactions between a user, a website and its ecosystem. Of particular interest here are the objects that are not immediately visible in the front-end, the end-user interface of the website, and which create relations with other actors on the web such as trackers. Roesner, Kohno, and Wetherall define a (third-party) tracker as "a website (like doubleclick.net) that has its tracking code included or embedded in another site (like cnn.com)" to "identify and collect information about users" (2012, p. 12).

Web bugs, beacons and other types of trackers embed the website in larger techno-commercial configurations on the web by establishing relations between websites and advertising networks, analytics companies and market research companies, amongst others. Detecting these relations requires moving beyond the user interface in order to detect the traces of these dynamic relations by engaging with the materiality of a website, the source code.

In this chapter, I draw from European media ecology which emphasizes the materiality of code and software of our contemporary media environment (Berry, 2012; Fuller, 2005; Goddard & Parikka, 2011). In this view, the source code of a website forms the object of the study of website ecology. The website's source code provides the material in which the relations with other actors become inscribed through dynamic third-party content, objects and features. This follows a perspective advocated by a number of authors (Ankerson, 2012; Brügger, 2008; De Souza, Froehlich, & Dourish, 2005; Marino, 2014) who engage with the materiality of new media by pointing to the source code as an important entry point for web historical analysis.

De Souza et al. propose to see the source code as "a social and technical artifact" in which aspects of software development have become inscribed (2005, p. 197). They draw from Latour's notion of inscription (1999)[1] to refer to "a process through which social practice and technological artifacts become inextricably intertwined" (2005, p. 197). They see "software artifacts as pure inscriptions" that can be used "to uncover the structure of software projects" and their development processes (2005, p. 197), an approach they refer to as "an 'archeology' of software processes" (2005, p. 206). Similarly, Megan Ankerson turns to the traces of software to engage with "the culture of software in constructing histories of the web" thereby bringing a "software studies lens to web historiography" (2009, p. 195). I build on De Souza et al.'s and Ankerson's approaches by seeing the archived source code as a document in which relations with third parties become inscribed and which that can be used to reconstruct historical techno-commercial configurations on the web.

TECHNO-COMMERCIAL ENVIRONMENTS: TRACKING ECOSYSTEMS

Trackers in the form of beacons and analytics can be implemented by webmasters to monitor the functioning of their websites or to collect data about their visitors. However, trackers can also come as a by-product of third-party functionality such as the Facebook Like Button on external websites which tracks Facebook users and non-Facebook-users across the web (Gerlitz & Helmond, 2013). Webmasters that employ website analytics, advertisements or social buttons therewith—intentionally or unintentionally—embed the website and its visitors in a tracking ecosystem.

Since the early days of the web, banner ads, cookies and other tracking web objects have been an integral part of the web. In October 1994, HotWired placed the first banner ads on its website which marked an important turning point for the web (D'Angelo, 2009). Another important development was the creation of ad networks connecting advertisers to webmasters (Gehl, 2014, p. 104). With the rise of ad servers to track and monitor ads on third-party websites, trackers have become an integral part of the interactions between websites and their ecosystem (Mayer & Mitchell, 2012). In addition, the number of advertising and analytical companies and type of tracking mechanisms has increased over the years as the result of an growing interest in the collection of user data for advertising purposes (Turow, 2011). Next, I will discuss what this means for the changing composition of the website.

THE WEBSITE AS AN ASSEMBLED UNIT

In the early days of the web, often referred to as Web 1.0, websites were considered to be fairly self-contained units since most content was stored on the same server (Mayer & Mitchell, 2012; Song, 2010, p. 251). Within Web 2.0, now more commonly referred to as the social web, websites are considered to be increasingly entangled in a networked context and shaped by third-party content and dynamically-generated functionality (Gehl, 2014, p. 103; Liu, 2004; Mayer & Mitchell, 2012).

This increasing modularity of websites is key to the changing nature of the website which, Alan Liu contends, can be understood as shifting from web pages as independent units to webpages which are filled with content from external databases (2004). Robert Gehl similarly argues that in Web 2.0 a website is assembled from third-party sources:

> a website is a 'mash-up' of top-down, incrementally altered architecture, bottom-up user participation and processing, and the lateral insertion of advertising, creating a coherent visual artifact out of these different streams. (2014, p. 103)

The website can be seen as an assemblage of modular elements that on the one hand enable interactions with other actors on the web and on the other hand permeate or redraw the boundaries of the website by setting up data channels for the exchange of content and data stored in external databases. Next, I will show that the website as an assembled object provides an important entry point for analyzing historical website ecosystems through web archives.

THE DETACHMENT OF THE WEBSITE ECOSYSTEM

To study previous states of the web, the web historian needs access to historical material which can be found in web archives such as the Internet Archive Wayback Machine (IAWM). However, web historian Niels Brügger argues, the archiving process actively shapes and determines how a website is archived and therefore what kind of reconstruction or historical analysis is possible (2009, p. 126). He argues that the effect of the arching process is that "in practice the website is almost always the basic unit in a web archive" (2013, p. 757). Brügger defines the website as

> a coherent textual unit that unfolds in one or more interrelated browser windows, the coherence of which is based on semantic, formal and physically performative interrelations. (2009, p. 126)

Web historians Foot and Schneider delineate websites as "groups of pages sharing a common portion of their URL" (2010, p. 69) where web pages are seen as "groups of elements assembled by a producer and displayed upon request to a server" (2010, p. 69). These definitions of the website as an object of study focus on the visible rendering of the website as a coherent yet assembled object. What we see in the archiving process is that archived website becomes detached from its larger context.

This may be seen in the archived websites in the IAWM, one of the largest available web archives. The IAWM, Richard Rogers argues, lends itself to 'single-site histories' or 'website biographies' as one accesses the archive by entering a single URL, the website's domain name (2013, p. 66). The focus on the single website shows how in the process of archiving, the website has been separated from its ecosystem. Web archives often privilege the content of websites over the search engine results they are part of, their Alexa rankings or their statistics, amongst others (Rogers, 2013, p. 63). Thus, in the archiving process the website is detached from the techno-social context it resides in (Weltevrede, 2009, p. 84).

While the website is often the main unit within web archives (Brügger, 2013, p. 756), the archived website's source code also contains elements that can be employed to "uncover parts of the web that were not preserved" (Samar, Huurdeman, Ben-David, Kamps, & de Vries, 2014, p. 1199). In what follows next I develop a novel method that moves beyond the single-site history by employing the code snippets of an archived website to reconstruct a website's ecosystem. My method addresses the conceptual and practical problem of the website as a bounded object which has troubled web archiving theorists (cf. Brügger, 2009; cf. Schneider & Foot, 2004). In shifting the focus from the content of the archived website to the code, different analytical opportunities present themselves.

ANALYZING HISTORICAL WEBSITE ECOSYSTEMS

In the source code of archived websites we can find the traces, the code snippets, of web objects such as trackers and other third-party content. Following Matthew Kirschenbaum (2003) and Megan Sapnar Ankerson (2009), I use the word traces to refer to the material evidences of software, in this case the tracker code. While trackers or tracking objects may not be archived their code traces allow for reconstructing the tracking networks that websites have been embedded in. Previous approaches in using aspects of a website's source code to study its environment include outlinks to other websites as one way to move beyond the single-site history. The HTML code for hyperlinks in an archived website's source code enables the reconstruction of past hyperlink networks through a historical hyperlink analysis.[2] Even though these websites may not have been archived themselves, the outlinks pointing to them allows for 'conjuring up' these websites (Stevenson, 2010) and map past states of the web or the blogosphere using the IAWM (Ammann, 2011; Ben-David, 2012; Stevenson, 2010; Weltevrede & Helmond, 2012). Following Elmer (2006) and Elmer and Langlois' (2013) call for employing other web objects for networking, I move beyond the hyperlink and focus on trackers as objects that entangle the website in a techno-commercial web environment.

Previous historical tracker studies include a longitudinal study on trackers on 1,200 websites between October 2005 and September 2008 (Krishnamurthy & Wills, 2009) and cookies and their (default) settings in different Netscape browser versions over time (Elmer, 2002). While web archiving has taken the first steps to attend to websites as part of hyperlink networks, little attention has been paid to the historical study of tracker networks so far.

My proposed methodology to analyze historical tracking networks builds on previous research to map tracking networks (Gerlitz & Helmond, 2013; van der Velden, 2014). In this chapter I further extend these methods to detect trackers in *archived websites* to analyze the tracking networks that websites have been embedded in over time. At the same time this methodology serves as a blueprint for developing further methods that focus on detecting and mapping other third-party objects such as social buttons in archived websites to study previous states of the web through website features and technologies to examine changes in the web's techno-commercial environments.

The methodology to create tracker networks is inspired by a digital methods approach of 'repurposing' the existing analytical capacities of tools and devices for research with the web (Rogers, 2013, p. 1; Weltevrede, 2016). Many tools on the web have a methodological approach built into them to achieve a particular functionality. An example of such a tool is the browser add-on Ghostery, which

> scans the page for trackers—scripts, pixels, and other third party elements—and notifies you of the companies whose code is present on the webpages you are visiting. Usually, these trackers aren't visible, and they are often hard to find in the page source code. (Ghostery, 2013)

Ghostery has an inbuilt method to detect trackers in websites that can be employed for research purposes. Instead of creating a new method or tool to find trackers, we can also repurpose the existing analytical capacities of Ghostery. Colleagues and I repurposed Ghostery and created the Tracker Tracker tool (Borra et al., 2012) to analyze and map the presence of trackers in a collection of websites.

Ghostery looks for patterns of trackers and matches them to a database of over 2,000 known trackers.[3] It uses simple string matching (matching a number of characters in a code string) and regex (regular expressions) as a method to detect and match the found tracker code against their database of trackers. For example, Ghostery looks for the presence of advertiser DoubleClick on a website by examining the website's source code for known DoubleClick patterns in Ghostery's tracker database, for example [ad.doubleclick.net] or [doubleclick.net/pagead]).

The main contribution of repurposing Ghostery—by building the new Tracker Tracker tool on top of it—is to detect and map *tracker networks*. While Ghostery has been developed as a plugin to detect and block trackers on *individual websites*, the Tracker Tracker tool is able to detect trackers in *collections of websites* and to create *a network view* of websites and their trackers. The Tracker Tracker tool scans URLs and outputs the name of the website, the tracker found, the tracker pattern and the tracker type in a .csv spreadsheet and .gefx file. This latter file, a Gephi graph, also contains the relations between the trackers and the websites in the collection, based on tracker presence, and can be used to visualize the network of websites and their trackers using the graph analysis and visualization tool Gephi (Bastian et al., 2009).

Scanning large collections of websites for trackers enables the mapping of tracking networks that websites are embedded in. Such an approach no longer focuses on the relations between websites, by reconstructing a network based on the visible outlinks found on the website, but instead focuses on the invisible connections established with trackers such as central ad servers and platforms in the backend. This approach, which looks at different devices to organize relations on the web, such as trackers, shows a specific view of the website's ecosystem. It allows for the reconstruction of a different network of connectivity operating in the back-end of a website by employing the data flows between websites and advertising, tracking and analytics companies as will be demonstrated in the following case study.

TRACING THE TRACKERS USING THE INTERNET ARCHIVE WAYBACK MACHINE

In this case study I develop a novel method to map the tracking ecology of the New York Times (NYT) website over time by using the Tracker Tracker tool in combination with the Internet Archive Wayback Machine (IAWM). I use the IAWM because it provides a valuable source for web historians because of its accessibility and scope. The IAWM contains over 464 Billion URLs and provides snapshots from a wide range of archived websites from 1996 until very recent.[4]

While trackers, or the websites issuing the trackers, may no longer exist or be in use, their code snippets—the code that enables the tracking—can still be found in archived websites within the IAWM. Trackers are visible in the archived website's source code because they are either 'hardcoded' into the source code or have become imprinted in the website's source code during the archival process.

An important finding is that Ghostery still detects trackers in archived websites when surfing through the IAWM with Ghostery enabled. When verifying the detected trackers, by manually comparing the source code of the archived website with the Ghostery database there is indeed a match with the found pattern [ad. doubleclick.net]. Many patterns are established on domain name [ad.doubleclick. net] or subpage level [doubleclick.net/pagead]) which means that even if the tracking technique changes, the tracker will still be detected if it is issued from the same domain or subpage. According to Ghostery's developers, trackers' issuing domains have hardly changed since they started developing the plugin, making it a suitable tool for historical research.[5] The question remains to what extent the Ghostery database contains old trackers. While the example of DoubleClick, which has existed since 1996, shows that such companies can be traced and detected in retrospect, the detection of old trackers relies on the assumption that tracker (sub)domains do not change over time. This means that the approach put forward here can only detect trackers that Ghostery currently has in its database and further research should therefore investigate old tracker patterns. Concerning new trackers, Ghostery operates a cumulative database and constantly adds new patterns of existing trackers to its database as well as new trackers.

What follows from the observation that Ghostery is still able to detect trackers in archived websites is that some of the functionality of the trackers resumes to exist within archived websites and that tracking companies continue to track users within the archived web. It also means that the Tracker Tracker tool—which is based on

Ghostery—works with the IAWM which makes it possible to detect and analyze a website's tracking ecology over time. Next, I will detail a method to do so.

Method

The object of study is the archived NYT website—or more specifically the archived NYT front pages. The NYT was chosen due to the site's centrality as a news source, its large number of visitors per day and the presence of a fair amount of trackers.[6] The selected time frame is 1996–2011, from the first (1996) to the final (2011) full year the NYT was archived in the IAWM at the time of the case study in December 2012. In a first step I set out to collect all the Internet Archive URLs for the archived snapshots from the NYT in the IAWM.

Instead of collecting all IAWM URLs manually, I have used the Internet Archive Wayback Machine Link Ripper tool (Borra et al., 2009) to automate the process. This tool retrieves the links of a website's archived snapshots at wayback. archive.org. The input is a URL [http://www.nytimes.com/] and the output is a text file which lists the IAWM URLs—the links of the archived snapshots. In case the IAWM has archived multiple snapshots of the website per day, only the first archived version of that day is retained and listed in the resulting text file. Since the advertising and analytical techniques that are implemented by the NYT's webmasters do not change on a daily basis, this does not affect the research setup. Table 9.1 shows the number of URLs collected by the IAWM Link Ripper tool per year.

Table 9.1: The number of IAWM URLs collected for the NYT website between 1996 and 2011 per year. The URLs were retrieved by the IAWM Link Ripper tool.

'96	'97	'98	'99	'00	'01	'02	'03	'04	'05	'06	'07	'08	'09	'10	'11
7	4	1	13	10	174	157	71	21	230	208	290	261	243	281	352

In a second step I used the Tracker Tracker tool to scan the IAWM URLs—the archived snapshots—for tracking technologies. The input is the list of IAWM URLs that was compiled in the previous step and the output shows the detected trackers per URL. The result file can be downloaded from the tool in CSV (spreadsheet), GEFX (Gephi) or HTML-format and contains the IAWM URLs, the tracker name, type and pattern that was detected. The type of trackers follows the categorization provided by Ghostery: Ad, Analytics, Beacon/Tracker, and Widget.[7] I then collected this detailed information in a spreadsheet. Figure 9.1 shows the number and type of trackers that have been detected in the archived snapshots of the NYT front page per year.[8]

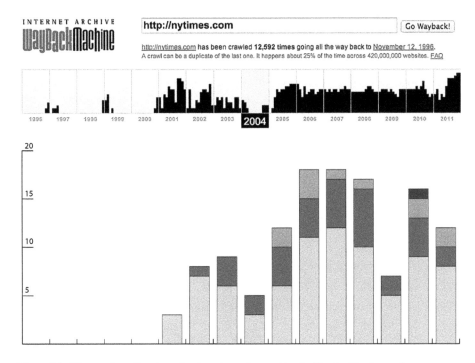

Figure 9.1: The number of trackers that have been detected by the Tracker Tracker tool per year on the archived NYT front pages in the IAWM between 1996 and 2011.

No third-party trackers have been detected between 1996 and 2000. As discussed previously, ad servers and trackers have been an integral part of the web since the mid 1990s, so I manually verified the data of this period by checking the source code for the presence of third-party trackers. In 1996 and 1997 the front page of the NYT is a clickable image map and does not contain any trackers. In 1998 the NYT contains a first-party tracker from RealMedia ads (now 24/7 Media) from the installed ad management platform Real Media on the NYT domain.[9] As of 2001 the NYT has started using a number of third-party advertising services: DoubleClick, LinkShare and Microsoft Atlas. The number of trackers increases per year and in 2006 and 2007 the NYT front page contains 18 unique trackers over that year. After 2007 there is a decline in the number of unique trackers which reflects the findings of the previously mentioned longitudal tracker study by Krishnamurthy and Wills who found an "increasing aggregation of user-related data by a steadily decreasing number of entities" (2009, p. 541). Further research could address this phenomenon by looking into whether this indicates media concentration. This would be a way to investigate how larger cultural, social and economic patterns on the web might be reflected in a website's ecosystem, such as increasing ownership concentration in the ad network industry.

Trackers in the form of widgets, which include social plugins such as Like, Share or Tweet buttons, are relatively absent from the results. This can be explained by the setup of the research design. In this study I focused on the front page of the NYT, whilst widgets such as social buttons are often not implemented on the front page but on the single-article page to like, share, and tweet an article. Figure 9.2 shows the diverse tracker environment the NYT website has been embedded in over the years.

Trackers on the New York Times 1996-2011

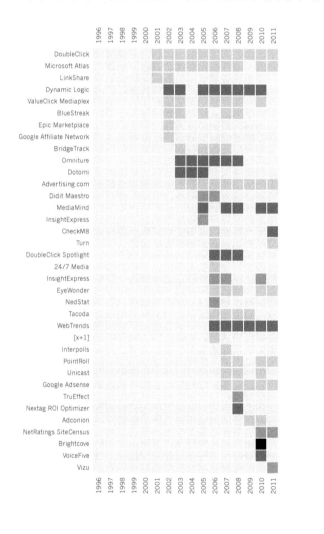

Figure 9.2: Names and types of the trackers that have been detected by the Tracker Tracker tool per year on the archived NYT front pages in the IAWM between 1996 and 2011.

This case study on the NYT has demonstrated how we can employ historical source code analysis to analyze the historical tracker environment of a website using the IAWM. As such it has put forward a way in which an individual archived website can be used to uncover the interactions between the website and its environment. One of the limitations of the case study is that the pattern of a specific tracker may change over time by using different scripts or tracking techniques (Orr, Chauhan, Gupta, Frisz, & Dunn, 2012). However, this case study has shown that in many cases patterns are established on domain name level and do not change significantly over time, e.g. [ad.doubleclick.com].

In future research the method presented in this chapter could be used to scan a larger set of websites and move beyond the front page of these websites to also detect social buttons. Scanning a large collection of archived websites over the timespan of 10 years would allow for reconstructing and analyzing the changing techno-commercial configurations of the web, for example by focusing on the changing infrastructural and economic underpinnings of the web with the rise of social media. This case study has demonstrated how a web historiographical approach may employ existing web archives to study a website's ecosystem over time in order to analyze historical states of the web using the website's archived source code.

WEB HISTORIES: RECONSTRUCTING PAST STATES OF THE WEB USING SOURCE CODE SNIPPETS

This chapter has aimed to contribute to the growing field of web historiography by putting the IAWM to new uses. One of the questions within this field is what kinds of web histories can be told using web archives. Dominant approaches focus on the history of a single site or a network of sites through historical hyperlink analysis because of the IAWM's focus on the unit of the website at the expense of the website's larger context (Ben-David & Huurdeman, 2014; Brügger, 2013; Rogers, 2013). I have shown how the code snippets of third-party objects in the archived source code can be used to address a common problem that web historians are facing: missing context. The archived source code contains information about a website's relationships with third parties and can provide an entry point for reconstructing a website's historical ecosystem. In this chapter I have developed and positioned *historical source code analysis* as a method to move beyond content analysis, single-site analysis, and hyperlink analysis of websites over time. Whilst the source code is useful to analyze a single website's development or content over time, I have outlined an approach for using it to explore changes in the composition of the web more broadly. As I have argued, the presence of third-party objects, scripts, and tools within a collection of websites can be employed for doing web history. The use of analytics, social plugins, and advertising, whose tracking capacities can all be detected via the Tracker Tracker tool, provides an important starting point to analyze the business strategies and economic underpinnings of websites and the web at large. That is, historical source code analysis enables empirically investigating infrastructural and economic changes on the web. Furthermore, such studies can also be of value for other areas of research, for example privacy researchers who wish to examine how techniques for gathering user data and the types of user data via websites have changed over time. Software studies scholars,[10] as also proposed by Ankerson (2009), may employ historical source code analysis to understand the commercialization of the web and the practices of web masters to investigate the web's underlying infrastructure and how websites, users and other actors on the web are connected. These are important issues to consider for understanding the foundations of how the web is built, organized and supported.

To do so, in this chapter I have proposed to reconceptualize the study of websites as website ecology. By developing a method which enables web historians to scan websites for trackers and other third-party objects over time, I have propositioned to add the study of historical website ecosystems to the field of web historiography.

ACKNOWLEDGEMENTS

I would like to thank Richard Rogers, Anat Ben-David, Carolin Gerlitz, Fernando van der Vlist, the reviewers, and editor Niels Brügger, for their feedback on earlier drafts of this chapter.

REFERENCES

Ammann, R. (2011). Reciprocity, social curation and the emergence of blogging: A study in community formation. *Procedia—Social and Behavioral Sciences, 22,* 26–36. doi:10.1016/j.sbspro.2011.07.053

Ankerson, M. S. (2009). Historicizing web design: Software: Style, and the look of the web. In J. Staiger & S. Hake (Eds.), *Convergence, media, history* (pp. 192–203). Abingdon: Routledge.

Ankerson, M. S. (2012). Writing web histories with an eye on the analog past. *New Media & Society, 14*(3), 384–400.

Bastian, M., Heymann, S., Jacomy, M. (2009). Gephi: An open source software for exploring and manipulating networks. *ICWSM, 8,* 361–362.

Ben-David, A. (2012). *Palestinian border-making in digital spaces.* Ramat Gan: Bar Ilan University.

Ben-David, A., & Huurdeman, H. (2014). Web archive search as research: methodological and theoretical implications. *Alexandria, 25*(1), 93–111.

Berry, D. M. (2012, September 23). *Life in code and software.* Retrieved April 21, 2013 from http://www.livingbooksaboutlife.org/books/Life_in_Code_and_Software/Introduction

Borra, E., Den Tex, E., Gerlitz, C., Helmond, A., Martens, K., Rieder, B., & Weltevrede, E. (2012). *Tracker tracker*. Amsterdam: The Digital Methods Initiative. Retrieved from https://tools. digitalmethods.net/beta/trackerTracker/

Borra, E., Weltevrede, E., Helmond, A., Stevenson, M., De Vries Hoogerwerff, M., & Rogers, R. (2009). *Internet archive wayback machine link ripper*. Amsterdam: The Digital Methods Initiative. Retrieved from https://tools.digitalmethods.net/beta/internetArchiveWaybackMachineLinkR ipper/

Brügger, N. (2008). The archived website and website philology: A new type of historical document? *Nordicom Review, 29*(2), 155–175.

Brügger, N. (2009). Website history and the website as an object of study. *New Media & Society, 11*(1–2), 115–132.

Brügger, N. (2013). Web historiography and Internet Studies: Challenges and perspectives. *New Media & Society, 15*(5), 752–764.

D'Angelo, F. (2009, October 26). *Happy birthday, digital advertising!* Retrieved from http://adage.com/ article/digitalnext/happy-birthday-digital-advertising/139964/

De Souza, C., Froehlich, J., & Dourish, P. (2005). Seeking the source: Software source code as a social and technical artifact. In *Proceedings of the 2005 international ACM SIGGROUP conference on supporting group work* (pp. 197–206). New York, NY: ACM. Retrieved from http://dl.acm.org/ citation.cfm?id=1099239

Elmer, G. (2002). The case of web browser cookies: Enabling/disabling convenience and relevance on the web. In *Critical Perspectives on the Internet*. Lanham, MD: Rowman & Littlefield.

Elmer, G. (2006). Re-tooling the network parsing the links and codes of the web World. *Convergence: The International Journal of Research into New Media Technologies, 12*(1), 9–19. doi:10.1177/1354856506061549

Elmer, G., & Langlois, G. (2013). Networked campaigns: Traffic tags and cross platform analysis on the web. *Information Polity, 18*(1), 43–56. doi:10.3233/IP-2011-0244

Foot, K., & Schneider, S. (2010). Object-oriented web historiography. In N. Brügger (Ed.), *Web history* (pp. 61–79). New York, NY: Peter Lang.

Fuller, M. (2005). *Media ecologies: Materialist energies in art and technoculture*. Cambridge, MA: MIT Press.

Gehl, R. (2014). *Reverse engineering social media: Software, culture, and political economy in new media capitalism*. Philadelphia, PA: Temple University Press.

Gerlitz, C., & Helmond, A. (2013). The Like economy: Social buttons and the data-intensive web. *New Media & Society, 15*(8), 1348–1365. doi:/10.1177/1461444812472322

Ghostery. (2013, October 1). Ghostery™ FAQs. Retrieved January 10, 2013 from http://www.ghostery. com/faq

Goddard, M., & Parikka, J. (2011). Unnatural ecologies. *The Fibreculture Journal, 17*. Retrieved from http://seventeen.fibreculturejournal.org/

Kirschenbaum, M. G. (2003). Virtuality and vrml: Software studies after Manovich. *Electronic Book Review* (The Politics of Information). Retrieved from http://www.electronicbookreview.com/ thread/technocapitalism/morememory

Krishnamurthy, B., & Wills, C. (2009). Privacy diffusion on the web: A longitudinal perspective. In *Proceedings of the 18th international conference on World Wide Web* (pp. 541–550). New York, NY: ACM. doi:10.1145/1526709.1526782

Latour, B. (1999). *Pandora's hope: Essays on the reality of science studies* (1st ed.). Cambridge, MA: Harvard University Press.

Liu, A. (2004). Transcendental data: Toward a cultural history and aesthetics of the new encoded discourse. *Critical Inquiry, 31*(1), 49–84.

Manovich, L. (2013). *Software takes command*. New York, NY: Bloomsbury Academic.

Marino, M. C. (2014). Field report for critical code studies 2014. *Computational Culture, 4*. Retrieved from http://computationalculture.net/article/field-report-for-critical-code-studies-2014

Mayer, J. R., & Mitchell, J. C. (2012). Third-party web tracking: Policy and technology. In *2012 IEEE Symposium on Security and Privacy (SP)* (pp. 413–427). New York, NY: IEEE. doi: 10.1109/SP.2012.47

Orr, C. R., Chauhan, A., Gupta, M., Frisz, C. J., & Dunn, C. W. (2012). An approach for identifying JavaScript-loaded advertisements through static program analysis. In *Proceedings of the 2012 ACM workshop on privacy in the electronic society* (pp. 1–12). New York, NY: ACM. http://doi.org/10.1145/2381966.2381968

Park, H. W. (2003). Hyperlink network analysis: A new method for the study of social structure on the web. *Connections, 25*, 49–61.

Postman, N. (1970). The reformed English curriculum. In A. C. Eurich (Ed.), *High school 1980: The shape of the future in American secondary education* (pp. 160–168). New York, NY: Pitman.

Roesner, F., Kohno, T., & Wetherall, D. (2012). Detecting and defending against third-party tracking on the web. In *Proceedings of the 9th USENIX conference on networked systems design and implementation* (pp. 12–12). Berkeley, CA: USENIX Association. Retrieved from http://dl.acm.org/citation.cfm?id=2228298.2228315

Rogers, R. (2002). Operating issue networks on the web. *Science as Culture, 11*(2), 191–213.

Rogers, R. (2013). *Digital methods*. Cambridge, MA: MIT Press.

Samar, T., Huurdeman, H., Ben-David, A., Kamps, J., & de Vries, A. (2014). Uncovering the unarchived web. In *Proceedings of the 37th international ACM SIGIR conference on research & Development in information retrieval* (pp. 1199–1202). New York, NY: ACM. doi:10.1145/2600428.2609544

Schneider, S. M., & Foot, K. A. (2004). The web as an object of study. *New Media and Society, 6*(1), 114–122.

Song, F. W. (2010). Theorizing web 2.0: A cultural perspective. *Information, Communication & Society, 13*(2), 249–275.

Stevenson, M. (2010). *The archived blogosphere: Exploring web historical methods using the internet archive.* Presented at the Digital Methods mini-conference, University of Amsterdam.

Turow, J. (2011). *The daily you: How the new advertising industry is defining your identity and your worth.* New Haven, CT: Yale University Press.

van der Velden, L. (2014). The third party diary: Tracking the trackers on Dutch governmental websites. *NECSUS. European Journal of Media Studies, 3*(1), 195–217.

Weltevrede, E. (2009). *Thinking nationally with the web: A medium-specific approach to the national turn in web archiving.* Amsterdam: University of Amsterdam.

Weltevrede, E. (2016). *Repurposing digital methods: The research affordances of platforms and engines* (PhD dissertation). University of Amsterdam, Amsterdam. Retrieved from https://wiki.digitalmethods.net/Dmi/RepurposingDigitalMethods

Weltevrede, E., & Helmond, A. (2012). Where do bloggers blog? Platform transitions within the historical Dutch blogosphere. *First Monday, 17*(2). doi:10.5210/fm.v17i2.3775

NOTES

1. Latour defines inscription as "a general term that refers to all the types of transformations through which an entity becomes materialized into a sign, an archive, a document, a piece of paper, a trace" (1999, p. 306).

2. Despite the fact that web archives are often incomplete, the proposed method does not require the linked website to be archived as well. The mere presence of the hyperlink pointing to it can be used to map the historical hyperlink network of a blogosphere, see the work of (Ammann, 2011; Ben-David, 2012; Stevenson, 2010; Weltevrede & Helmond, 2012).

3. See: https://www.ghostery.com/our-solutions/ghostery-browser-extention/ 1 [Accessed January 10, 2016].

4. See: https://archive.org/web/ [Accessed January 23, 2016].

5. On May 30, 2013 I visited Ghostery's office (Evidon Inc.) in New York City and interviewed Ghostery's developers about their tracker database and the plugin's technical functionality.

6. See http://www.alexa.com/siteinfo/nytimes.com and http://www.alexa.com/topsites/category/Top/News [Accessed January 12, 2013].

7. See: http://www.knowyourelements.com/#tab=intro [Accessed January 12, 2013].

8. There are a number of gaps in the available IAWM data from 1996 to 2000 and in 2004 data is missing for the months April–September which may explain the sudden 'decline' in trackers in 2004.

9. First party trackers are issued from the same domain as the website "that the user has voluntarily interacted with" whilst third-party trackers are issued from a different domain than the website, indicating involuntary interactions with an external actor (Mayer & Mitchell, 2012, p. 413). In this chapter a tracker refers to a third-party tracker, indicating a connection with an external actor.

10. My proposal for historical source code analysis can also be seen as a contribution to Critical Code Studies (CCS), an approach aligned with software studies and platform studies which analyzes the code layer of software (Marino, 2014). It specifically addresses a concern expressed by Matthew Kirschenbaum during the 2011 HASTAC Scholars Critical Code Studies Forum that "by focusing on the analysis of code snippets, CCS could potentially abstract code from its larger software constructs" (2014). The approach put forward here uses code to direct the attention back to these larger software constructs of the web such as tracking ecologies.

CHAPTER TEN

THE changing digital faces OF science museums

A diachronic analysis of museum websites

ANWESHA CHAKRABORTY AND FEDERICO NANNI

INTRODUCTION

In recent years, web history (Brügger, 2010) has started to receive substantial attention in internet studies and digital humanities, and its theories and methods have been applied to political science research (e.g. Ben-David, 2015; Foot, Schneider, Dougherty, Xenos, & Larsen, 2003) as well as cultural and social history (e.g. Milligan, 2015). Inspired by this academic development, this chapter is intended to be a starting point to discuss how prominent scientific institutions develop their websites over a period of time to communicate better with their visitors. More specifically, this work presents the formulation of a methodology for using websites as primary sources to trace and examine activities of scientific institutions through the years. This is achieved in three steps: first, we diachronically analyse snapshots of pages of select museum websites from the Internet Archive, the most important and comprehensive web archive (Howell, 2006).[1] Then, we combine this analysis with interviews of the current website managers and with resources available on the live web.

The choice to study museums was prompted by the fact that these institutions are perceived by the civil society as authoritative custodians of artifacts, culture and heritage. This is true for science and technology museums as well, which have the additional task of communicating specialised (and often less understood) branches of knowledge. In the last 20 years the World Wide Web has become ubiquitous and websites have affirmed themselves as one of the first points of communication with museums (Wilson, 2011). However, from our research it has become apparent that little work has been done so far on using websites as primary resources to trace the history of the representation of scientific institutions on the web. Thus, the goal of our research is to understand how science museum websites have transformed over time and what these changes imply in the larger context of growing functions of websites.

The three case studies we have chosen include some of the most prominent science museums in Europe: the Science Museum, London; the Deutsches Museum, Munich and the Museo Nazionale della Scienza e della Tecnologia (hereafter, Museo della Scienza), Milan. We chose the Museo della Scienza to carry out the first round of interviews because of our spatial proximity to the museum.[2] At this stage, we also felt the need to include a few more representative examples, and thus we selected the Deutsches Museum and the Science Museum, which regularly feature among the most visited science museums in the world.[3] The rationale for selecting a number of cases is to examine a similar set of institutions (in this chapter, museums of history of science). These institutions have increasingly been providing greater number of hands-on activities alongside the traditional displays of artifacts to encourage visitor participation. This is also reflected in how websites have changed through the years.

In this chapter we present a periodisation of the phases of significant structural and functional changes of the websites. The chapter chronicles what the websites have done since they were digitally born; what have been the milestones in terms of their development and the trajectory they are pursuing for better communication and relations with the public. It is important to point out that this work does not intend to offer a comparison of the three museums; rather the idea is to use a set of case studies to demonstrate our methodology, which focuses on the analysis of websites as primary sources for studying the recent history of scientific institutions.

IMPORTANCE OF MUSEUM WEBSITES

While there is little attention paid to websites as primary sources in museum studies, they have not been overlooked in discussions on the vast potential of digital domains in improving communication. Morrison (2006) states that a museum these days is not just the building, the collections and the staff, but also the website. Museums can connect with their visitors by providing them with more tools for personalized visits to the institution through their websites (Bowen, Bennett, & Johnson, 1998; Bowen & Filippini-Fantoni, 2004). Marty (2007) argues that websites also boost attendance to the physical museum, and that a museum needs to have an effective and well-designed website, in order to justify its rationale, attract visitors, showcase its importance in the social life of a specific area and a nation. Day (1997) and Cunliffe, Kritou, and Tudhope (2001) posit the argument that the specific goals and objectives of the museum should be reflected on the website. One such goal is preservation of artifacts and Mason and McCarthy (2008) argue that a strong relationship can be ascertained between museums and computers and other digital tools over the last two decades, created to preserve data and digitize collections for better storage.

Online resources can augment engagement facilities of museums (Wilson, 2011). This is not just limited to websites, but also downloadable apps and interactive exhibits. Davies (2007) and Yasko (2007) argue that the virtual space is in fact an extension of the physical space with enhanced opportunities for visitors to interact with objects in the museum, with access to digitized collections and virtual tours. With greater presence in social media, museums have also started communicating directly with their potential audiences by posting videos, updating information related to exhibitions, and discussing recent developments in the fields which are a part of the core exhibits of the museum. A very good example of this is the website of the California Academy of Sciences which gives access not just to the content of the museum exhibits but also to all the recent breakthroughs in the world of science.[4] The institution also maintains active Facebook, YouTube and Twitter accounts, which are used to constantly communicate with audiences from around the world making them aware of cutting-edge research in traditional and new scientific disciplines.

It is fascinating that one of the most succinct explanations of the potential of websites is to be found in an early document of the Museo della Scienza, back in 1995.[5] The document proposed certain characteristics that a successful website must possess, which are still relevant today even with the continuous advancements in the field of web technologies. These features include: dynamism (the ability to update information at a swift pace), hypertextuality (the possibility of creating linkages between articles and web pages both internally and externally), interactivity (considered as the most important ingredient for the success of the website) and the use of direct voice (the need to address the visitors informally).

As mentioned earlier, while there is a growing body of research on web history and some specifically focusing on museum websites, the history of these websites have largely been neglected by museum studies. Mason and McCarthy (2008) astutely observe that discourses about new technologies generally are presented in overtly theoretical and under-historicized styles. Where we depart from Mason and McCarthy is however when they claim, quoting Henning, that new media "like old media, is best understood as 'a means to organize and structure knowledge and visitor attention, not as a means of communication or a set of devices'" (Henning, 2006, p. 303: Mason & McCarthy, 2008, p. 64). Our position, following communication theories, is that new media not only help in structuring knowledge, they embody information through technologies that are user-enabled and friendly. In new media theories, technology has increasingly been conceptualized as performative, conversational and primarily as a space where "perspectives are accommodated rather than stifled by an imposed ordering." (Srinivasan, 2013, p. 206) As we will see in the diachronic analysis of the selected websites, museum professionals have been aware of the performative and conversational aspects of new technologies.

In the following section we present the different sources we employed in our analysis of the changes in the layout, content and structure of the selected websites. In particular, the use of snapshots from the Internet Archive is discussed in detail.

SOURCES AND METHODS

In order to conduct our analysis, we employed three types of primary sources. First of all, we used snapshots of websites preserved by the Internet Archive, as these materials hold the potential of presenting the changes in layout, structure and contents of a website through time. Secondly, we conducted a series of interviews with the people who are managing the websites at present. By combining these sources, our goals were *(a)* to obtain a comprehensive perspective on the evolution of science museum websites and *(b)* to understand the reasons behind specific changes and decisions. We expanded our analysis further by adopting resources available on the live web. The live web includes the current version of the website and the presence of the museum on social media. In the following paragraphs, the reliability and potential of the different primary sources introduced above will be explained further.

Web archive materials

During its first 25 years, the World Wide Web has been constantly growing and today it presents the vastest collection of primary evidences of our past ever to have existed. However, at the same time, the web has also transformed constantly without leaving any trace (Brügger, 2005) and this has made its preservation and diachronic study extremely challenging for scholars.

Since the second part of the Nineties, initiatives have been taken by private (Lyman & Kahle, 1998) and public (Gomes, Miranda, & Costa, 2011) actors to preserve the web for future research. Currently through its Wayback Machine the Internet Archive offers the largest collection of preserved pages (Lepore, 2015). Moreover, in the last decade web archive materials have been already used by media studies scholars, historians and political scientists for a large variety of research (e.g. Ben-David, 2015; Dougherty et al., 2010; Foot et al., 2003; Hale et al. 2014; Milligan, 2012; Nanni, 2017, in press). These different studies have revealed the great potential of web archives in offering new/different perspectives on our recent past.

In this work, we focused on a qualitative analysis of the web histories of the three websites introduced in Section 2. The preliminary step of this analysis was to create a collection of all the snapshots of the websites available on the Internet Archive. This was accomplished by using the Wayback Machine. We initially focused on studying the homepages of these websites over time, as they offer a general over-view of the structural organization and highlight which subsections were considered highly relevant at specific points in time (for example, the ones listed in the sidebars). During this analysis we identified, in a coarse-grained fashion, all major changes in the structure and the layout of the homepages. Next, we examined the transitions between the layouts of each website, more specifically, how layouts changed over time and what were the main modifications. This helped us in recognizing, for instance, the subsections which remained linked to the homepage after a layout change, those which were removed and those subsections which were introduced.

After having performed this coarse-grained analysis of the three websites, we then examined the obtained results in order to detect *(a)* similar patterns in how the overall layout and structure changed over time, *(b)* correlations with other studies on the topic (e.g. Schweibenz, 2004) and *(c)* evidences of how new technologies (e.g. Twitter em-beddable timelines) were integrated into the museum websites. The results of our fine-grained study helped us defining the narration and periodization of the three science museum websites, presented in the section 'Diachronic Analysis of the Websites' Past'.

Oral histories

As previously emphasized, while reconstructing our past will rely increasingly on born digital materials, they are extremely difficult to preserve in their integrity. For this reason, although web archives will continue to be recognised as a relevant source in historical research in the next decades, a key role will be played by recording and preserving oral memories.[6] In fact, while snapshots from the Internet Archive can provide the 'what' of the website, i.e. they can help reconstruct the changes in the website's structure diachronically, oral memories will give us a better understanding of the 'how' and 'why' of those changes. These direct sources will, therefore, explain the rationale behind the changing architecture of the websites.

For our work we conducted oral interviews with the digital teams of the museums we chose as case studies. A set of qualitative, open-ended questions were emailed to the website managers of the three museums, which were aimed at understanding the evolution of the websites.[7] The qualitative data gathered from the interviews with Paolo Cavallotti (Head of Digital, Museo della Scienza, Milan), John Stack (Digital Director, Science Museum Group, UK) and Annette Lein (Head of Online Media, Deutsches Museum, Munich) will be discussed in conjunction with the findings of the in-depth analysis of the snapshots from the Internet Archive and of the live web.

The live web

While web archive materials and oral memories help us in reconstructing the changes in websites over time and in discovering the reasons behind specific transformations, materials available on the live web will also play an important role for future web historical research. The live web reveals the current role of websites in the museum's organization and management (e.g. attracting international visitors and promoting temporary exhibitions). Additionally, by combining materials from the websites and from social media pages of those institutions (such as Facebook, Youtube and Twitter profiles), we can make reasonable assumptions about the digital interactions between users and institutions that have been established in recent years, outside the digital space of the museum websites. While materials from social networking websites will play a fundamental role in helping researchers to better understand the multidirectional communication in the first decades of the 21st century, it is important to remember that their suitability for historical analysis is currently under scrutiny, as preservation (Zimmer, 2015), computational (Webster, 2015) and reliability (Brugger, 2015) issues have to be considered and debated.

DIACHRONIC ANALYSIS OF THE WEBSITES' PAST

We conducted in-depth analysis of the three science museum websites introduced in Section 2, adopting the combination of methodologies described in Section 3. Based on the results of the analysis, we propose a periodisation to track significant changes in the structure and functions of the websites, by dividing the timeline into four macro-phases.[8] The first phase covers the second part of the Nineties, when the websites were set up, primarily to provide information about location, collections and activities. The second comprises the years between 2000 and 2006, when a growing focus on the 'virtual museum' and on the importance of interactions with digital representation of objects presented in museums could be detected. The third phase includes the years between 2007 and 2010, when the focus shifted from creating sophisticated version of the physical museum on the web, to forging better alliances with potential visitors through blogs and similar participatory platforms. Given the extraordinary growth of social networking websites that has been prevalent in the last decade, we consider museums now fully entering the fourth phase (2011–present), when the majority of the interactions and the dialogue with the user takes place on Facebook and Twitter and the website purports to be an extremely advanced digital interface to the collections and archives.

While this periodization has helped us shaping the diachronic narration of the changes in science museums websites over time, these phases should not be considered as watertight compartments because many old features continue to make appearances in the new versions. The periodisation is intended to show how websites can be traced as new historical sources, which are in a state of constant modification.

The 'leaflet' museum website

The early use of the website as an information leaflet of the museum corresponds with Schweibenz's (2004) analysis of the typologies of museum websites, in which he describes the first category as the 'brochure museum'. The definition of this type is given thus "[...] this is a website, which contains the basic information about the museum, such as types of collection, contact details, etc. Its goal is to inform potential visitors about the museum." This is, in other words, the initial identity of the museum website as described by Annette Lein of Deutsches Museum in the personal interview. Paolo Cavallotti of the Museo Scienza concurs: "The idea was to present the museum and its objects and collections. The website's main function is to present the museum aesthetically."

The following paragraphs present the results of our analysis of the early years of the three websites. In these years, the main goal of the websites was to function as a digital leaflet for the museum, in order to reach and attract potential visitors. In fact, materials presented on the websites include detailed textual descriptions of the museum's collections and information regarding temporary exhibitions, often available in more than one language.

The Museo della Scienza has been online since 1995, with an essential informative interface on the activities of the museum, its collections and the opening hours.[9] As it can be noticed from Internet Archive's snapshots, the first version of a more extended service was presented as early as in 1997: a 3D graphic interface was developed "in order to transmit the idea of an overwhelming variety of information".[10] The homepage provided general information about the museum, its activities and on temporary exhibitions, both in Italian and English. Hyperlinks and descriptions of other international institutions, such as the Science Museum in London and the Deutsches Museum in Munich, were offered.[11]

By studying the new contents that were added over time, we noticed that the museum offered a series of introductory guidelines for its users on topics such as the 'Internet' and the 'web', in the second part of the Nineties. Teaching how to use new technologies (e.g. how to send emails) was also a key aspect in the collaboration between the museum and schools, as described in the 'Scuole attività' (school activities) page.[12]

At the end of the Nineties a first experimental version of 'Leonardo Virtuale', a virtual tour of the museum, was presented online. This development marked the first step of the museum towards establishing a different presence online compared to the initial 'leaflet', and presenting its website as a parallel (digital) collection, which could be explored by users directly from home.

A similar path, focused on providing an overview of the collection and a series of practical information, could be detected in the initial years of the London Science Museum website. The goal of the museum for its website, mentioned in the two reports published between 1998 and 1999, was to attract more visitors to the physical museum (by improving the structure and the usability of the website) and to improve its role for educational purposes.[13] Reading the first report, we also noticed that the interest of the museum was to develop a solution to offer a different browsing experience to different users.

In 1997, the Deutsches Museum website offered a similar homepage with several pieces of information, both in German and in English. From news regarding the museum, to descriptions of special exhibitions to courses and seminars offered, this website could be identified as the paradigmatic version of Schweibenz's brochure website discussed earlier. Moreover, a multimedia section (available in 1997 under the rubric 'dioramen') offered interactive demonstrations of specific expositions, videos and other contents. Great attention was paid to describe its archive devoted to the history of science and technology, one of the most important in Europe. Part of the catalogue was presented online and could be directly consulted by users. As pointed out by Annette Lein in the interview, in this early version of the website, "[…] the aim was to provide information for visitors and to present the exhibitions online with text and photos worldwide. Other main topics were: calendar of events, a list of people working in the museum, a glance at archives, library and research institute, feedback form, contact."

Figure 10.1: The Deutsches Museum website in a snapshot from 1998.

At the end of the Nineties, the leaflet type of museum website encountered a major overhaul in terms of image and content, aided greatly by the changes in software and hardware technologies available to web managers. This phenomenon, together with the development of websites that permitted interactive tours of digital reconstructions of museum collections, signalled the beginning of a new phase. John Stack, the Digital Director of the Science Museum Group summarises this transition thus: "There is a general trend of museums initially thinking of their websites as a way to promote a visit to the museum. There is then an increase in considering the website as a destination in its own right and of therefore producing content for it such as digitized collections and other online resources."

The rise and fall of the virtual museum

During the first part of the 2000s, a common trend characterized the efforts that the three museums focused on their digital space. Moving from a conception of the website as a series of pages where pieces of information regarding collections and archives were presented, they started experimenting with virtual reality. The goal was to offer new experiences to the user who would have the opportunity of interact with the collections directly from home.

In 1999, the Museo della Scienza introduced a virtual museum called 'Leonardo Virtuale', created in collaboration with the Polytechnic of Milan. Using this software, users could 'walk' and 'fly' through the different rooms of the museum and explore its collections. Visitors had the possibility of meeting and chatting with other guests and following a virtual guide. An innovative choice was to adopt Webtalk, a technology developed by the Hypermedia Open Center (HOC) of the Polytechnic of Milan based on VRML (Virtual Reality Markup Language) and Java, which guaranteed a real time interaction between different users.

Figure 10.2: The virtual museum 'Leonardo Virtuale' on the website of Museo della Scienza.

In 2001 the London Science Museum also introduced the 'Exhibitions online' section. Similar to a virtual museum, in this case visitors could explore the different collections from their desks, from Babbage's machine to Marie Curie and the history of radioactivity. Moreover, interaction with a series of objects was offered (for example, the possibility of exploring the Apollo 10 module).[14]

The potential of the web as a place to interact with digital collections gave museum practitioners the chance of experimenting new forms of education. For example, the 'Learn and Teach' section of the Science Museum presented several pieces of information for family and school classes and offered a series of activities that could be conducted from home.[15]

Giving users the possibility of interacting with digital objects was a fundamental aspect of the changes in the Deutsches Museum website as well. As early as in 1998 a 'Museum Multimedial' was created with a link available on the homepage. During the following years this page offered a large variety of resources:[16] from dioramas to live-cameras, from video-clips to interactive demonstrations.

Even though all three science museums showed ample interest in offering interactive collections online (e.g. in the form of virtual tours), the realisation of the virtual version had to face serious technological impediment, which contributed to the demise of the trend of creating virtual museums. First of all, the majority of internet connections were not sufficiently fast and stable to fully support the usability of these services. Secondly, 3D graphic reconstructions were usually not accurate enough to be considered a real substitute to a visit to the museum. Discussing the diminishing popularity of the concept of the virtual museum, Cavallotti comments on the strategy adopted by Museo della Scienza: "This concept was very popular some years ago. But the museum's website team does not want to make a difference between the virtual and physical museum. The team uses digital tools to talk about the physical museum."

While the goal of creating a virtual experience of visiting the real museum have subsided during the second part of the last decade, the interest in digitizing content and presenting them in interactive ways to the user has remained, as is evident in new digital projects taken up by both the Deutsches Museum and Science Museum. The Deutsches Museum Digital project, as described by Lein, will provide online access to the entire collection of objects of the museum, and to the archives and the library.[17] Stack mentions that while they do not have a plan for a full-scale digital museum, they are participating in the Google Cultural Institute Gallery View Project. So will the early trend of virtual museums make a comeback with these kinds of current collaborative projects? Lein's observation tells us otherwise, as she makes a sharp distinction between the virtual museum and the digital museum. While the former as a trend has subsided, the latter has gained popularity as it can ensure better opportunities to interact with the museum online, due to multiple digitised collections being granted open access. Furthermore, the digital museum consists of the website as well as the communication taking place on social media managed by the museum team.

The outreach-museum website: ensuring greater engagement

While the virtual museum as a trend had started waning by the middle of the 2000s, increased attention was being paid by website managers to present collections in innovative ways (e.g. enhancing digital collections and accurately describing them in dedicated blogs) and to improve communication and dialogue with the users. In museum studies literature, this was the period of increasing number of scholarly works being written about the concepts of participatory designs in museum exhibits, and co-participation of visitors in determining the content inside the museum space. Among them, *The Participatory Museum* (Simon, 2010) by Nina Simon explains in detail how greater visitor participation can be achieved. She argues that authority over content should be shared between the museum and its visitors, citing O'Reilly's definition of Web 2.0, "an application that gets better the more people use it."[18] Following the greater focus on more inputs from the public as emphasised by Web 2.0 theories, the websites examined in this chapter show similar structural changes at this stage of the decade to accommodate more voices.

Figure 10.3: The homepage of the Science Museum in a snapshot from 2007.

Museums have offered snippets of information regarding their collections and new exhibitions to their users, in particular through newsletters, since the Nineties. However, during the second part of the 2000s there was a greater focus on communicating through blog posts and podcasts to go beyond the traditional authoritative role of these institutions. An excellent example was the Science Museum's 'Antenna', a constantly updated resource for science news. Blogs describing the collections were also developed, as 'Stories' from the Science Museum and "Der Blog das Deutsches Museum" shows. The second one, which has been regularly updated since 2009, has been mainly written in German, highlighting their target users.

While blog posts represent a continuation of newsletters and updates regarding collections, an alternative way of presenting the museum online is to employ social networking sites to share photos and videos. In 2006 the Science Museum opened a Flickr account that was intensively used until 2015 (more recently the museum started using Instagram for sharing pictures and short videos). Between 2007 and 2008, interest in YouTube resulted in the three museums opening accounts, where they have been constantly sharing interviews and videos regarding exhibitions. In the last years, the possibility of assuring multidirectional dialogue between museums and users has become one of the central aspects of the online activities of our three case studies, as evident from the activities on the social media profiles of the three institutions. We thus propose that these websites are now entering a new phase, where their social media profiles have become the most frequented spaces to directly interact with visitors.

The social-media website: managing large networks of communication

Science museums have been constantly trying to improve communications with their visitors since Nineties, through emails and online forums in order to improve interaction with visitors. This could be seen, for example, in the 'Let's Talk' section of the Science Museum in 2002.[19] The aim of this section was to answer questions, to create discussion forums about scientific themes and to receive specific feedbacks.

More recently however, these institutions decided to use two of the most frequented social networking websites (Facebook and Twitter), which allow many to many communication. Since 2011, all three museums have been using Twitter and Facebook for greater engagement with users. On social media, the Museo della Scienza and the Deutsches Museum are primarily communicating with their national audience, as can be noticed by the language of the posts and tweets.[20] The Science Museum, which was actively using both Facebook and Twitter already in 2009, represents a good example of how to use social media to communicate with the visitors using specific thematic news, hashtags and photos. The digital department has also launched a mobile version of the website, to cater to a very large audience who frequent the web using their phones.

In recent years, while social media interactions are being managed carefully, the website has returned to be an extremely advanced digital presentation of the institutions and their collections. Attention has been paid to develop online scientific games, interactive apps and thematic sections. At the same time, prominent links to the social media pages are always present on the homepage. Lein observes: "Facebook, YouTube, Twitter are the important social media channels—the press office is responsible for the accounts. We closely work together, plus there is the Museum Blog.[21]" Stack's comment about the strategies of the London Science Museum sums up those being adopted by leading European science museums to upgrade their facilities, which are reflected online and offline: "We are looking at increasing digitization of collections, using digital media to tell the stories of the collections and to engage audiences with contemporary science through social media."

Given that social media is gradually becoming the main dialogic space for museums and visitors, we also need to consider that content generated in these networking spaces will not necessarily be completely available to the museum for specific analyses. In fact, while large amount of user-generated data in these social networking sites can help museums to engage better with the public (e.g. by carrying out large scale visitor surveys), efforts have to be made to obtain them from the parent companies. The history of museum websites in the recent future will not only be contained in the preserved snapshots of their website's pages, but also will be found on the walls and the tweets shared among interested groups.

CONCLUSION

The purpose of this chapter has been to offer an initial contribution towards the formulation of a methodology for studying websites as primary sources to trace activities of scientific institutions through time. Documents and snapshots preserved in the Internet Archive can help us trace how the websites have evolved over the years, while interviews with the people who manage them can provide useful insights into the reasons behind specific choices as to why certain changes were made. The live web also has to be consulted as it helps us track the current versions of the sites, and their linkages with other social networking sites. The use of all three methods together is important when reconstructing the digital past of the websites, especially in order to address reliability issues discussed intensively in web history literature, i.e. the fact that archived websites are "re-born digital materials" (Brügger, 2012).

Apart from contributing to the methodology of studying websites through time, this chapter also proposes a periodisation of museum websites in four macro phases, namely the leaflet museum, the virtual museum, the outreach museum and the social-media museum. Our findings show how these institutions, traditionally viewed as authoritative, top down entities, have constantly worked towards developing websites that go beyond being informative, which have in turn become the central node of an interactive, multidirectional communication between the museums and their visitors.

REFERENCES

Ben-David, A. (2015). What does the web remember of its deleted past? An archival reconstruction of the former Yugoslav internet. Two-day Conference at Aarhus University, Denmark.

Bowen, J. P., Bennett, J., & Johnson, J. (1998). Virtual visits to virtual museums. In D. Bearman & J. Trant (Eds.), *MW98: Museums and the web conference*, Toronto: Archives & Museum Informatics

Bowen, J.P. and S. Filippini-Fantoni (2004). Personalization and the Web from a museum perspective. In D. Bearman & J. Trant (Eds.), *Museums and the web 2004 proceedings*, Toronto: Archives & Museum Informatics.

Brügger, N. (2005). *Archiving websites: General considerations and strategies.* Aarhus: The Centre for Internet Studies.

Brügger, N. (Ed.). (2010). *Web history.* New York, NY: Peter Lang.

Brügger, N. (2012). Web historiography and internet studies: Challenges and perspectives. *New Media & Society*, 15(5), 752–764.

Brügger, N. (2015). A brief history of Facebook as a media text: The development of an empty structure. *First Monday*, 20(5).

Cunliffe, D., Kritou, E., & Tudhope, D. (2001). Usability evaluation for museum web sites, *Museum Management and Curatorship*, 19(3), 229–252.

Davies, A. (2007). Virtual museums: Out of this world. *Museums Journal* (July), 34–35.

Day, A. (1997). A model for monitoring web site effectiveness. *Internet Research: Electronic Networking Applications and Policy*, 7(2), 109–115.

Dougherty, M., Meyer, E. T., Madsen, C. M., Van den Heuvel, C., Thomas, A., & Wyatt, S. (2010). *Researcher engagement with web archives: State of the art* (August 1, 2010). Joint Information Systems Committee Report, August 2010. Available at SSRN: https://ssrn.com/abstract=1714997

Foot, K., Schneider, S. M., Dougherty, M., Xenos, M., & Larsen, E. (2003). Analyzing linking practices: Candidate sites in the 2002 US electoral Web sphere. *Journal of Computer-Mediated Communication*, 8(4).

Gomes, D., Miranda, J., & Costa, M. (2011). A survey on web archiving initiatives. *Research and Advanced Technology for Digital Libraries*, 2011, 408–420.

Hale, S. A., Yasseri, T., Cowls, J., Meyer, E. T., Schroeder, R., & Margetts, H. (2014). *Mapping the UK webspace: Fifteen years of British universities on the web.* Proceedings of the 2014 conference on Web Science, Association for computing machinery, Bloomington – Indiana university.

Henning, M. (2006). *New media.* In S. Macdonald (Ed.) *A companion to museum studies.* Oxford: Blackwell

Howell, B. A. (2006). Proving web history: How to use the Internet Archive. *Journal of Internet Law*, 9(8), 3–9.

Lepore, J. (2015). The Cobweb: Can the Internet be archived? *The New Yorker*, 34–41.

Lyman, P., & Kahle, B. (1998). Archiving digital cultural artifacts. *D-Lib Magazine*, 4(7).

Marty, P. (2007). Museum websites and museum visitors: Before and after the museum visit. *Museum Management and Curatorship*, *22*(4), 337–360.

Mason, D. M., & McCarthy, C. (2008). Museums and the culture of new media: An empirical model of New Zealand museum websites. *Museum Management and Curatorship*, *23*(1), 63–80.

Milligan, I. (2012). Mining the "Internet graveyard": Rethinking the historians' toolkit. *Revue de la Société historique du Canada* [Journal of the Canadian Historical Association], *23*(2), 21–64.

Milligan, I. (2015). *Welcome to the GeoHood: Using the GeoCities web archive to explore virtual communities.* Two-day conference at Aarhus University, Denmark.

Morrison, J. (2006). Cultural websites: Making the net work. *Museums Journal* (September), 24–27.

Nanni, F. (2017, in press). Reconstructing a website's lost past: Methodological issues concerning the history of www.unibo.it. *Digital Humanities Quarterly*.

Schweibenz, W. (2004). Virtual museums: The development of virtual museums. *ICOM News Magazine 3*, 3.

Simon, N. (2010). *The participatory museum.* Santa Cruz: Museum 2.0.

Srinivasan, R. (2013). Re-thinking the cultural codes of new media: The question concerning ontology. *New Media & Society*, *15*(2), 203–223.

Webster, P. (2015). Will historians of the future be able to study Twitter? Retrieved from http://peterwebster.me/2015/03/06/future-historians-and-twitter/

Wilson, R. J. (2011). Behind the scenes of the museum website. *Museum Management and Curatorship*, *26*(4), 373–389.

Yasko, J. (2007). Museums and web 2.0. *Museum News* (July-August), 43–47)..

Zimmer, M. (2015). The Twitter archive at the Library of Congress: Challenges for information practice and information policy. *First Monday*, *20*(7).

NOTES

1. Links of analyzed snapshots have been indicated as footnotes.
2. One of the authors carried out a period of research at the Museo della Scienza in early 2015.
3. See for instance http://museumplanner.org/worlds-top-10-science-centers/
4. http://www.calacademy.org/ and http://www.calacademy.org/explore-science
5. https://web.archive.org/web/20041217025646/http://www.museoscienza.org/INTERNET/prog1995.htmhttps://web.archive.org/web/20041217025646/http://www.museoscienza.org/INTERNET/prog1995.htm
6. The importance of oral memories for web historical research has been emphasized both by Ahmed AlSum and Federico Nanni at IIPC 2015: https://www.youtube.com/watch?v=AHrxvRWf9OM
7. https://drive.google.com/file/d/0B3qiRI3zLcHtWFlHRFBYenlpc1U/view?usp=sharinghttps://drive.google.com/file/d/0B3qiRI3zLcHtWFlHRFBYenlpc1U/view?usp=sharing
8. The idea of presenting the changes in the website in phases is inspired by the categories presented in Schweibenz's (2004) article on the development of museum websites. These categories include: the brochure museum (early website type which provides information for potential visitors), content museum (website which presents museum collections and allows visitors to explore them online), learning museum (website that provides context-oriented information about objects to enhance learning), and virtual museum (website which presents a version of the physical museum with digital collections). It must be noted here that Schweibenz's article, which was published

in 2004, could not have envisioned the recent changes in the web, specifically the social media explosion.

9. https://web.archive.org/web/20001012004412/http://www.museoscienza.org/INTERNET/sito.html

10. https://web.archive.org/web/20001012004412/http://www.museoscienza.org/INTERNET/sito.html

11. This confirms further the strong linkages between the museums and explains further our choice of their websites as case studies.

12. http://web.archive.org/web/19990903174023/http://www.museoscienza.org/SCUOLE/Default.htm

13. http://web.archive.org/web/20000418181553/http://www.sciencemuseum.org.uk/usage/index.html

14. http://web.archive.org/web/20021002123300/http://www.sciencemuseum.org.uk/on-line/apollo10/intro.asp

15. http://web.archive.org/web/20021001232233/http://www.sciencemuseum.org.uk/education/families/online.asp

16. http://web.archive.org/web/20021019104649/http://www.deutsches-museum.de/mum/start.htm

17. http://www.deutsches-museum.de/forschung/deutsches-museum-digital/http://www.deutsches-museum.de/forschung/deutsches-museum-digital/

18. See http://www.participatorymuseum.org/chapter3/

19. http://web.archive.org/web/20021004110407/http://www.sciencemuseum.org.uk/lets_talk/index.asp#

20. Cavallotti mentions that the Museo Scienza has hired a social media specialist on a part time basis from 2015.

21. http://www.deutsches-museum.de/de/blog/

Web archives AS historical source

CHAPTER ELEVEN

Users, technologies, organisations

Towards a cultural history of world web archiving

PETER WEBSTER

If 2015 marked the elapse of 25 years since the birth of the web, 2016 marked the 20th anniversary of web archiving: of systematic attempts to preserve web content and make it accessible to scholars and the public. As such, the time is ripe to make an initial assessment of the history of the movement, and the patterns into which it has already fallen. Although there have been short sketches of this history (Brown, 2006, pp. 8–23; Brügger, 2011, pp. 29–32), this chapter represents the first attempt to document the subject at length. In the space available, it could not be hoped to provide an exhaustive account of the activities of diverse organisations and individuals in many countries. The chapter attempts to draw the main contours of a landscape, the details of which may be filled by other more local and thematic studies. The timing is particularly significant since several of the pioneers of web archiving have reached or are approaching retirement, and so this study uses interview evidence as a supplement to written documentation.

Some notes on scope are necessary. The story of the technical evolution of web archiving is a complex one, reflecting the sheer speed of the evolution of the web itself and the technological 'arms race' in which the community has been engaged, in order to develop and maintain tools that can keep pace. The task of preserving web content has also necessitated fresh thinking about digital preservation as a discipline (Day, 2006). This chapter, however, leaves these questions aside, to concentrate on what might be termed the cultural history of the movement. It does not address the question of how web archiving has been carried out, but *why, by whom*, and *on whose behalf.*

Historians have for long known that, in order to interpret archival materials properly, it is first necessary to understand how that archive came into being. Why is a particular object to be found, and not another? What does the archive seek to document, and whose interests does it serve? The last very few years have seen a very welcome growth in interest in the archived web among scholars (see, for example, Brügger & Schroeder, 2017). However, that interest is not yet accompanied by the necessary familiarity with how the archived web came into being, and to be thus familiar is arguably even more important in this context than for traditional paper-based archives. Older distinctions with which historians are familiar—between published document, 'grey literature' and institutional records—have become blurred, as have those between personal and institutional publication. As a result, it has become less clear where the responsibility for preserving which types of content lies among the established institutions in the library and archives field. In addition, the archived web resource is unlike the live version from which it was derived in subtle and complex ways that do not apply to print publications or to manuscripts (Brügger & Finnemann, 2013, pp. 74–76). If this chapter serves to orient users as to some of the questions they should be asking of their sources, and of the institutions that provide them, it will have achieved its aim. It dwells on certain projects and organisations as illustrative of more general trends. Proceeding in a broadly chronological order, it begins where most narrations of the story have begun, with the Internet Archive.

THE INTERNET ARCHIVE (1996–)

Insofar as the general public are aware of web archiving at all, it is likely that the Internet Archive and its Wayback Machine is the thing they know. This is hardly surprising, since the Archive is amongst the earliest systematic attempts at web archiving, operates at a global scale, and gives unrestricted access to its content via the Wayback Machine. By contrast, the majority of other web archives restrict their collections either by geography or by subject matter, and (in the case of many of the national libraries) are required to impose restrictions on access, due to the legal frameworks under which they operate.

The story of the Internet Archive is relatively well-known (see Kimpton & Ubois, 2006; Livingston, 2007, pp. 274–278). The Archive's founder, Brewster Kahle, had already developed the Wide Area Information Server, acquired by AOL for a multi-million dollar sum. In 1996 he founded two organisations: the Internet Archive, as a not-for-profit organisation (with Bruce Gilliat), and Alexa Internet, the business model of which was based on the analysis of data describing usage patterns online. (Alexa was also later sold, this time to Amazon.) The early holdings of the Archive were composed of the content first collected by Alexa, although over time the Archive began to capture content in its own right. In 2001 the Archive launched the Wayback Machine, the first browser-based access mechanism to archived content. The software on which the Machine was built, also known as Wayback, remains the most widely used means of enabling access to archived web pages. Similarly dominant have been the successive versions of Heritrix, the web crawler application built by the Archive to enable the capture of content. By 2006 the Archive had already collected some 50 billion individual web pages and was serving 70,000 visitors per day; at the time of writing it held some 472 billion archived objects (Kimpton & Ubois, 2006, p. 203).

The achievement of the Internet Archive is an extraordinary one. From the very beginning Kahle was aware of the many technological and legal obstacles in the path of successful web archiving: obstacles which even now still preoccupy the web archiving community. Despite this, the Archive pressed ahead with archiving, motivated by both the fragility of web content and the rate at which it which disappeared, and by the possibilities offered to users in the future (Kahle, 1997). This was in line with a realisation in the mid-1990s of a need to avoid the period becoming known as "a digital Dark Ages" exacerbated by the euphoria and cultural amnesia of the newly emerging internet industry, an "epoch of forgetting" (Kuny, 1997, p. 1, citing Umberto Eco). The Internet Archive remains the only web archive for a substantial majority of national domains.

Recent years have seen a significant growth in mainstream press coverage of web archiving, and of the Internet Archive in particular. As a result, Kahle has had something of the status of a hero thrust upon him, as shown by the 2015 campaign to promote him as the new Librarian of Congress. The Archive is headquartered in San Francisco, and in one sense its story is a classic Californian story: of an entrepreneur with a disruptive idea, creating an organisation the history of which is characterised by (in the words of a well-informed observer) "the dual themes of visionary experimentation and whimsy" (Scott, 2015). This story of the Archive has tended to obscure other streams of web archiving activity, carried out by different kinds of organisations acting in response to different drivers. It is to these other streams that we now turn.

NATIONAL LIBRARIES

At the same time that the Internet Archive was founded, national libraries on three continents were also taking their first steps towards systematic archiving of the web. In Canada, the issue was first discussed in 1994 by the Executive Committee of the National Library of Canada (now part of Library and Archives Canada), leading to the Electronic Publications Pilot Project which reported in 1995. The Library's historic remit included the duty "to collect, preserve and promote access to Canada's published heritage", now understood to include publications in whichever format, whether print, physical storage media such as disks, or delivered via the internet. (National Library of Canada, 1996).

The National Library of Australia, under the National Library Act of 1960, had a similar remit to maintain a comprehensive collection of materials relating to Australia and the Australian people. As in Canada, it was seen as a natural extension of that remit to take in material made available via the internet, and the PANDORA project was established in 1996, with harvesting of content beginning the following year. Faced with the need to obtain permission from the owners of websites to harvest their material, and a simple lack of resources, the NLA took a pragmatic decision to take a selective approach from the beginning (Koerbin, 2004, pp. 1–2; 2016).

This selective mode has been one of two patterns into which national library archiving has subsequently fallen, often although not always on a permissions basis. As such, many collections of web material exist, created by decisions by subject experts as to scope and importance, and structured variously by content type (such as blogs, or news media), by theme (such as climate change), or by events, such as elections. In fact, several web archiving programs have begun with election collections, since consensus about their importance is relatively easy to achieve. In 1996 the Internet Archive collected the sites of candidates for the presidency of the United States, in partnership with the Smithsonian Institution, and in 2000 collected sites related to the election on behalf of the Library of Congress (Kimpton & Ubois, 2006, pp. 202–203). In Denmark, a test case was provided by the 2001 municipal elections (Brügger, 2016).

In Sweden, the Royal Library had been responsible for collecting, preserving and providing access to Swedish printed publications since 1661. As in Canada and Australia, the archiving of the web as a distribution mechanism closely analogous to publication was viewed as a natural extension of that remit. As a result, the Kulturarw3 project was begun by the Royal Library in 1996. In contrast to the Australian case, the Swedish project took a comprehensive approach, for several reasons: because it was more cost-effective than a selective approach, since the latter involved the deployment of human effort on a very large scale, and also because "[o]ne doesn't know what information future generations will consider important" (Arvidson, Persson, & Mannerheim, 2000). This agnosticism about the relative potential value of different kinds of content has been a common theme in subsequent comprehensive web archiving.

At this point, the history of web archiving becomes enmeshed with the larger history of systems of legal deposit. Several states have centuries-old systems of legal deposit that entitle organisations such as national libraries to receive copies of everything published within that jurisdiction. In nations where print legal deposit was already in force there have been moves to extend that legal framework to cover non-print content. One of the first nations to implement a new law was Denmark, in 1997, although in 2004 it was to be substantially revised and its scope widened. The relevant act for New Zealand was the National Library Act of 2003, which coincided with the Legal Deposit Libraries Act in the United Kingdom (Elliott, 2011; Field, 2004; Larsen, 2005). Several other nations have followed suit, including France in 2006 (Aubry, 2010).

To be sure, the implementation of these schemes varies between nations. The types of content that are covered have varied, with exclusions applied to audio-visual content in the UK, for instance. The national web sphere has been defined in various ways: by country-code Top Level Domains, by domain registration, by the physical location of the hosting server, by the intended audience, and by language, or by some combination of those criteria. However, from the point of view of the present cultural history, there were certain key similarities between the contexts in which these frameworks have been formed.

The user of web archives has reason to be thankful for the existence of a net-work of national libraries with a mission to preserve published heritage at a large scale. Without this network, with its long-established channels of communication and co-operation, users would be even more reliant on the Internet Archive than they already are. At the highest level, there was international collaboration from the first, in the shape of a working group on non-print legal deposit set up by the Conference of Directors of National Libraries, that worked between 1994 and 1996 (Field, 2004, p. 90). The International Internet Preservation Consortium, formed in 2003 by the Internet Archive and a nucleus of national libraries, has been of vital importance (Illien, 2011). However, the location of this effort within institutions so steeped in print culture has tended to shape that effort in particular and not always helpful ways.

Denmark first revised its legal framework to allow the Royal Library to collect non-print content in 1997. However, in relation to online content, the revised law applied only to materials that had the character of print publications, and thus excluded the bulk of the web. The inadequacy of this approach soon became ap-parent to the libraries concerned (Henriksen, 2016; Larsen, 2005, p. 81). The same point for scholarly users was brought home forcibly in 1999 to one media studies specialist, Niels Ole Finnemann of Aarhus University, when the website about which a graduate student was about to submit a thesis was suddenly and radically changed (Finnemann, 2015). This event was in part responsible for a press release by Finnemann and his colleague Niels Brügger, announcing their intention to work towards the establishment of a Danish web archive. This catalysed the formation of a partnership with representatives of the Royal Library in Copenhagen and the State and University Library in Aarhus which led in turn to the establishment of netarkivet.dk, the Danish web archive (Brügger, 2016).

At this stage (2002), there was an institutional basis for archiving of the Danish web, but not yet the legal backing. In the process that then led to the revised legislation in 2004, the Danish case is highly unusual in that the interests of researchers were represented, by the presence of Niels Ole Finnemann on the committee that helped draft the legislation. The law when passed also stipulated that there be a standing editorial committee, including researchers, to guide and inform the development of netarkivet.dk (Larsen, 2005).

A common feature of most web archiving backed by legal deposit legislation is some sort of restrictions on the access afforded to the end user of the archive. In cases where archiving is limited to a single copy of a work in a particular institution, it is possible to see the ghost of the print legal deposit paradigm: a curious paradigm to apply to the web. It is also in the development of these restrictions that one can see most clearly the interplay of the interests of the three key stakeholders: the libraries, the owners of the content (and the established media companies in particular) and the end user. In different contexts greater or lesser emphasis has been placed on the different reasons for restricting access: copyright and the rights of content owners to exploit their intellectual property; the risk to the libraries of republishing libellous material or other content that is in breach of the law; and the treatment of sensitive personal data relating to individuals. Naturally much of the process leading to new legislation was not documented publicly, but from those accounts that have emerged it would seem that in at least some cases the influence of the larger commercial publishers has weighed disproportionately heavily.

One such account is that of Andrew Green, former Librarian of the National Library of Wales and participant in the highly protracted process that led from the initial discussions over non-print legal deposit in the UK in 1997 to the final implementation in 2013. Green noted a "mutual suspicion—sometimes bordering on hostility" between librarians and publishers, particularly the news media companies. The latter were part of an industry on the defensive against commercial pressure, "and defensiveness often breeds aggression, and it is no surprise that newspaper owners, who are under most market pressure, proved the least tractable interlocutors" (Green, 2012, p. 105). In Green's account, even after the 2003 Act restricted access to library premises, thus removing any significant threat to prevailing business models, the publishers pressed for further restrictions. As a result, at the time of writing, users of the Legal Deposit Web Archive in the UK are permitted to print only a small proportion of an archived page, may not make digital copies of any sort, and may not consult an archived resource simultaneously with any other user at the same library: this last restriction being the single-copy model of print legal deposit combined with commercial pressure to produce a manifest absurdity.[1]

The full history of the development of non-print legal deposit must of course wait until minutes of private meetings become publicly available. When that story is told, it will require an articulation with the histories of other movements in media and publishing, including the Open Access movement for scholarly literature, and the radical disruption in traditional markets for news, both print and broadcast (for which see, for example, Burns & Brügger, 2012; Ji & Waterman, 2014). Indeed, the story may be one of a clash of cultures, between owners of valuable intellectual capital and advocates of freer dissemination of the products of human effort, in which librarians have found themselves in a perhaps somewhat surprising alliance with some of the rhetoric surrounding Silicon Valley and the argument that "information wants to be free". For now it is reasonable to note, with Andrew Green, that delays in the process leading to the implementation of non-print legal deposit have led to the loss of very significant bodies of content from the most formative years of the live web, for which users must rely almost entirely on the Internet Archive (Green, 2012). In addition, the fact that the Danish case is so exceptional in having a strong representation of academic users from the very beginning shows the degree to which the voice of the end user has been relatively neglected in the midst of often confrontational negotiations between libraries and publishers.

WEB ARCHIVING AS THE CORPORATE RECORD

Thus far, this chapter has been concerned with organisations making archival copies of other organisations' content: either as part of a national responsibility for the published record or—as in the case of the Internet Archive—in pursuit of a more generalised philanthropic goal. The second half of the period under discussion saw a further strand of web archiving activity emerge in response to quite different drivers: the archiving by organisations of their own content. Within this broad movement there have been several distinct streams.

Scholars of politics and government have noted the simultaneous shift in many countries towards the delivery of government services on a 'digital by default' basis, particularly since 2011 (Lips, 2014). In some contexts, this has necessitated a reinterpretation of the traditional demarcation between official publications (usually considered part of the published record), and public or government records, traditionally managed in paper form and the responsibility of a national archival administration. The dividing line became especially hard to see clearly as government activity online widened from the simple delivery of documents to include general communication and the conduct of transactions between state and citizen via web interfaces.

In by no means all countries have national archives engaged with web archiving: in some cases the task has been left in the hands of other organisations. Two examples, one from the USA and one from Europe, will illustrate where such engagement has taken place. The National Archives of the United Kingdom were among the earliest to institute a comprehensive program for archiving government sites. This was a consequence of two movements within government: a 1999 decision that all newly-created public records were to be stored and retrieved digitally by 2004, and a target set (first for 2008, then for 2005) that all services to business and to the citizen should be delivered online. In consequence, it was determined that the websites used to deliver those services should perforce be considered as public records, and not just documents delivered via those services. The UK Government Web Archive was formally founded in 2003 after a period of experimentation begun in 2001 (Brown, 2006, pp. 178–179).

In the USA, the responsibility for government web archiving has been shared between institutions, and in different combinations at different times. Some of the earliest government web archiving took place not under the auspices of the National Archives and Records Administration (NARA), but as part of the Federal Depository Library Content Partnerships Program. This was a continuation of an established tradition of distributed collection of government publications by federal deposit libraries, under the overall direction of the Government Printing Office. The priority was the websites of federal agencies that had ceased operation, such as the Advisory Commission on Intergovernmental Relations, archived in 1996 by the Libraries of the University of North Texas (Advisory Commission on Intergovernmental Relations [ACIR], 1996; Hartman, 2000, 2016). In 2000–2001 the NARA first took a single snapshot of federal government websites for the USA in connection with the end of the presidential term of Bill Clinton, followed in 2004 by a similar collection at the end of the first term of George W. Bush. Quite separately, the NARA has also been harvesting Congressional websites since 2006. However, in 2008 the NARA issued guidance that placed responsibility for preservation of federal agency web estate back in the hands of individual agencies (National Archives and Records Administration [NARA], 2008). As a result, the 'end of term' collection in 2008–2009 and in 2012–2013 was carried out by a group of agencies in collaboration: the Library of Congress and the Government Printing Office (from within government) and the University of North Texas, the California Digital Library (part of the University of California) and the Internet Archive.[2]

Governments have not been the only kind of organisation that have wished to archive their own web content. Since the mid-2000s universities, schools, churches, commercial organisations and many other organisations besides have done so. However, few of these organisations have chosen to create a full web archiving programme within their own walls, since the costs in IT infrastructure are considerable, and the specific skills required often in short supply. As such, the growth of a small but global group of organisations providing web archiving services has made outsourcing an option. The Internet Archive for a time provided such contracted services, for instance to the National Archives of the UK from 2003. The Internet Archive was also instrumental in the foundation of the European Web Archive in Amsterdam in 2004, a non-profit organisation providing similar services in Europe (Brown 2006, pp. 18, 180–181). The European Archive became the Internet Memory Foundation, offering web archiving services via its Internet Memory Research subsidiary. In 2006 the Internet Archive itself also launched its Archive-It service, delivered via a web application allowing easy management of the process by its clients.

These two services—Internet Memory Research and Archive-It—at the time of writing remain the two principal outsourcing services for the creation of web archives that are available freely online to end users. Both organisations have been heavily involved in the wider development of the web archiving community, with a significant degree of crossover of personnel. One of the founders of the European Archive was Julien Masanès, who had previously led the web archiving program at the Bibliothèque nationale de France from 2000. Masanès had been one of the instigators of the IIPC, and also of the series of conferences known as the International Web Archiving Workshop, which ran annually from 2001 to 2010.[3]

The same period saw the inception of attempts to provide web archiving services commercially. One early example of this was Hanzo Archives, incorporated as a limited company in the UK in 2005 by two former members of the web archiving program at the British Library, Mark Middleton and Mark Williamson, with Julien Masanès as a member of the board of directors (Hanzo Archives, 2006). Since that time, several other firms have been set up to serve the market, including amongst others Pagefreezer (Netherlands and Canada) and Aleph Archives (Switzerland, USA and Canada). It is more difficult to assess how widely these services are used, since one of the distinguishing features is that the archive is closed to everyone but the staff of the client. The value proposition is also articulated in different terms to that by Archive-It and Internet Memory Research, being in terms of enabling corporations to meet legal requirements in relation to disclosure of information, and as a defence against litigation. Already by 2005 there were cases coming to courts around the world that involved the use of archived web pages as evidence ("Keeper of expired web pages," 2005).

RESEARCH-DRIVEN ARCHIVING

The availability of outsourcing services, and in particular Archive-It, enabled a wide range of organisations to enter the web archiving arena. One particularly significant group are those scholarly organisations, mostly universities, who have begun to archive content in support of their library content development: a form of archiving in close articulation with the needs, known or inferred, of particular groups of scholars. This movement has proved particularly strong in the USA. One early example is that of Columbia University in New York, which (as well as archiving its own content) has created research collections on subjects including human rights (from 2008) and religious life in New York City (from 2010). The former is a project of the Center for Human Rights Documentation and Research which, although located within the Columbia University Libraries, engages directly in education and research activities as well as acquiring collections for research. One of the selection criteria is the relevance of the content to "current research, teaching and advocacy" (Centre for Human Rights Documentation and Research [CHRDR], 2016).

Examples of this kind of subject-based archiving are relatively few outside the USA, but one example, and possibly the earliest of all, is DACHS, the Digital Archive for Chinese Studies. DACHS was a joint venture between two specialist Sinological institutes, in the universities of Heidelberg and Leiden, although it began first in Heidelberg. Although the project was and is managed by librarians on an operational level, the initial impetus was directly from academics and first expressed in 1999; archiving began in 2001. Perhaps unsurprisingly, there was a keen sense of the unusual fragility of the Chinese web, given the political situation in that country and the widespread use of censorship even at that time, and so the archive focussed specifically on social and political discourse. There was also a realisation that the Internet Archive and other large scale projects could not be expected to capture content for any particular subject area at the optimal depth and frequency, and so specialist organisations would have to meet that need. To aid selection, the project also drew on the the accumulated knowledge of a distributed group of collaborators—scholars and 'netizens' both within and outside China some of whom were active participants in the discourses concerned. This model of distributed participant curation is one that has rarely been emulated elsewhere, and even in this case the resources required to construct and maintain such a network have proved significant (Lecher, 2006, 2016).

ACTIVIST ARCHIVING

It may become clear after further research that the few years either side of 2010 saw a shift in the way in which the story of the web was understood by at least some of its users. According to this new narrative of web history, the individualistic spirit that had characterised the early years had given way to an increased colonisation of the web by authoritarian governments, corporate lobbyists, and technology companies with overreaching ambition (see, for instance, Jeanneney, 2007; Morozov, 2011). In place of a web with many relatively small publishers on the one hand and archivists on the other, there were now three kinds of participant: large content organisations, the individual users who entrusted their content and data to them, and the archivists charged with keeping the record.

All of the web archiving programmes examined so far have indeed been pro-grammes: planned activity carried out by organisations in line with their wider mission and purpose. In part because of the scale at which these programmes have operated, and the relative accessibility of the archived content, they have tended to be more prominent. There is, however, an important strand of web archiving activity that tends to be overlooked as a result: the work of individuals and small groups, responding to a particular cause. One such is the Dale Askey Archive, concerning the 2012 libel suit against the academic librarian Dale Askey, then of McMaster University in Canada, which raised questions of freedom of speech and the appropriate use of the law of libel. Members of the Greater Toronto Chapter of the Progressive Librarians' Guild, seeing a fast-developing online event which would not be captured by the periodic crawls of the Internet Archive or other institutions, came together as individuals to begin capturing key discussions of the case. Using a combination of open source tools, the Dale Askey Archive was sub-sequently made publicly available. Even though in 2012 all the major components of the web archiving landscape were in place, there were still other ways for the librarian, acting personally but guided by "the professional ethics of libraries and archives, to choose a community to document, preserve, and support" (Milligan, Ruest, & St. Onge, 2016).

The #freeDaleAskey team were clear that their work was within the remit of the librarian and archivist, broadly conceived, and not a call to the profession to become citizen journalists or community activists. There has however been a strand of web archiving which approaches such a status, the most prominent example of which has been the Archive Team. In 2008 Jason Scott noted the readiness of corporations to discontinue online services that were no longer profitable, often with the loss of user-generated content of significant value both to its creator and to later scholars. Motivated by the shutting-down of AOL Hometown in late 2008—which Scott described as an 'eviction' of people from their webspace—the volunteer-run Archive Team was created (Scott, 2008, 2011). Its most public case followed in 2009 with the closure of Geocities by Yahoo, at which several million individual websites disappeared in an instant, but of which the Archive Team, a "loose collective of rogue archivists, programmers, writers and loudmouths ded-icated to saving our digital heritage" were able to capture a subset, numbering in the millions (Archive Team, 2016).

In one sense, both the Archive Team and the Dale Askey campaign represent a return to an approach closer to that of the Internet Archive than of the national libraries. A rapid response was required in order to save content that would not be archived by any of the existing institutional programmes. It was a pragmatic approach, characterised by a willingness to press ahead and archive content despite some risk relating to breaches of copyright law: risks which national libraries, by their nature, rarely contemplate taking. Both ventures were motivated by a sense of public duty, and a particular political and social vision of the kind of space that the web should be. They also represent a response to a new configuration of stakeholders after Web 2.0: publishers, users who create content, and archivists who set out to document the relationship and (at times) to redress the balance of power between them. This new articulation of interests was significantly different from the binary library-publisher relationship that so profoundly shaped the development of non-print legal deposit.

WEB ARCHIVING IN 2016 AND THE FUTURE

If the history of web archiving is now a story of 20 years, from 1996 to the time of writing, then by the mid-way point of 2006 the movement had taken its present institutional shape. The International Internet Preservation Consortium had been established, giving a global point of reference for the community of web archiving practitioners. The two key technologies—Heritrix for large-scale crawling, and Wayback for replay of content—were both in general use. Comprehensive legal deposit frameworks for web harvesting had been formulated and put into force in several countries. Outsourcing services had become available for organisations to archive their own content, or (in the case of research-driven archiving) the content of others for research purposes. Significant publications attempting to survey the whole scene had also begun to appear (Brown, 2006; Brügger, 2005; Masanès, 2006).

I have attempted to show that the shape of each of these component pieces of that organisational pattern was a product of the interplay between institutions, their perception of their mission, and the interests (sometimes competing) of the various stakeholders in each context. A larger study (which the topic would certainly merit) would be able to tease out the complexities of these relationships in each national situation, and the growth and influence of the global web archiving community. Its approach might be exhaustive where the current chapter can only be selective, and would involve a very significant programme of oral history interviews.

Missing from this picture, in 2006, was the researcher, as the end user of the archive. Although the Association of Internet Researchers was well established, having begun to hold its annual conferences in 2000, there was yet little engagement with the archived web as an object of study.[4] There were, to be sure, scholars beginning to use the archived web (Brügger, 2005; Foot & Schneider, 2004), but in relative isolation. Possibly the first international conference to take up the theme took place in 2008 on the fringes of the Association of Internet Researchers conference in Copenhagen; several of the papers were subsequently published (Brügger, 2010). The first PhD from within the social sciences and humanities to use the archived web was that by Meghan Dougherty, a student of Kirsten Foot at the University of Washington (Dougherty, 2007).

Understandably, the attention of the web archiving community in the early years was focussed on developing the necessary tools to capture web content, the mechanisms by which that data might be preserved, and the organisational work of integrating web archiving in existing and often ancient institutions. If some of the access mechanisms have not served all the possible uses that researchers might have wanted, this was understandable under these circumstances, and given the small number of researchers with whom libraries and archives could engage.

Happily, recent years have seen a growing interest, both amongst researchers and from institutions engaged in web archiving, in collaborating in order to inform both selection decisions and the development of access services. This was prefigured by the Danish collaboration noted above, and by webarchivist.org, a collaboration between researchers at the State University of New York, the University of Washington, the Library of Congress and the Internet Archive, which began in 2001 and continued until 2010 (Foot, Schneider, Xenos, & Dougherty, 2003). More recently, other examples include the collaborative curation project named Researchers and the UK Web Archive that ran between 2010 and 2011 (Webster, 2010), and the two projects in the UK to co-design a new search interface for British Library data (with acronyms of AADDA and BUDDAH) which between them ran between 2011 and 2015.[5] It is to be hoped that the next 20 years are characterised more and more by just this collaboration between archivists and their users.

ACKNOWLEDGEMENTS

The author should like to thank Helen Hockx-Yu, Ian Milligan, the editor and the anonymous peer reviewer for their comments on this chapter, as well as those who commented on a draft made available online for review.

REFERENCES

Advisory Commission on Intergovernmental Relations. (1996). Homepage, now in University of North Texas Digital Library. Retrieved May 4, 2016 from http://digital.library.unt.edu/ark:/67531/metadc800/

Archive Team (2016). Homepage. Retrieved May 3, 2016 from http://www.archiveteam.org

Arvidson, A., Persson, K., & Mannerheim, J. (2000). *The Kulturarw3 Project: The Royal Swedish web archive—An example of 'complete' collection of web pages.* Paper given at 66th Council and General Conference of the International Federation of Library Associations and Institutions (IFLA), Jerusalem. Retrieved April 15, 2016 from http://archive.ifla.org/IV/ifla66/papers/154-157e.htm

Aubry, S. (2010). Introducing web archives as a new library service: The experience of the National Library of France. *LIBER Quarterly, 20*(2), 179–199.

Brown, A. (2006). *Archiving websites: A practical guide for information management professionals.* London: Facet.

Brügger, N. (2005). *Archiving websites: General considerations and strategies.* Aarhus: Centre for Internet Studies.

Brügger, N. (Ed.). (2010). *Web history.* New York, NY: Peter Lang.

Brügger, N. (2011). Web archiving—Between past, present and future. In M. Consalvo & C. Ess (Eds.), *The handbook of internet studies* (pp. 24–42). Chichester: Wiley-Blackwell.

Brügger, N. (2016). Interview with the author, March 14, 2016.

Brügger, N., & Finnemann, N. O. (2013). The web and digital humanities: Theoretical and methodological concerns. *Journal of Broadcasting and Electronic Media, 57*(1), 66–80.

Brügger, N., & Schroeder, R. (Eds.). (2017). *The web as History: The first two decades.* London: UCL Press.

Burns, M., & Brügger, N. (Eds.). (2012). *Histories of public service broadcasters on the web.* New York, NY: Peter Lang.

Centre for Human Rights Documentation and Research. (2016). Human Rights Web Archive. Retrieved May 5, 2016 from http://library.columbia.edu/locations/chrdr/hrwa.html

Day, M. (2006). The long-term preservation of web content. In J. Masanès (Ed.), *Web archiving* (pp. 177–199). Berlin: Springer.

Dougherty, M. (2007). *Archiving the web: Documentation, display and shifting knowledge production paradigms* (PhD thesis). University of Washington.

Elliott, A. (2011). *Electronic legal deposit: The New Zealand experience.* Paper given at conference of the International Federation of Library Associations and Institutions (IFLA), San Juan, Puerto Rico. Retrieved April 1, 2016 from http://www.ifla.org/past-wlic/2011/193-elliott-en.pdf

Field, C. D. (2004). Securing digital legal deposit in the UK: The Legal Deposit Libraries Act 2003. *Alexandria, 16*(2), 87–111.

Finnemann, N. O. (2015). Speech at tenth anniversary of Netarkivet.dk, Aarhus, June 2015.

Foot, K., & Schneider, S. (2004). The web as an object of study. *New Media & Society, 6*(1), 114–122.

Foot, K., Schneider, S., Xenos, M., & Dougherty, M. (2003). Opportunities for civic engagement on campaign sites. Retrieved June 22, 2016, from https://web.archive.org/web/20080201083014/http://politicalweb.info/reports/engagement.html

Green, A. (2012). Introducing electronic legal deposit in the UK: A Homeric tale. *Alexandria, 23*(3), 103–109.

Hanzo Archives (2006). Annual company return, 1 April 2006. Retrieved June 22, 2016, from https://beta.companieshouse.gov.uk/company/05410483/

Hartman, C. N. (2000). Storage of electronic files of federal agencies that have ceased operation: A partnership for permanent access. Retrieved June 14, 2016 from http://digital.library.unt.edu/ark:/67531/metadc181693/

Hartman, C. N. (2016). Interview with the author, 21 April.

Henriksen, B. N. (2016). Interview with the author, 15 April.

Illien, G. (2011). Une histoire politique de l'archivage du web. *Bulletin des bibliothèques de France, 2.* Retrieved December 1, 2013 from http://bbf.enssib.fr/consulter/bbf-2011-02-0060-012

Jeanneney, J.-N. (2007). *Google and the myth of universal knowledge: A view from Europe.* Chicago, IL: Chicago University Press.

Ji, S. W., & Waterman, D. (2014). The impact of the internet on media industries: An economic perspective. In M. Graham & W. H. Dutton (Eds.), *Society and the internet: How networks of information and communication are changing our lives* (pp. 149–163). Oxford: Oxford University Press.

Kahle, B. (1997, March 1). Preserving the internet: An archive of the internet may prove to be a vital record for historians, businesses and government. *Scientific American.* 276 (3), 82–83.

Keeper of expired web pages is sued because archive was used in another suit. (2005, July 13). *New York Times,* p. C (L).

Kimpton, M., & Ubois, J. (2006). Year-by-year: From an archive of the internet to an archive on the internet. In J. Masanès (Ed.), *Web archiving* (pp. 201–212). Berlin: Springer.

Koerbin, P. (2004). *Managing web archiving in Australia: A case study.* Paper given at IWAW (International Web Archiving Workshop), Bath (UK), 2004. Retrieved May 1, 2016 from http:// iwaw.net/04/

Koerbin, P. (2016). Interview with the author, May 4, 2016.

Kuny, T. (1997). A digital dark ages? Challenges in the preservation of electronic information. Paper presented at the 63rd Council and General Conference of the International Federation of Library Associations and Institutions (IFLA), Copenhagen. Retrieved May 1, 2016 from http://archive. ifla.org/IV/ifla63/63kuny1.pdf

Larsen, S. (2005). Preserving the digital heritage: New legal deposit act in Denmark. *Alexandria, 17*(2), 81–87.

Lecher, H. (2006). Small scale academic web archiving: DACHS. In J. Masanès (Ed.), *Web archiving* (pp. 213–226). Berlin: Springer.

Lecher, H. (2016). Interview with the author, April 20, 2016.

Lips, M. (2014). Transforming government—By default? In M. Graham & W. H. Dutton (Eds.), *Society and the internet: How networks of information and communication are changing our lives* (pp. 179–194). Oxford: Oxford University Press.

Livingston, J. (2007). *Founders at work. Stories of startups' early days.* Berkeley, CA: Apress.

Masanès, J. (Ed.) (2006). *Web archiving.* Berlin: Springer.

Milligan, I., Ruest, N., & St. Onge, A. (2016). The great WARC adventure: Using SIPS, AIPS and DIPS to document SLAPPS. *Digital Studies/Le Champ Numerique,* 2016. Retrieved June 14, 2016 from https://www.digitalstudies.org/ojs/index.php/digital_studies/article/view/325/412

Morozov, E. (2011). *The net delusion: How not to liberate the world.* London: Allen Lane.

National Archives and Records Administration. (2008). Web harvest background information [15 April]. Retrieved June 14, 2016 from http://www.archives.gov/records-mgmt/memos/ nwm13-2008-brief.html

National Library of Canada. (1996). Electronic Publications Pilot Project (EPPP). Summary of the final report. Retrieved April 22, 2016 from http://epe.lac-bac.gc.ca/100/200/301/nlc-bnc/eppp_ summary-e/ereport.htm

Scott, J. (2008). Eviction, or the coming datapocalypse. Retrieved May 1, 2016 from http://ascii. textfiles.com/archives/1617

Scott, J. (2011). Presentation at Personal Digital Archiving conference [Internet Archive]. Retrieved April 1, 2016 from https://archive.org/details/PDA2011-jasonscott

Scott, J. (2015). The case for #DraftBrewster. (n.d.). Retrieved April 11, 2016 from https://medium. com/@textfiles/the-case-for-draftbrewster-abca1fd3cf71

Webster, P. (2010). Using the UK Web Archive. Retrieved June 22, 2016 from https://peterwebster. me/2010/12/03/using-the-uk-web-archive/

Wellman, B. (2011). Studying the internet through the ages. In M. Consalvo & C. Ess (Eds.), *The handbook of internet studies* (pp. 17–23). Chichester: Wiley-Blackwell.

NOTES

1. As engagement manager for the UK Web Archive at the time the 2013 regulations came into force, when making public presentations I was often met with little short of incredulity from users when outlining these restrictions.
2. The End of Term Web Archive may be accessed at http://eotarchive.cdlib.org.
3. The proceedings of IWAW are available at http://iwaw.net.
4. For a periodisation of the discipline of Internet Studies, see Wellman (2011). In the case of the Association, an important milestone was a workshop on the fringes of the 2004 conference in London, at which scholars engaged with members of the IIPC. See, for instance, the paper given by Alex Halavais, at http://alex.halavais.net/blogs-and-archiving (retrieved June 16, 2016). I am grateful to the anonymous reviewer for drawing this meeting to my attention.
5. The project blogs may be found at http://domaindarkarchive.blogspot.co.uk/ and http://buddah.projects.history.ac.uk/.

CHAPTER TWELVE

Revisiting THE World Wide Web AS artefact

Case studies in archiving small data for the National Library of Australia's PANDORA Archive

PAUL KOERBIN

INTRODUCTION

In acknowledging, celebrating and reflecting upon the first 25 years of the World Wide Web emphasis will naturally and rightly be given to the innovations and initiatives that have made the web possible and led to the way it has transformed life from the late 20th century onwards.

While naturally in the shadow of these achievements, the outcomes of the programs established to preserve the content of the web should not be overlooked. In studying a quarter century of web history it is notable that for 20 years of that period there have been active web archiving programs collecting and sustaining the preservation of at least representative samples—the artefacts—of the web. Given the web's earliest public manifestation as predominantly a publishing medium it is not surprising that among the early web archiving initiatives are those established by national libraries with mandates to collect their national publishing culture.

This chapter presents short case studies of examples of early preserved web artefacts from one such national library web archiving initiative, the National Library of Australia's PANDORA Archive established in 1996. That year perhaps represents the signal year for web archiving since it also saw the establishment of the Internet Archive. As the largest and most ambitious of all web archiving programs—and the most notable web archiving initiative established outside the national library and archives communities—the Internet Archive maintains a critical resource not only for understanding the web as cultural artefact generally but also to support the analysis of the artefacts of other archives such as PANDORA. While the objective of this chapter is to reflect upon research issues in respect to early archived content, it also serves to highlight the fact that no single archive resource can deliver all that current and future researchers require.

THE WEB AS ARTEFACT

The Internet Archive has had a profound effect on the web archiving community over the first two decades of web archiving history by its ambition and by its technical developments for web harvesting (Heritrix), archive file management (WARC) and archival content playback (Wayback). Indeed the starting point for this chapter is a paper published shortly after the establishment of the Internet Archive by the founding directors, Brewster Kahle and Peter Lyman, who characterised the objective of web archiving as a process of archiving digital cultural artefacts (Lyman & Kahle, 1998). Recognising digital cultural artefacts as "still being shaped by experimentation and practice" they distilled the significant differentiations of digital cultures from other cultural artefacts, among which were:

- Things   occupy spaces while digital documents are "electronic signals with local storage but global range";
- Digital   documents are both ubiquitous (because of their global range) and a universal medium by virtue of their "size and ability to represent culture expressions in all other media";
- Digital   documents are at once tangible (the "representation in code") and intangible (the code is meaningless unless transmitted and represented); and,
- Digital   objects are not the property of cultural elites for the "medium is profoundly democratic".

The characterisation by Lyman and Kahle remains fundamentally true for the web today; but it is also reflective of the early web as essentially a medium of digital 'documents'. Over the two decades since actions to preserve the web began the functionality of the web has expanded from largely a publishing medium to a communication (including publishing) medium based on dynamic interaction. Indeed the pervasive characteristic of the web as it has emerged and become part of all aspects of our lives is its relentless *present*; what Douglas Rushkoff (2014) calls 'present shock', where the continuity between event and response is lost and initial action and feedback is virtually indistinguishable—where all seems a simultaneous *now*. Though it was always more than a publication medium the web now is a cultural space for communication, interaction and publication (and indeed conscious redaction or 'un-publishing')—it is, in short, the space for making and expressing culture in the present. Content of course lingers on the web and while it does so it remains part of the culture in the present. Even while web content is being accessed it may continue updating, regenerating and reconstituting. Moreover, since it exists in the present tense it remains in constant expectation of change or even ostensible oblivion with a facility and finality that hardly finds comparison in the world of physical artefacts. All web content is ephemeral and merely apparent *in potentia*.

Oral tradition scholar John Miles Foley has suggested the internet—or the 'eAgora' as he characterises it—is in fundamental respects closer to oral traditions (the 'oAgora'). Like oral tradition the internet (and this is certainly true of the web specifically) ontologically depends upon networks and pathways and emergent culture (Foley, 2012, pp. 68–69). Online culture like oral culture is powerful as a lived space but it is also fundamentally without perspective. The web as a thing engaged with is without history; as a living thing is has no taphonomy—the defining and described processes and conditions pertaining to the survival of artefact.[1] While the web is built upon its preceding iterations it only ever really exists in the current manifestation or performance in which the user engages with it. To construct a history, to build a perspective, we need therefore to establish the texts and initiate the taphonomic process—the 'tAgora' in Foley's conceptualisation. While being as essential in the electronic tradition as the oral tradition, capturing texts has its limitation, as Foley writes:

> Texts derive their actual and perceived value from resisting change [...] [however] unless we redefine cultural reality as a still photograph of one moment in time and space as experienced by a single observer from a unique perspective, texts will always remain partial solutions. They will always do their explaining via analytical fragmentation rather than holistic embodiment. (Foley, 2012, p. 68)

As Foley goes on to say, we need an ever accumulating collection of texts. So to have a sense of the culture as played out on the web we must look to the accumulation of web artefacts. This is the role of the web archive, to create these texts or artefacts that calibrate the history of the web, however incompletely and inadequately.

Brügger (2010a, p. 33) puts this succinctly suggesting the analytical object 'website' as a "mediated textual artefact". Therefore, to approach even the most basic website history requires "writing the history of this mediated textual entity as it appears on the web or in a web archive".[2] This textual artefact is only ever potential on the web and only becomes actual in the static textual space, 'tAgora' (in Foley's terms), of the web archive.[3] Indeed the objective of the web archive is necessarily counter-intuitive to the ontology of the web: that is to say, the archived material (by definition as a text) is the static (if taphonomically susceptible) preservation artefact of what was once (and may continue to be) the dynamic and live entity. However, through this process—the accumulation of the texts in the archival context—the history of websites becomes epistemologically tangible and meaningful.

SMALL DATA AND GREY LITERATURE

Midway through the second decade of the 21st century increasingly researchers such as digital historians are looking to 'big data' to analyse social activities and cultural output. Computational techniques applied to large data sets enables efficient and powerful data analysis.[4] There is no doubt that web archives provide great potential for programmatic analysis; but data sets that are not collected for a specific research purpose with custom metadata to support that purpose are likely to disappoint or fail to adequately meet researchers' needs. Rarely can collecting institutions, particularly those with a broad collecting remit, resource the metadata creation and full discovery suites—search, browse, visualization and programmatic—that would cater to all researcher requirements.

The 'early' web archive collections, such as the National Library of Australia's PANDORA Archive, will disappoint big data researchers not only in the extent of the data and available metadata but also in the selection decisions made. While the selection objectives may be comprehensive, realising such an ambition is never really possible. Even large scale harvesting does not capture every resource at every possible moment in time. All web archives to a greater or lesser degree can only suggest comprehensiveness. Selective web archives may try to be broadly representative but collecting emphasis will most certainly be given to specific types of material deemed to have higher value because of its uniqueness and content substance. Moreover, even the best collecting ambitions may be thwarted by technical and legal constraints that prevent collecting selected material.

So, while web archives certainly provide the potential for big data analysis, what they deliver effectively now—with the historic corpus of archived material—is small data and intellectual content. Much of this content may be considered grey literature. This is a contestable term, though it may generally be understood as the output of non-commercial publishers including government, academia, business and industry.[5] In the online world there is a vastly increased amount of this material available since publishing is simplified and, as Kahle and Lyman noted, ubiquitous and democratic. This is critical material for web archives to collect since so much of this material represents the research texts for the development of social, political, economic and cultural policy. This includes the plethora of documents, reports, submissions and commentary produced by governments, think-tanks, peak bodies, lobby groups, political candidates and pundits. It also extends to self-publishing (including blogs) and increasingly social media.

Curated collecting of this material is important to facilitate timely collection—material published online may be of more cultural or social significance at a particular time—and to ensure the completeness of the content with sufficient context (for example, the preliminary reports, discussion papers and submissions as well as a final report). Such material may not represent the statistical and graphical potential of programmatically analysed big data sets, but is critical for understanding the development of the public policy and practice that affects us all.[6]

WHAT IS WEB ARCHIVING?

It is all too easy in discourse about web archiving to assume a common understanding of what we mean by web archiving (and the tangible output of this, the web archive). The terminology is now long and well established. The earliest web archiving programs including both the Internet Archive and the PANDORA Archive adopted the term 'archive'. However, in respect to national library initiatives this can be very confusing when national archival institutions have legislated archive responsibilities distinct from that of the national library, as is the case in Australia. Moreover, the ostensible straightforwardness of the terminology is prone to various understandings of meaning; for example, whether connoting a formal archival process or simply a storehouse. In the national library context perhaps 'collection' is a more accurate term, since it implies curation, but neither does it encapsulate the full understanding of the web archive.

Brügger rightly points out that web archiving should not be equated merely to web harvesting. He suggests the definition as the "deliberate and purposive preservation of web material" (Brügger, 2010b, p. 349). Brügger's definition is intended to encompass more than the actual artefacts harvested from the web (the web harvesting process) and to include material published in other forms (e.g. print media) that inform the history of the web. Such a breadth of material is undoubtedly important for the historian of the web, though it may not be clarifying in understanding more precisely what we mean in regard to web archiving programs.

What we do need to understand is that web archiving is a process and a *commitment* to the sustainable preservation of web artefacts. Fundamentally it requires a strategic purpose with a long term objective. This is another reason national libraries have been in the vanguard of sustainable web archiving, since the strategic purpose to collect, preserve and provide access is enshrined in the statutory function of the institution.[7] There is much that is required in terms of technologies, systems, policies, procedures and resources to make archiving more than merely harvesting and storing.[8] Not the least is the *sine qua non* purpose of archiving and preservation: sustainable long term access. Without access preservation is little more than a costly and meaningless storage burden. Access may come in forms that range from open to limited, individual to programmatic, available now or be a future objective—but it must be the objective.

THE PANDORA WEB ARCHIVE: CASE STUDIES OF ARCHIVED ARTEFACTS

The early history of the PANDORA Archive is well documented and need not be retold here.[9] In looking back at some specific examples of early archived content my purpose is neither to proclaim the virtues of the small data archiving approach nor to specifically criticise it. My objective is certainly to highlight the value of having such early collected artefacts and to consider some aspects in regards to how they came about and how they might be understood.

Experiencing the times: the 2000 Sydney Olympic Games collection

The 2000 Sydney Olympic Games declared by then President of the International Olympic Committee, Juan Antonio Samaranch, as 'the greatest Games ever' was also the first to have a major web presence. It is also the first Olympic Games to have its web presence systematically archived for posterity. While traces of the preceding summer Olympics held in Atlanta in 1996 (which coincided with the dawn of web archiving activity) survive in the Internet Archive they not easily found since the Wayback Machine is yet to offer full text searching. Consequently the 2000 Sydney Olympic Games website collection is of significance as a collection not only collected but also curated at the time. Timely curation has obvious benefits since curators can be attuned to the emergent culture surrounding the event. However it does not necessarily ensure a thorough collection since technical, legal and resource constraints still have an impact on what can be achieved.

The PANDORA Archive's 2000 Sydney Olympic Games collection consists of 137 websites and the collection for the subsequent 2000 Paralympic Games adds another 14 sites to the general Games coverage collected for the Archive.[10] Most harvesting activity took place in the period immediately leading up to and during the Games which were held in September 2000. Some content was collected earlier, most significant being the official site of the Sydney Organising Committee for the Olympic Games (SOCOG) which was first collected in January 1998. That site was harvested two more times in the lead up to the Games (in January and May 2000) and 22 more times during September and October 2000 including every day of the competition.

The curatorial objective was to identify, select and capture a broad coverage of websites that would reflect issues of the moment as identified by curators who were attentive not only to the online target media but also to broadcast and print media at the time. So for example there are a number of anti-Olympic and satirical websites such as *Shame 2000*[11] and *Silly 2000*, both of which aped and subverted the design of the official SOCOG site. The Sydney Olympics was promoted as the 'Green Games' and this is documented by the inclusion of such websites as *Green Games 2000, Green Games Watch 2000* and *Greenpeace Australia Olympic Campaign*.

Sites collected covered a broad range of perspectives and topics including sites relating to arts and culture, business involvement, merchandising, logistics, security, venues, tourism and travel.[12] Frivolous material that nevertheless captured the spirit of the Olympics as played out in Australia was also included; notable being the fan website for the 'Rampaging' Roy Slaven and H.G. Nelson[13] creation and unofficial Olympic mascot 'Fatso the Wombat'. Also included were early examples of the now familiar doodling on the Google logo; in this case by cartoonist Ian D. Marsden who created a series of Google Kangaroo Doodles. A browse through the sites also permits the experiencing of some of the 'state of the art' web technologies of the time, for example the 'in your face' full screen Flash splash page for the Shell Australia sponsorship website.

To achieve the objective of a broad coverage of representative sites significant curator effort was required for securing the permissions (copyright licences) to collect, preserve and continue to make accessible the selected sites. This was necessary as legal deposit provisions for digital online material did not exist in Australia at the time. While onerous and limiting, since licence permission may not be forthcoming from publishers, the licences obtained allowed not only the collection and preservation actions but also open access to the archived material. As sites belonging to a number of major and international companies (including Fuji Xerox, Shell, VISA, Fosters, Telstra) were involved this was not always straightforward and in some cases (for example in respect to an Eastman Kodak site and an NBC site) the necessary permissions were not able to be obtained and significant sponsor websites were not therefore included in the final collection. The reasons for such omission will not be evident or transparent to researchers.[14] The PANDORA workflow system (PANDAS) records the selection, including the original URL, and with this metadata it is possible to locate the content in the Internet Archive, though the timeliness of the archiving in the Wayback Machine may only be serendipitous. While systematic and curated web archiving is not comprehensive—certainly in these early web archiving efforts—the recording of metadata (even for, or especially for, failed collecting outcomes) can be important to facilitate research in the Internet Archive (or potentially other archives that expose their content to access).

The 2000 Sydney Olympics collection does not replay the exact experience of the web in September 2000. This is not 'time travel'—a regrettably over-used description in respect to web archives. But it does give something of the experience when the context is understood. Where a collection like this does fall short is in adequately explicating that context since, for the most part, the researcher is merely presented with the artefacts. Much therefore remains for the researcher to do. For example, the researcher will understand that this collection documents an international event before the advent of social media—Twitter, YouTube, Facebook are noticeably absent from the content. Understood in this context, the collection provides evidence and something of the experience of how public voices were expressed around such major events before the dominance of interactive social media.

The reflected presence (and surprising persistence) of the ephemeral— the election website *jeff.com.au*

One of the more obvious and pertinent yet most difficult questions asked of the web archivist is: what websites have you not archived? If the question can be answered at all it is only by recourse to evidence from other documentary sources, from curatorial metadata or from an analysis of links within collected material. Such evidence might tell us something of the missing resource, certainly the fact of its absence, and may even provide some reflected experience of the absent material if not the ability to re-experience the actual website. The following case study demonstrates both the precariousness and resilience of web material in that most ephemeral manifestation—the election campaign website.

The ephemeral and dynamic nature of the web means that we can never be sure that everything that appears on the web leaves a trace. As suggested earlier, the electronic medium of the web corresponds more closely to an oral world than a text world in the absence of the recorded artefact. As with oral culture the timeliness of the recording event (the archiving event) is critical to the survival of specific cultural experience. Election campaigns, which began to be played out on the web from the second half of the 1990s, epitomise the ephemeral web.

The *jeff.com.au* website was launched in August 1999 by the then Premier of Victoria, Jeff Kennett, for the state's upcoming election campaign. The website was not able to be collected at that time yet 13 years after it disappeared from the web it was able to be added to the PANDORA Archive, partly through chance and partly as a result of the knowledge and memory of the website arising from the web archiving curatorial process and record.

The website was described at the time of the launch as "the symbol of politics in the information age" and "the basis of the most advanced political campaign ever seen in Australia and possibly the world".[15] The site certainly drew attention receiving substantial newspaper coverage as well as major billboard and poster advertising. Newspaper reports at the time detailed many of the features of the website including the opportunity to email Jeff, subscribe to Jeff's newsletter and view Jeff's diary and play Jeff's Election Strategy and Grand Prix games. In Australian political campaign history it was certainly an important and historic website being the first of the political party campaign websites to aggressively promote the personality of the leader and to actively engage with the electorate.[16]

Reaction to the *jeff.com.au* website included the creation of websites responding to the web campaign both satirically and seriously. Given that the *jeff.com.au* site was not archived at the time this was all the more useful since some of these reaction sites were able to be collected for PANDORA. Such sites gave an impression— subsequently recorded in the archive—of the look of the original *jeff.com.au* since they copied the design. The *realjeff.com* site has a fractured image on the splash page parodying the original site. Another site, the 'official unofficial' www.Jeff.coma site also parodied[17] the original site including the 'state of the art' high bandwidth and low bandwidth options splash page of the original (although on the parody website this lead to exactly the same page).

Perhaps the most interesting of all the reactions to the *jeff.com.au* site was that by former Kennett staffer Stephen Mayne[18] with his "Independent Candidate Against Corruption" website (later to be called *jeffed.com!*). In the version of this website archived on 27 September 1999 Mayne asserts that *jeff.com.au* was "shut down for political reasons"—that is, Kennett lost the election.

Election campaign websites, particularly party websites promoting the person of the leader, invariably and without ceremony revert (or redirect back) to the standard party political website soon after the election date. The 1999 Victorian state election was held on 18 September and Victorian Labor Party's Steve Bracks was sworn in as Premier on 20 October. On the evidence of Mayne's website archived on 27 September 1999 *jeff.com.au* had already disappeared by that date, being active therefore for no more than one month. The Internet Archive provides no archived version of the *jeff.com.au* website. Its earliest extant crawl of the site is dated 13 October 1999 (more than two weeks after the site was known to have disappeared) and, consequently only retains a redirect file to the *liberal.org.au* website. On the evidence of the Internet Archive's collection, the domain remained a proxy for the website of the Victorian Division of the Liberal Party for two more years before lapsing.[19]

In the case of *jeff.com.au*, the PANDORA Archive failed to archive the site due to strict adherence to permission protocols. On this occasion the Internet Archive also failed to archive the website since the harvester evidently did not take a timely snapshot during the few weeks the website was active. Nevertheless, by collecting websites that were a reaction to *jeff.com.au* (as well as retaining something of the back story in the curator workflow systems) reflected evidence was collected that, added to the evidence from print media and printed ephemera (such as posters), would give researchers a sense of the experience of the website.

Since we knew so much about the *jeff.com.au* and because of its political and cultural significance it became the exemplar website in answer to the question posed at the beginning of this section: what websites have not been archived? However, as a result of a blog post published in August 2012 about this loss of this significant election material a copy of the site was located; moreover, it was complete with even the games component functional![20]

Adding content to the PANDORA Archive that had disappeared from the web 13 years previously was unprecedented. Practical considerations include the matters of permissions, provenance and date-stamping of the archived instance (copy). Much of this is necessarily recorded in the PANDORA management system and other administrative records. For the benefit of researchers a note was added to the access page to the archived version. Adding the copy of the website to the archive was not complicated technically as the PANDAS workflow system has the facility to upload content from a local drive. However this process created an archived 'instance' with the system applied date-stamp of the upload date not the date of the original copy of the website. To establish a probable provenance it was necessary to use internal evidence from the website pages indicating it was originally copied around 17 or 18 September 1999. The instance date in the PANDORA Archive however appears as 5 November 2012 the date it was uploaded to PANDORA. The use of 'title entry pages' as access screen for each archived website provides for public notes to explain such discrepancies.[21]

Calibrating time: continuity and the dating of websites in the archive

The previous case study raised the issue of establishing the dating of both the living website and its artefactual remnant in a web archive. The dynamic delivery of content and the persistent 'now' of the web along with the ever present ability to 'unpublish' material with as much—perhaps greater—facility as publishing it mean that the artefacts of web archiving 'snapshots' become critical time calibrations of the live web. Web archives establish the chronological dimension of the web.[22]

To mark the 20th anniversary of the world's first website CERN (The European Organization for Nuclear Research) launched a project to restore the ostensible first website address. Specifically this meant, in the first instance, restoring the original URL and the files that were there at its earliest iteration. More than that, they also aimed to restore machine names and IP addresses to their original state and finally to have the first web address—http://info.cern.ch/—as a destination at which the beginnings of the web would be preserved for the future.

This posed the question as to whether such a resurrection of the original files, machine names and IP addresses really constitutes *the actual* first website. What does the re-creation of a virtual artefact mean? There is evidence to suggest this site disappeared, was indeed lost to living web culture, years ago. The Internet Archive's Wayback Machine again provides an interesting perspective. The earliest archived instance of the 'first web address' accessible in the Wayback Machine dates from 10 December 1997 and displays the reasonably helpful message page explaining the "error you have just encountered". So the address did exist at this time but not the content. A year later when Wayback again collected the page at this address the information is more informative saying: "sorry, the hypertext and WWW information is no longer available on the info.cern.ch site. The physical machine no longer exists". Then, from January 2002 until August 2006, the URL makes no appearance in Wayback. When it does reappear it presents a greeting by Tim Berners-Lee welcoming us to *info.cern.ch* "the website of the world's first-ever web server". Which is how it has remained, with only a little bit of a style make-over, until 30 April 2013 when the project to reconstitute the website and server was announced. So, perhaps the site just went missing for a while, the best part of a couple of decades; but when it returns to the live web is it the original site or a replica, a re-creation or a new site—or some hybrid of all these?

The project to reconstitute the first web page at CERN certainly puts into focus some very basic issues that web archive curators confront and which are certainly pertinent to those who would study the history of the web. For a start, how do we establish the age of the site? Copyright dates may be a guide to identify when old content was produced but can be no more than that—a guide. Dates indicating the last modification or last update of a web page are more helpful in establishing the age of the page. Other dates and content within the page may help to establish context to determine when a page was last updated. This may work sufficiently for the earliest content we have, when websites were considerably more static and stable documents; however, it does not work so clearly with the dynamic delivery and updating of content characteristic of websites today. The date of archiving (or more correctly, the date of harvesting or collecting) that defines an archived instance in the web archive—typically included in the archived resource's URL as well as associated metadata—while not able to define the age of a site at least creates a point from which its age may be projected. In other words, is it only at the time that the 'live' website is made a static textual artefact in an archival context that we can actually establish a chronological status for the web content.

When looking into the PANDORA Archive to find the earliest websites—and try to answer another common question: 'what is your oldest website?'—the discoveries are moot in what they reveal. For example, the website of the 'virtual proceedings' of *CybErg 1996* (the first international Cyberspace Conference on Ergonomics) was selected for preservation in PANDORA in February 1997. At this time the National Library of Australia was still developing its harvesting systems and it would be three years before it implemented the first version of the web archiving workflow management system (PANDAS). The first archived version of this site carries the date stamp 15 August 2000. Without any other evidence we may assume that was indeed the date it was harvested—the date of the artefact. However the website itself proffers evidence of being the site as it *was* in late 1996. The copyright date is 1996—the conference was held in September 1996—and there are no other indications on the site of a later 'updated' or 'modified' date. There is other evidence in the text, for example the exhortation to have orders for hard copy proceedings placed before 31 October 1996. This would add evidence to suggest the version, collected in August 2000 was most probably unchanged from the website of late September to early October 1996. But, for research purposes, how should this website actually be dated? Should it be by the evidence of the content, that is 1996; or the provenance of the artefact, that is 2000?

The earliest archiving date stamps for PANDORA content date from mid-1997, though content was certainly collected before that time. The reasons are complex and relate to the 'proof-of-concept' approach taken to the development of the web archiving program at the National Library. Collecting content for PANDORA began before fully formed workflow systems and infrastructure were developed and implemented. To illustrate this point, one of the earliest sites collected for PANDORA was the short-lived science fiction site *Mindgate*, which carries the archiving date of 25 June 1997 although it was almost certainly one of the sites collected earlier in 1997 or even late 1996. The copyright dates are stated as 1995 and 1996 and there are no later update or modification dates to challenge the supposition that this site, as it survives in the archive, is as it was in 1996.

What, then, is a feasible candidate for the oldest archived Australian website, based on the evidence of the web archived artefact? Probably this is *The Australian Observer*, the *soi disant* first Australian online news magazine "compiled by professional journalists specifically for an Internet audience". It appears to have had a short life between 1995 and 1996. The first issue from May 1995 is found in the PANDORA Archive with the archived date stamp of 31 May 1995 which predates the establishment of the PANDORA Archive itself! This anomaly is explained by the fact that this website content was manually downloaded at the time of publication by staff at the State Library of New South Wales (SLNSW) who in a rather Pirandellian dilemma were subsequently in search of a web archive. This content was added to PANDORA when the SLNSW began participating in the program some years later. This does also illustrate the need to be circumspect and cautious in regard to the provenance of archiving date stamps in isolation.[23]

But perhaps we are being distracted from the real point of collecting small data and we should actually look to the content of the archived publication, knowing at least that the artefact does date to the period on or shortly after May 1995. The archived website allows us with a reasonable sense of chronological accuracy to observe how little the serious subjects of social discourse have changed over more than two decades. From the May 1995 issue of Australian Observer the issues covered include: "greenhouse gases: are they really killing the earth? [...] Aborigines and Australia's hidden shame [...] The new cold war between East and West [...] Can newspapers survive on the net?"[24]

CONCLUSION

Developments in web archiving must and will strive to improve the technical processes employed to collect web materials so as to collect on a scale to sufficiently represent comprehensiveness, to retain as much functionality and media elements as possible and to strengthen the collection and stainability of relevant metadata. Such development will promote the opportunities of web archives as big data repositories. Nevertheless, we should not lose sight of the fact that web archives are also constituted of individual artefacts of content that provide primary evidence of culture as played out on the web. In presenting case studies of early archived content from one of the worlds earliest selective web archives I have sought to demonstrate how web archiving creates artefacts removing them from the 'live web' and, in doing so, initiating taphonomic processes that compromise the original (at the very least in the removal of a living context) and influence the state in which researchers necessarily encounter the artefact in the archive. That is, web archive collections exist subject to resource, technical and legal constraints and are framed by curatorial policies, decisions and, indeed, opportunities. Involved and complex stories are often behind the inclusion (or omission) of content in the web archive. Because web archivists are both actively responsible for the processes and responsive to the circumstances—such as the legal, technical and resource constraints—by which these digital artefacts come into being and are maintained, they also have the opportunity (and perhaps responsibility) to tell these stories so that researchers will be more informed in understanding and interpreting the content they find.

ACKNOWLEDGEMENTS

The author would like to thank the editor and anonymous peer reviewer for their comments on the original draft for this chapter; and acknowledge his colleague David Pearson who first introduced him to the concept of taphonomy.

REFERENCES

Brown, A. (2006). *Archiving websites: A practical guide for information management professionals*. London: Facet Publishing.

Brügger, N. (2005). *Archiving websites: General considerations and strategies*. Aarhus: The Centre for Internet Studies.

Brügger, N. (2008). The archived website and website philology: A new type of historical document? *Nordicom Review, 29*(2), 155–175.

Brügger, N. (2010a). Website history: An analytical grid. In N. Brügger (Ed.), *Web history*. New York, NY: Peter Lang.

Brügger, N. (2010b). The future of web history. In N. Brügger (Ed.), *Web history.* New York, NY: Peter Lang.

Foley, J. M. (2012). *Oral tradition and the internet: Pathways of the mind.* Urbana, IL: University of Illinois Press.

Koerbin, P. (2004). Managing web archiving in Australia: A case study. In J. Masanès & A. Rauber (Eds.), *Proceedings of the 4th International Web Archiving Workshop* (IWAW'04). Bath, UK: International Web Archiving Workshop. Retrieved March 14, 2016 from http://www.iwaw.net/04/

Koerbin, P. (2010). Issues in business planning for archival collections of web materials. In M. Collier (Ed.), *Business planning for digital libraries: International approaches* (pp. 101–111). Leuven: Leuven University Press.

Koerbin, P. (2012). PANDORA past, present and future: National web archiving in Australia. Transcript of talk given at the Seminar Kebangsaan Sumber Electronik Di Malaysia, Penang (Malaysia). Retrieved March 14, 2016 from http://www.nla.gov.au/content/pandora-past-present-and-future-national-web-archiving-in-australia

Lawrence, A. (2012). Electronic documents in a print world: Grey literature and the internet. *Media International Australia, 143,* 122–131.

Lawrence, A., Houghton, J., Thomas, J., & Weldon, P. (2014). Where is the evidence? Realising the value of grey literature for public policy and practice. Melbourne: Swinburne Institute for Social Research. Retrieved March 14, 2016 from http://apo.org.au/research/where-evidence-realising-value-grey-literature-public-policy-and-practice

Lyman, P., & Kahle, B. (1998). Archiving digital cultural artifacts: Organizing an agenda for action. *D-Lib Magazine, 4*(7/8). Retrieved March 14, 2016 from http://www.dlib.org/dlib/july98/07lyman.html

Marsanès, J. (Ed.). (2006). *Web archiving.* Berlin: Springer.

Meyer, E. T., Thomas, A., Schroeder, R. (2011). *Web archives: The future(s).* Oxford: Oxford Internet Institute. Retrieved March 14, 2016 from http://apo.org.au/resource/web-archives-future

Milligan, I. (2016). Lost in the infinite archive: The promise and pitfalls of web archives. *International Journal of Humanities and Arts Computing, 10*(1–2), 78–94.

Pearson, D., & Connah, G. (2013). Retrieving the cultural biography of a gun. *Journal of Conflict Archaeology, 8*(1), 41–73.

Rushkoff, D. (2014, January 15). How technology killed the future: Presidents—and the rest of us—can't get anything done anymore. *Politico Magazine.* Retrieved March 24, 2016 from http://www.politico.com/magazine/story/2014/01/how-technology-killed-the-future-102236

van de Sompel, H., Nelson, M. L., Sanderson, R., Balakireva, L. L., Ainsworth, S., Shankar, H. (2009). Memento: Time travel for the web. *arXiv:0911.1112.* Ithaca, NY: Cornell University. Retrieved March 14, 2016 from http://arxiv.org/abs/0911.1112

Webb, C., Pearson, D., & Koerbin, P. (2013). "Oh, you wanted us to preserve that?!" Statements of preservation intent for the National Library of Australia's digital collections. *D-Lib, 19*(1–2). Retrieved March 14, 2016 from http://www.dlib.org/dlib/january13/webb/01webb.html

NOTES

1. Taphonomy arises from the study of decaying organisms and their processes of fossilization. As a study of such process and the biases they present in respect to the preserved object, taphonomy

is employed by archaeologists in regard to biological remains. Taphonomy has also been applied to the study of inorganic archaeological artefacts such as artillery objects in the study of conflict archaeology (Pearson & Connah, 2013). By extension, web archives present artefactual evidence for the digital archaeologist that also comes with biases resulting from the processes that led to the objects being removed from the 'living' web to be held in the digital archaeological *locus* of the web archive. Studying taphonomic processes as they apply to digital materials may well assist us in how we interpret those artefacts. For example, the processes involved in harvesting and preserving content from the live web for the web archive involves biases resulting from technical, resource and curatorial constraints. Knowledge of such conditions may be usefully applied to the development of strategies and policies for preservation intent (Webb, Pearson, & Koerbin, 2013).

2. In one of the most critical studies regarding web archiving, Brügger (2008) provides a detailed examination of why archived websites may be viewed as a new type of historical document representing a unique, re-created and often deficient version of the original, being neither the surrogate of the original nor a mere copy. He characterises web archiving as an active process, wrought of methodological deliberation, that does not stop with the creation of the version since preservation exigencies may determine that we see archived versions differently in the future to the way they appear at the time of collecting. Brügger rightly points out that we can only determine the appearance the original from the archived with varying degrees of probability.

3. In Brügger's characterisation: "any archived website is a reconstruction that does not exist in a stable form before the act of archiving, but is only created through the archiving process on the basis of web elements" (Brügger, 2008, p. 171).

4. See for example Milligan (2016).

5. This general definition derives from 1997 the Grey Literature Conference, Luxembourg as quoted by Lawrence (2012).

6. On the research value of grey literature see Lawrence, Houghton, Thomas, and Weldon (2014).

7. This is certainly the case in Australia where these functions are mandated in the *National Library Act*, 1960.

8. For full length studies on all aspects of the operation of web archiving see Brown (2006), Marsanès (2006), and Brügger (2005). For the business planning with specific reference to the PANDORA Archive see Koerbin (2010).

9. See especially Koerbin (2004) for a case history of the early development; Koerbin (2012) for a later overview and future prospects; and Web et al. (2013) for preservation intent statements.

10. All the archived websites for the 2000 Sydney Olympic Games collection can be viewed at http://pandora.nla.gov.au/col/4006 and the Paralympic Games collection at http://pandora.nla.gov.au/col/4007.

11. 'Shame' was a political cry of the time particularly in reference to the Australian government's treatment of Indigenous people and asylum seekers. The archived *Shame 2000* website presents an interesting preservation case study since an active script on the page tries to identify obsolete browsers to display the website consequently not allowing access to the content. An interim workaround was implemented in PANDORA to make two versions accessible in current browsers. The Internet Archive copies, the earliest of which dates three months after the completion of the Games, are also not accessible at the time of writing due to the browser identification script.

12. Included in this category is the Ansett Australia website. Ansett was the official airline for the Games and was to suddenly cease operations the following year.

13. Roy Slaven and H.G. Nelson are a popular comedy duo who parody Australia's obsession with sport.

14. For example, was an omission due to lack of resources, the absence of necessary permissions or because of technical constraints associated with collecting or rendering the content?

15. The words are those of the Liberal Party of Victoria's Director Dr Peter Poggioli as reported in *The Age* newspaper on 26 August 1999.

16. Subsequent election campaigns have followed this personality focus, prominent examples being the 'Team Beattie' campaign by the Queensland Labor Party for the 2004 Queensland Election and the 'Kevin07' campaign by the Australian Labor Party for the 2007 Australian federal election. These campaign sites typically redirect the political party's established URL during the campaign period to the specific campaign URL (e.g. www.alp.org.au replaced by www.kevin07.com or www. queenslandlabor.org with www.teambeattie.com).

17. The parody including changing the common domain element of the URL from '.com' to '.coma'.

18. Mayne in the aftermath of the election campaign subsequently established *Crikey* in early 2000 and which is now the longest running independent online political commentary publication in Australia.

19. The domain reappeared in 2005 as the website of a completely different 'Jeff'.

20. The harvest was made using the offline browser software Teleport Pro. The technologies used to collect websites is beyond the scope of this chapter however PANDORA content has been collected using a number of softwares including the Harvest Indexer, WebZip and HTTrack. The National Library's other web collections the Australian Government Web Archive and the Australian domain harvests use the Heritrix harvester. The proliferation of harvesting approaches and technologies has considerable implications for the management, preservation and delivery of web archive content.

21. This public note can be viewed and the archived website accessed through the PANDORA 'title entry page' available at: http://nla.gov.au/nla.arc-15037

22. The Memento framework with its promise of 'time-travel' (van de Sompel et al., 2009) by linking web archive content to live content through a browser application is an implementation intended to make this chronological dimension a functional reality in the context of the live web.

23. Especially since the date-stamp was manipulated in this specific case to reflect the assumed collection dates.

24. The Internet Archive's earliest version of this site dates from October 1996 and includes only the final issue of the publication. The Wayback Machine evidence indicates that by late 1997 the domain (www.aobserver.com.au) had disappeared only to reappear after a hiatus of nearly 15 years in July 2013 as The *Aussie Observer* still proclaiming itself again as "Australia's first online news magazine" though bearing no resemblance to the copies archived from 1995 to 1996. By mid-2015 it had again disappeared.

CHAPTER THIRTEEN

Looking back, looking forward

10 years of development to collect, preserve, and access the Danish web

DITTE LAURSEN AND PER MØLDRUP-DALUM

INTRODUCTION

In 2005, a new legal deposit law was passed in Denmark, and archiving the Danish web became mandatory. The intention of the law was to collect data on the entire publicly available Danish part of the internet, using three different yet complementary collection strategies: broad crawls three to four times per year, selective daily crawls of frequently updated websites, and event crawls (Andersen, 2006; Schostag & Fønss-Jørgensen, 2012). With this law, Denmark became one of the first countries in the world that mandated legal deposit of dynamic web materials.

In this chapter, we look back on 10 years of archiving the Danish web. We ask: How can a web archive be understood and how can its development over time be studied? More specifically, we investigate the archive and the archive's development over the last 10 years from three perspectives: legal, technical, and curational. Based on data and behind-the-scenes stories from the Danish web archive, we demonstrate how the three perspectives frame how web archives develop over time and will continue to develop. We contend that a web archive's history is pertinent to all users of the archive and that all three perspectives are relevant for a web archive's history. Since a web archive is an altered mirror of the history of the web, users should be aware of its heterogeneous and changeable character when using it.

Therefore, users need to examine the archive in light of the changes it undergoes. An archive's history is particularly relevant in order to evaluate it as a source.

This history of the archive is an altered mirror of the history of the web, because the web archive is a recomposition as a technical and legal object (which history you can retrace), the web archive is not a reflection of the living online web, and researchers should be aware of that. It very well shows that both in time and in space, several (technical and legal) logics of archiving are superimposed into one big collection that is actually heterogeneous. Thus, this chapter sheds important light on problems of transparency and exhaustivity raised by web archives, and allows the reader to go beyond the black box of web archiving. We suggest that the authors make this more explicit in the methodological and discussion sub-chapters, which somehow read like the technical determinations are above all other problems.

METHOD

For this study, we used a multiple-method approach, combining traditional qualitative methods with new quantitative data-mining methods. Qualitatively, we interviewed staff members and managers who have worked or still work with the web archive. We reviewed all internal documentation of the archive placed on wikis and servers, and we reviewed all publications from the archive.[1] Based on this review, we created a timeline for the archive (Appendix A) and a cluster of possible themes for further exploration. We then selected some of the themes for data mining and for further investigation (interviews) in an iterative process.

The most time consuming task turned out to be the data mining. Basically the web archive is not yet ready for data mining and quantitative analysis and we had to experiment and invent things we needed for the analysis described in this text. We also knew that without the data mining, we could not have produced most of the information this text is based upon. Data mining skills and supporting systems are both essential when looking at web archives. The amount of data gathered from the world wide web is a constraining factor for doing qualitative research.

One of the authors has had many years of working with software development on the UNIX and Linux platforms which gave us the necessary competencies to utilise existing data manipulation tools; to acquire the necessary competencies for performing the included descriptive statistics and data visualisation in R; to develop new, albeit one-shot, Java and Python programs. We also had the opportunity to run our analysis and data mining jobs on some, at that time, unused Linux servers at the library without which no analysis could have been done in this amount of data.

The challenge of the amount of data to mine is always related to the amount of time and hardware available. Initially, we decided to use the first broad harvest of each year from 2005 until 2015. Although the total archive stores more than 650 TB of data, the 10 broad harvests still total around 250 TB, which is unmanageable for the available analysis system and resources. We further reduced the data by looking at just the metadata for these harvesting jobs. When an object is harvested from the web, a single line that describes this single harvested object is stored. This is information such as the reported document type, referring URL, date, and time. Limiting the data this way decreased the data sample to 4.5 TB or an estimated 5 billion URLs, which is manageable. To mine this data, we applied three methods: simple UNIX[2] commands, java programs written for some of the more intensive tasks, and descriptive statistical analysis using R.

We accessed the data through an ordinary NFS mount from our servers and used a Java program written for the specific task of extracting the metadata and aggregating this data by counting the three properties: MIME types, sizes, and HTTP response codes—more on those properties later. We then used standard UNIX tools like awk, sed, cut, etc. to clean the data and perform some quality assurance. After those processes the data was finally at a size that could be handled on a regular desktop computer. We then used R for visualising our extracted data and, very importantly, discuss the validity of it. We had to explore the data as uncharted territory, and we had many discussions about what we found. A great challenge was that nobody knows what the data is supposed to look like. This can be illustrated with an example: When we first started to look at the archive, we counted harvested terabytes over time, and the year 2010 showed a big decrease, an outlier compared to the other years as illustrated in Figure 13.1. We went to a key employee for an explanation, and he said that 2010 was a bad collection year. Based on this information, we accepted the graph. However, weeks later, another employee said, "This doesn't look right." Thus, we looked into the curational documentation for the 2010 harvest. We learned that 2010 was a bad year in several ways, but nothing as big as we had observed. Moreover, the harvesting went wrong after the first crawl, so it could in no way explain the big drop in our analysis, which was based on the first crawl. We then went through our data extraction routines again, and we discovered an error. When we had corrected the error, the big decrease disappeared as illustrated in Figure 13.2.

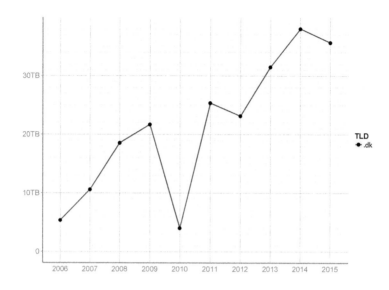

Figure 13.1: Amount of data harvested from the .dk TLD with an error in the 2010 data analysis.

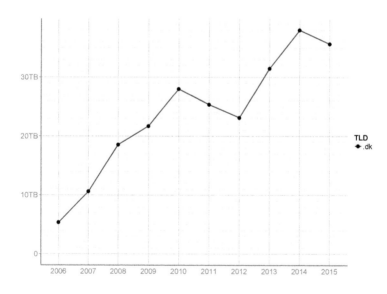

Figure 13.2: Amount of data harvested from the .dk TLD.

Another challenge is the mere size of the data. As can be observed in almost every account of data science projects, data preparation consumes an incredible amount of time even without the complication of dealing with data that we do not know what should look like, such as data for which we have no prediction model or explanatory hypothesis. We spent several months reducing and preparing the data for this analysis project, and even after we reduced the data, we still had terabytes. For example, the metadata file for the 2015 broad harvests consists of 800 million lines. Running a simple line count on UNIX on the available hardware takes an hour. This means that one of the diagrams, which has 10 data points, would take 10 hours to re-generate, which is not a very exploratory-friendly process. Fortunately, we had access to a small cluster of UNIX servers for the tasks that were more hardware intensive. However, computing in parallel added a new level of complexity.

LEGAL PERSPECTIVE: COLLECTING AND ACCESSING WEB MATERIALS

The legal history of the Danish web archive is the first perspective that demonstrates how a web archive is not a direct reflection of what actually happened on the online web. The legal framework is a key component of what has been collected in the archive and how it has been made accessible over time.

The 2005 law mandated that the two Danish national libraries must collect web pages within the Danish Top Level Domain .dk, and websites directed at Danish citizens. With this law, Denmark became one of the first countries in the world with a legal depository of dynamic web materials. However, the 2005 law was not the first legal deposit legislation regarding Danish internet material. The previous legal deposit act of 1998 imposed on the two Danish national libraries mandated that they collect published and completed work on the web, such as monographs, journals, in the form of e.g. .pdf documents, but not the actual sites (Jacobsen & Hielmcrone, 2005). In the period until 1998, an online form with which publishers of web-based works could register their publications with a URL pointing to the document was available. The document and related information were then downloaded by national libraries. This method provided 32,926 documents in 1998–2004 (Henriksen, 2005), and the collection is open to the public today through Statens Netbibliotek.

In the years before 1998, the archive collected nothing. However, in 1987, the top level domain .dk was created. Then, the number of .dk domains grew from 49 in 1987 to 70 in 1988 (Storm, 1988). In these early years of the Danish web, the domains were mainly used by companies and organizations in Denmark (Storm, 1988), and the number of domains grew slowly (this analysis is more elaborated in Brügger, Laursen, Nielsen, 2017). However, from 1998 to 2005, when the archive collected only manually registered documents, the Danish web grew from a few to half a million web domains (in press). Some of these domains may have still been alive in 2005, but some websites were not. Netarkivet has subsequently acquired examples of material from before 2005, and it is now incorporated in the archive as a special collection. Thus, in reality, the Danish web is several different archives in one: two archives each with their own legal framework, one from 1998 to 2005 and one from 2005 and onward, and special collections donated to the archive after it was created.

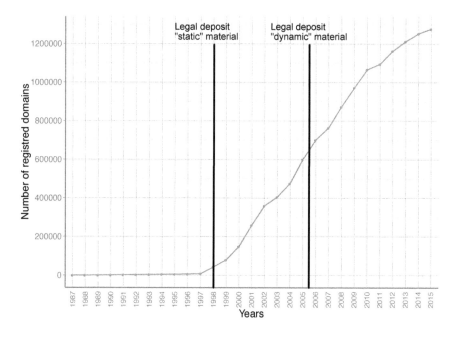

Figure 13.3: Chart of the development of .dk domains.

The legal framework is also a key component of how the web materials in the archive have been made accessible over time. The 32,926 documents collected in 1998–2004 are available to the public today through Statens Netbibliotek. However, the archive from 2005 onward is open only to researchers who are conducting specific research. This is due to the Act on Processing of Personal Data. A revised clause in the deposit law from 2005 discusses the possibility of widening access to users other than researchers, while obeying the act on personal data protection. However, this clause was first postponed in 2008 and then in 2011 dropped completely when it was realized that automated methods could not be used to locate and block data protected by this act. This still applies today. The plan is to combine automated and manual screening of the archive in the future to widen access. This is not possible to do for the entire archive but might be possible for parts of the archive, for instance, news sites and government sites. Once they are screened, the archive can make them available to anybody, on premises and maybe, at a later stage, online for students. However, new and future methods may, in their own ways, open up access. For example, controlled data mining is—at least in principle—possible for anybody, as long as they get access only to the results because such results stand a better chance of being screened by curators.

TECHNICAL PERSPECTIVE: CREATING A WEB ARCHIVE

Technical settings are also key component of what has been collected in the archive and how it has been made accessible over time. First, we discuss the technical framework in relation to collecting web materials. The technology behind parchment, books, and other classical storage media for knowledge and cultural information is very detached from the content. When a scholar performs a study based on books, he or she knows that the book contains all there is. If a page is missing, the scholar can either see the torn remainder or perhaps see a jump in the page numbers. The technology driving the World Wide Web is very tightly interwoven with the actual content. This also applies to the web archive itself. A user does not know whether the archive harvested everything or only a fraction. One cannot know which part of a website is in the archive. State-of-the-art technology is used to create systems that can harvest and host web pages of the ever-changing World Wide Web. In this section, we describe some of the technological challenges involved in creating a web archive.

When a web browser or, more relevant for this discussion, a web harvester, requests a web page, the harvester receives a code that explains the response to the request, the HTTP response code. If this code is 200/OK, everything went fine, and the web page was received and can be rendered for the user or stored in the archive. If no web page or other resource exists at the requested URL, the web server responds with code 404/Not Found. Another code is 301/Moved Permanently, which means the requested web page has been moved permanently to another URL, and additional requests should go to the new URL, which is included in the response.[3] A variant of the 301/Moved Permanently code is the code 302/Found: The request should be redirected to another URL, but in contrast to the 301/Moved Permanently code, additional requests for this resource should still go to the original URL.

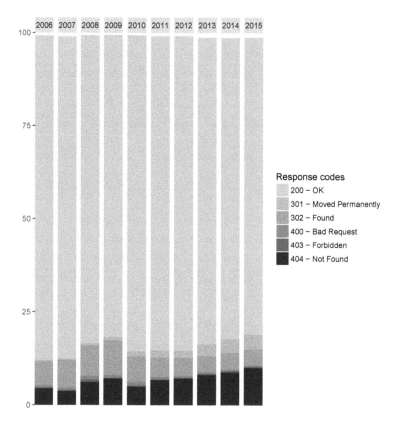

Figure 13.4: Number of harvested documents relative to the total count for each harvest and grouped by HTTP response codes.

Figure 13.4 shows these codes as they have been received in the last 10 years. A slight increase in the number of error codes is observed in Figure 13.4. Such an artefact can be attributed to several domains or systems: It could be a defect in the archive or the data extraction process from the archive, it could have been introduced by the harvesting process, it could also be an artefact existing on the living web,—or it could be a combination of two or more of the above. To focus on this artefact, we present Figure 13.5, which shows the same data as in Figure 13.4 except the successful requests have been removed to focus on the error codes.

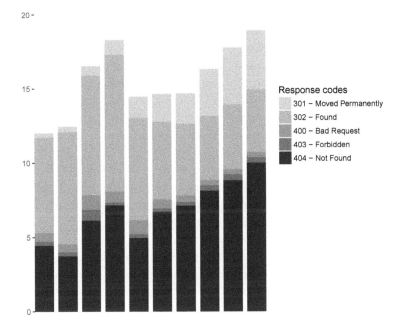

Figure 13.5: Number of harvested documents relative to the total count for each harvest and grouped by HTTP response codes.

We see the three major codes: 301/Moved Permanently, 302/Found, and 404/Not Found. At the present, there is no model for the dynamics of the web. However, there is a plausible explanation for the observed patterns. A standard web page has its own unique URL, and most web pages also contain a number of outgoing links to other pages, images, movies, and so on. When the web was young, these outgoing links were written verbatim in the page's HTML code, creating what is now known as static web pages. Today, most web pages are created dynamically at the time of the request. A server or the JavaScript in the web browser writes the HTML code returned in a 200/OK response.

When a web harvester requests a page at a URL, the harvester can receive the code 302/Found and use the received URL to jump to the actual dynamically created web page. Therefore, an increase in 302/Found responses could be interpreted as an increase in the dynamic web, but we see a decrease. Does that mean the dynamic web is going away? Well, we also see an increase in 404/Not Found responses; that is, harvesters request an increasing number of nonexistent pages or resources. When a web harvester receives a web page, the harvester parses the code of the page to create lists of referenced URLs to use for the next requests. These links are often calculated by the web browser on the fly, which is very difficult for a web harvester to mimic and would lead to many miscalculations and subsequent 404/Not Found responses. This knowledge lends itself to the following hypothesis: The web is actually becoming increasingly dynamic, but we are becoming worse at harvesting it by calculating the wrong URLs for subsequent requests. How does that affect the use of the Danish web archive? One conclusion, given that the hypothesis is true, could be that the archive separates itself increasingly from the live web the archive tries to preserve.[4] Any research using the archive should be very careful in taking onto account artefacts such as this one. For example, the number of documents and the data harvested might not represent what is actually on the web, and this should be kept in mind when using the archive. Another obvious artefact in Figure 13.5 is the steady rise in permanently moved pages, 301/Moved Permanently. This is an example of a feature of the archive that might also be a feature of the web. Further investigations must be performed that go much deeper into the harvesting system itself. Could the existing numbers be used to suggest implications for the archive due to this artefact?

Figure 13.6 shows the amount of data harvested grouped by the different response codes, and as expected, successfully captured pages make up most of the received data. When a browser requests a nonexistent document, that is, receives a 404/Not Found response, the browser actually receives data in the form of a 404 page. For the first broad harvest in 2015, 404 pages totaled 1.5% of the collected data. The 1.5% corresponds to 85 million pages or more than half a terabyte of data. With four broad harvests a year, that sums to two terabytes a year used for these, in essence, error messages. This analysis clearly shows that the applied systems could be improved to harvest the dynamic web. To do that, the core system is continuously being enhanced, and in fall 2015, the fifth major version of the NetarchiveSuite was released. One of the new features in this release was a shift from Heritrix 1 to Heritrix 3, the core harvesting system. In addition to these scheduled and incremental enhancements of NetarchiveSuite, Umbra from Archive-It and Crawljax are now being evaluated as alternative harvesters. These systems are based on browser technologies and thus stand a better chance at keeping up with new technologies on the web. They could be used for general broad harvests and extraordinary or custom web harvests.

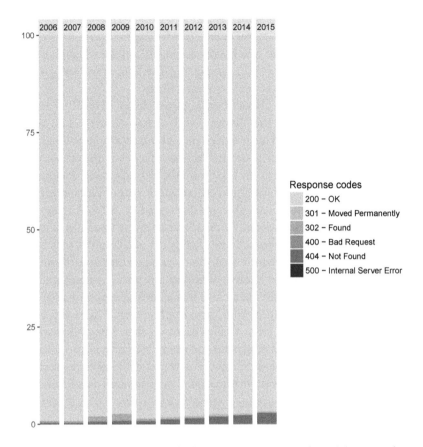

Figure 13.6: Amount of data harvested relative to the total amount for each harvest and grouped by HTTP response.

TECHNICAL PERSPECTIVE: ACCESSING A WEB ARCHIVE

When the web archive opened in 1999, access was possible through only a single computer located at the Royal Library. This computer was named the Monk Machine (Jacobsen & Hielmcrone, 2005), as in "you need to come to the cloister to access the information." This computer provided a discovery system for the harvested web pages and printed hard copies of the pages. In the following years leading up to the passage of the new legal deposit law, a completely new software suite for harvesting the internet was developed. This new NetarchiveSuite system went live in 2005, just in time for the signing of the law. NetarchiveSuite also had an access module called the ViewerProxy. This module was created as a tool for curators and was very closely tied to the technical concepts of the harvesting process and the archive. The module was not intended as a general discovery tool for researchers. In 2012, NetarchiveSuite was enhanced with integration in the Wayback Machine, which made the archive much more accessible to researchers. It enabled them to browse the historical web, for example, the timelines of websites, without the technical knowledge needed to use the ViewerProxy.

In the summer of 2015, the Danish Net Archive celebrated its 10-year birthday, and during that celebration, the Net Archive Search system was launched as a birthday present for the archive. This search engine is built on a large Solr index that lets users perform almost always sub-second full-text queries in the complete web archive. The index is not limited to the texts from the harvested web documents as it also covers many other data sources and properties. For example, a query could return .pdf documents written in Arabic and harvested in 2014. A query could return HTML pages from the national TV broadcast company that links to its competitor's website. All these properties can be aggregated into complex search terms thus creating a combination or hybrid of qualitative and quantitative research and all in real time, facilitating an explorative discovery process. The newest addition to the list of access possibilities for the archive was launched in autumn 2015. The Danish e-infrastructure corporation DeIC and the State and University Library began establishing a computer cluster facility based on close integration with the Danish cultural heritage archives in general and the web archive in particular. The computer cluster facility is primarily for liberal arts and will enable researchers in these fields to ask all types of quantitative questions using modern data science techniques. It will be possible to use existing open source tools to conduct link analysis, natural language processing, machine learning, image analysis, audio analysis, etc. The facility provides access to several tools for quantitative analysis on very big data sets, such as data that exceeds billions of rows. The available tools are a spreadsheet-like tool for semi-structured data, an advanced drag-and-drop text analytics tool for unstructured data, plus the implementation of a highly distributed and parallel extension to R. In addition to these easily accessible tools, the facility also makes it possible for researchers to use arbitrarily advanced tools written in most computer languages, by themselves or with collaborators. In the coming years, we hope to provide an integrated environment using these systems, creating an extensive platform for doing research on the historical web. This environment should facilitate qualitative and quantitative research and enable researchers to (1) browse the Wayback Machine doing qualitative research (get an idea of a corpus and refine the research subject), (2) search and aggregate data in real time using the Net Archive Search (perhaps even define a corpus based on a specific search), and (3) perform a highly quantitative analysis of the created corpora on the cluster facility by using modern methods for big data analysis, data mining, machine learning, etc.

CURATIONAL PERSPECTIVE: VIDEO MATERIALS IN THE ARCHIVE

The last perspective is the curational perspective. Curational practices also affect collection practices over time. We illustrate this perspective with an example about video in the archive. The following figure shows the relative number of media types in the Danish web archive: video, text, images, and audio.

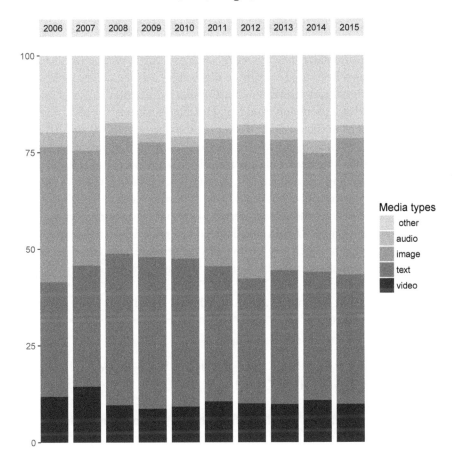

Figure 13.7: Amount of data harvested relative to the total amount for each harvest grouped by media type.

The diagram shows that the relative amount of video remain about the same over the years. However, the diagram covers up curational practices with video over time. In 2007, curators noticed a growing amount of video related to the general election in Denmark that year. For instance, several candidates and several parties had their own YouTube profiles. A manual curational effort made it possible to collect this video material. However, in 2008, video was present on many of the archive's selective sites, and with an individual solution required for each site, the curators could not keep up with the manual work involved. Moreover, technologically, streaming took off, which is even more difficult to collect. Thus, the diagram is a reflection of what curators managed to collect and not a reflection of the amount of video material on the Danish web. The effort in 2007 showed a slight increase, but since 2008, the relative amount of video material has remained the same.

In 2012, the archive produced a new tool for collecting YouTube videos. Over the years, the archive used screen filming to capture content from Second life (in 2012) and other game-like universes, such as Lego Universe (in 2010). This technique has also been used to capture live web television, for example, content produced by a broadcast television company during election nights. Finally, the archive also received a donation from DR, Denmark's national broadcasting corporation, of videos from their website dr.dk published between 2010 and 2015. From a curator's point of view, this is typical. Curators do what they can to capture what they can, and their practices and opportunities change over time. However, from a user's point of view, the archive is in disarray because some video materials are kept not in the main archive but in a special collections archive that is not always accessible to users. Thus, the video materials in the archive do not reflect the amount of video materials on the Danish web. Instead, the materials in the archive is more a reflection of what has been possible to collect. Therefore, when researching video, users should consider materials harvested in the main archive, materials captured in a special collection by a special tool, donations in special collections, and videos with non-digital origins, that is, web materials that ended up as video even though they were not created that way.

CURATIONAL PERSPECTIVE: DANISH WEB DOMAINS AND WEB DOMAINS OTHER THAN ON .DK

We show how curational practices affect the collection with another example, Danish web domains on .dk and Danish web domains other than on .dk.

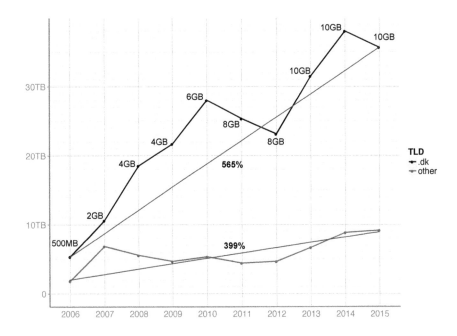

Figure 13.8: Total amount of data harvested for each harvest from the .dk and outside the .dk TLD respectively.

The diagram in Figure 13.8 shows Danish web domains on .dk and Danish web domains other than on .dk. The upper red line shows how many terabytes the archive has harvested during each year's first broad crawl, from approximately 6 TB in 2006 to 35 TB in 2015. However, this is not a reflection of what was on the live web since curational practices have had a direct effect on how this line looks. First, the archive sets an upper harvest limit for domains during each broad crawl. This limit is set because most domains can be captured within this limit. The upper harvest limit has changed over the years from 500 MB in 2006 to 10 GB in 2015. Therefore, the size of the broad crawl increased from 10 TB in 2007 to 19 TB in 2008 probably because the archive raised the upper harvest limit for domains from 2 to 4 GB. The following year, the upper harvest limit was not raised; thus, the increase in terabytes was only from 19 to 22 TB. Second, the archive uses global filters. Global filters are set to avoid overloading Danish web servers and to protect against crawler traps.[5] The use of global filters might explain the drop from 28 to 24 TB a year from 2010 to 2012: Although the archive raised the upper harvest limit from 6 to 8 TB, the archive harvested less.

The lower line on the diagram displays Danish web content on domains other than .dk. A dramatic increase from 2006 to 2007 is seen. Again, this can be explained by curational practices. In 2007, the archive used automated methods to locate Danish content outside .dk. For example, a GeoIP program was used to determine if a domain was placed on a server placed in Denmark (Jacobsen, 2008). The archive identified more than 38,000 relevant domains, and they were added to the crawler. Then, over the following years, the increase is not nearly as high (399%) compared to the increase in .dk (565%), perhaps because the archive did not use automated methods to identify Danish materials on domains other than .dk during that period. Likely, there are more and more Danish web materials outside .dk. In 2006, seven of the top ten largest domains that were harvested were on .dk while 10 years later only two from .dk were on that same top ten. This could be a sign that the size of materials outside .dk is growing. Moreover, a research project in the archive revealed that in 2012 there were 91.751 Danish domains outside .dk that were not found in the archive at the time (Zierau, 2015). In that way, the archive is not a complete version of what was once online but a reflection of curational practices.

DISCUSSION: ARCHIVES AS SOURCES

The Danish internet continues to grow, and the Danish web archive will face great challenges in terms of collection, preservation, and accessibility. In relation to collecting materials, the harvesting tools must be able to capture the increasingly advanced content. The archive will need to use customized crawler tools to capture advanced content; one type of crawler cannot do it alone. The archive will also need to use automated methods, for instance, to locate Danish materials outside .dk or to perform quality control. Only comprehensive data-mining analyses can help the archive learn about the whole archive and improve harvesting technologies. At the moment, specialized collection systems for e-books, e-newspapers, and e-music have been established, while at the same time, better automated methods for general collecting are being developed. To preserve the data, systems must be developed that can scale to volume, differentiate collections, and manage data under controlled conditions, for example, by keeping data on different types of storage media in geographically separate copies. The number of users and the demands they make to access the material continue to grow. This demand requires robust, secure, and user-friendly systems.

An archive's particular history is relevant for all users of the archive because archives are never neutral, objective, and impartial. Just as a camera and a camera operator produce representations that are highly coded, web archiving shapes what it records. And archives change over time. Therefore, users need to examine the archive in light of the changes it undergoes. An archive's history is particularly relevant in order to evaluate it as a source. First, the scope of the archive is relevant. Does it extensively or marginally cover the research topic? What years are covered? What are the collection strategies? For instance, if one wants to study newspapers behind paywalls, one would want to know whether newspapers behind paywalls are included in the archive. Second, the quality and exhaustivity of the collection is relevant. For instance, if one wants to study banner ads, one would want to know that technical challenges have hindered a complete collection. Quality is related to authenticity, ie. to what degree the records are what they claim to be. Quality is also related to authority. Who collected the material, and what are the experience and credentials of the institution or people who created the source? In short, the story of an archive is relevant for the trustworthiness of the archive, which is what kind of conclusion can be drawn based on the archive and how useful the archive is. In other words, users of the archive should be aware of how well the archive support their research question.

CONCLUSION

In this article, we investigated the Danish web archive over 10 years from three perspectives: legal, technical, and curational. We have shown how each perspective affects how the archive looks today, how it has developed, and how it will develop. Legislation is a continuous process that shapes what we collect and how we collect it, and it shapes how we can create access. Technical settings develop on the live web as well as within the archive, and the archive has a hard time keeping up with development. However, when it comes to new ways of accessing the collection, the future looks bright. From a curational perspective, we have seen that practices are not consistent over time—and they should not be, because the world around us is evolving. The three perspectives are intertwined, and there are other perspectives.

The findings and arguments in this chapter have implications for researchers. First, the three perspectives are pertinent for users of all web archives since these perspectives frame how archives develop over time and will continue to develop. When using an archive as a source, researchers should understand the legal framework, technological settings, and curational practices and understand how that shapes and has shaped the collection. Research questions should then be framed accordingly. For instance, investigating the development of the amount of video over time or the development of dynamic content is not a very good idea in the Danish archive, because this content has not been captured very well. Thus, research questions should be formulated in a way that can be backed up with appropriate data. In addition, tools are not value-free. When using the tools of the archive, one should be aware of each tool's possibilities and limitations. Finally, results should be double-checked and backed up by other sources, if possible. Because the amount of data is so large and the data is in disarray, it can be hard to get a sense of whether a finding is valid.

The findings and arguments in this chapter also have implications for archives. Archivists and curators typically know their archive very well, and they have a great communication task in telling users about its actual content. Archivists need to disseminate their knowledge and illustrate what type of research questions can be asked. Curators should also demonstrate the pros and cons of different access tools. In addition, the quality control of an archive is more than ever very relevant. Since nobody knows what the data is supposed to look like, it is all the more important to compare the content with what other archives archive and their tools. Finally, this chapter was written to celebrate the Danish web archive's 10th birthday, but archives does not have to have a birthday to take a step back and look at their archive, their collections, their tools, and their practices. Working on a continuous basis with analysis, with or without researchers, the archive will make itself better for all.

REFERENCES

Andersen, B. (2006). DK-domænet i ord og tal. *DF Revy, 4,* 4–7. Retrieved from http://rauli.cbs.dk/index.php/revy/article/viewFile/995/1006

Brügger, N., Laursen, D., & Nielsen, J. (2017). The development of the Danish web 2005–2015. In N. Brügger & R. Schroder (Eds.), *The web as history: The first two decades.* London: UCL Press.

Henriksen, B. N. (2005). Webarkivering. In E. K. Nielsen, S. B. Larsen, & N. C. Nielsen (Eds.), *Kommunikation erstatter transport: Den digitale revolution i danske forskningsbiblioteker 1980–2005: festskrift til Karl Krarup* (pp. 637–656). Copenhagen: Museum Tusculanum Press.

Jacobsen, G. (2008). Erfaringer med høstning af det danske net 2005–2008. *DF Revy, 8,* 12–15. Retrieved from http://ej.lib.cbs.dk/index.php/revy/article/view/2291/2276

Jacobsen, G., & Hielmcrone, H. v. (2005). Den digitale pligtaflevering. Fra UBIS og lovrevision (1997) til Kulturarvsrapport (2003). In E. K. Nielsen, S. B. Larsen, & N. C. Nielsen (Eds.), *Kommunikation erstatter transport: Den digitale revolution i danske forskningsbiblioteker 1980–2005: festskrift til Karl Krarup* (pp. 269–287). Copenhagen: Museum Tusculanum Press.

Schostag, S., & Fønss-Jørgensen, E. (2012). Webarchiving: Legal deposit of Internet in Denmark. A curatorial perspective. *MDR, 41,* 110–120. doi:10.1515/mir-2012-0018

Storm, K. F. (1988). DKnet. *DKUUG-nyt, 18,* 13–19. Retrieved from http://www.dkuug.dk/wp-content/themes/dkuug/arkiv/dkuug-nyt-018.pdf

Zierau, E. (2015). Identifying national parts of the internet. Retrieved from http://netpreserve.org/sites/default/files/attachments/2015_IIPC-GA_Slides_13b_Zierau.pptx

APPENDIX A: TIMELINE NETARKIVET

1997: Legal deposit 'published work'

1997: KB&SB acquires a collection system for web publications at Uni-C

1998–2004: 32.926 netpublications collected (Jacobsen & Hielmcrone, 2005)

1999: Access established on premises (munkemaskine)

2000: Cataloguing of published work is discontinued

2000: First press coverage with support from KB&SB of establishment of a national web archive (Jyllands-Posten)

2000–2001: Nordic Webarchive Project

2001–2002: Pilot project Netarchive.dk

2003: KB founding member of IIPC

2003–2004: The Nordic countries create a requirement specification for an open source harvester and two developers are sent to San Francisco to develop it with the Internet Archive

2003–2004: Project Netarchive.dk—implementation of production system

2004: Netarchive.dk offers a 'web time machine' as a wedding gift to Frederik, Crown Prince of Denmark, and Mary Donaldson, with an event harvest of their wedding

2005: Legal deposit 'electronic materials'

2005: Netarchive.dk in operation

2005: KB IIPC membership transferred to Netarchive.dk

2005: First event harvest (local elections)

2005: First snapshot harvest

2005: First harvests of selective sites

2006: Deduplication in operation, saves 40% storage

2006: QA made possible within the system

2006: Relaunch website netarkivet.dk

2006: SB&KB join EU project PLANETS (Preservation and Long-term Access through Networked Services)

2006: Video conference systems established at SB and KB for internal cross country meetings

2006: First meeting Editorial Advisory Board

2007: First researchers are given access to the archive ('electronic materials')

2007: Survey: Webarchiving Internationally: Interoperability in the Future?

2007: Online notification form published at netarkivet.dk

2007: Release of open source NetarchiveSuite Curator Tool

2007: First workshop NetarchiveSuite with participants from 10 european institutions

2007: Wiki established for internal documentation

2007: Internal workshop on automated blocking of sensitive personal data

2007: First dialogue with Facebook about harvesting Danish open profiles

2007: Research project Integration of non-harvested web data into an existing web archive

2008: Study of password-protected sites; harvesting begins of selected domains

2008: Heritrix-GUI released for Netarchive Suite

2008: Inclusion of 38.000 domains outside .dk

2008: Harvesting of ebooks begins

2008: Recommended number of selective sites reached

2008: Workflow and documentation of selective sites established

2008: The French National Library (BnF) and the Austrian National Libraries (ONB) join NetarchiveSuite development project

2009: Inclusion of .dk 2000–2004 collected by Internet Archive

2009: First Ph.D. student graduates with a project based on the archive

2009: First on demand harvest

2010: First screen filming (Second life)

2010: First IIPC collaborative collection (Winter Olympic Games)

2010: SB/KB founding members of Open Planets Foundation

2010: Netarchive.dk participates in international work on Report for IOS on "Statistics and Quality Issues for Web Archiving"

2010: Special collection ftp harvesting of ebooks begins

2011: Wayback access available for researchers via FirePass

2011: Special collection on Games begins

2011: Revision of Legal Deposit law, section on regular revision of the law is dropped

2011: Daily manager position reduced to part-time job

2012: Relaunch website netarkivet.dk

2012: Special collection of selective sites' news by email begins

2012: Digital Humanities Lab infrastructure project launched

2012: Special collection on YouTube videos begins

2012: Four snapshot harvests in one year are completed for the first time

2012: Netarchive.dk joins RESAW (Research infrastructure for the Study of Archived Web Materials)

2013: Special collection of Apps begins (games)

2013: Research and development project Cross media production and communication

2013: AutoScreenFilming tool in operation

2013 WARC files in operation

2013: Research and evaluation project Harvesting the digital Music Revolution—the Case of Sys Bjerre

2013: Access on premises established for master students in their final year

2013: Special collection of published text messages begins (novels)

2013 Netarchive.dk develops a solution which makes selected electronic publications from ministries and official agencies open access via persistent links from The Administrative Library's catalogue

2014: Indexing for full text search of the full archive begins

2014: First internal meeting including all employees of the archive (24 employees)

2014: Research and development project Legal deposit outside the TLD .dk

2014: Research and collection project European Song Contest, held in DK

2014: Coordinating management group established

2014: Wayback access available for researchers via Citrix

2015: Pilot project on collection of digital news papers

2015: Pilot project on collection of digital music

2015: Netarchive.dk celebrates its 10th birthday with the RESAW conference (Research Infrastructure for the Study of Archived Web materials)

2015: Full text search available for researchers

NOTES

1. http://netarkivet.dk/om-netarkivet/publikationer/
2. e.g. wc –l <file name>
3. A complete list of the possible HTTP response codes are listed on Wikipedia at https://en.wikipedia.org/wiki/List_of_HTTP_status_codes.
4. This comes as no surprise to the curators of the archive, and many resources are put into keeping the technology of the harvesting system in line with the technology driving and producing the web we are trying to harvest.
5. Crawler traps are places on the net where the web crawler gets caught up in downloading an infinite number of pages. A typical common crawler trap is a calendar application, wherein one can surf around a calendar with links to, for example, the next day, next month, and next year. This means that a crawl could keep running for a very long time, finding 'new' URLs that it had not encountered previously.

CHAPTER FOURTEEN

Usenet AS A web archive

Multi-layered archives of computer-mediated communication

CAMILLE PALOQUE-BERGES[1]

Funny how those 30 year old posts read exactly the same as today's posts.[2]

INTRODUCTION

Librarians and researchers working with born-digital archives face now more than ever the issue of excess in the normative, stabilization process of collecting and standardizing documents for heritage purposes. Among other excesses, the web generates and carries records of computer-mediated communications (CMC), which have not yet become the focus of institutions' appraisal process of web archiving (Niu, 2012)—and attempts to do so have been paved with challenges, as shown by the example of the American Library of Congress archiving of Twitter (Zimmer, 2016).[3]

CMC exceeds the web not only in terms of protocols, formats and software, but also in terms of history. CMC's prototypical genre, email, was one of the first applications of computer networks for human communication in the early 1970s, and is an object of research in humanities and social sciences at least since the 1990's (Baym, 1995; Wellman, 2001).[4] In this chapter, I consider the web as a critical environment for bringing out and building the heritage value of CMC. Lisa Gitelman has outlined a similar argument in *Always Already New* (2006): digital networks' data and artifacts participate in writing the history of the web. Studying the case of Usenet archives on the web unfolds a critical history of the social web itself. Following the methodology of code and software studies, my analysis positions the issue of born-digital heritage within a "Software as Service" paradigm (SaaS). In line with Erickson & Kelty's study of legacy in a layered software environment (2015), I ask how the use and analysis of Usenet archives can unlock the constraints of their hosting information systems. I suggest a multi-layered approach to include network experiences, both technical and cultural, through the unifying lens of the web. CMC web archives are analyzed through different levels of hardware and software infrastructure, formal and natural languages for communication purposes. Thus, stratification is of analytical interest in terms of literal description, metaphor and methodology. Ultimately, the heritagization of CMC on the web raises the issue of an economy of use, both technical and social: how do web archive services handle the complex perspectives of CMC systems and contents? What role do web users and researchers play within these services?

The case of Usenet is exemplary. Born in 1979, Usenet's newsgroups put a social spin on the pre-existing "electronic conferences" (Quarterman, 1990). Attracting a great deal of the connected international academic community and beyond, acting as a place to contribute knowledge and opinions as a "net citizen" (Hauben & Hauben, 1997), Usenet reached its peak of popularity in the early 1990's as one of the most popular places for early internet adopters to establish what was then-called "virtual communities" (Rheingold, 1993).[5] The content of Usenet was not systematically preserved, however, until the first commercial Usenet providers appeared during the web era, leading to the commodification of what was considered public knowledge into private corporate hands (Hauben, 2002). I explore the genealogy of Usenet archives on the web, and show that they were deployed in a vernacular fashion: whether handled by user communities for memory purposes, or developed as an incentive in the information and communication services of the new web economy, the archiving of Usenet both anticipated and adapted to the evolution of the social and technical environment of computer networks. Then, I will demonstrate the multi-layered structure of these archives and examine their potential analytical and preservation purposes.

A GENEALOGY OF USENET HERITAGIZATION ON THE WEB

It is important to assess the role of internet communities in the web archival and heritagization of CMC in general and Usenet in particular. Initial users of CMC and handlers of their archives, they were also used as targets for strategies of web services developments in the new digital economy. Through this critical genealogy, I discuss how users challenge attempts by web services at appropriating internet history and memory.

CMC heritage in internet historical communities

Before the web, internet-based CMC was mostly comprised of email, mailing-lists and newsgroups, stemming from the design of occupational CMC (Computer-Supported Collaborative Work, or CSCW). Histories of the internet agree that CMC played a central role in the development of the internet (Abbate, 1999; Brunton, 2013; Flichy, 2007; Hafner & Lyon, 1998; Hauben & Hauben, 1997; Rheingold, 1993; Turner, 2006). CMC user communities pioneered amateur archiving through the management of their own records. The web made it easy to open and make these archives accessible to the public. Popular mailing-lists managers such as Listserv or Sympa include automated services that embed archives as hypertext on a web page. Prominent organizations in the internet's technological development (IETF, RIPE or W3C for instance) have been operating such web-based archives. The Internet Engineering Task Force (IETF), responsible for internet technical standards, took one step further in 2012 by issuing a Request for Comment (RFC n°6778) for "Email List Archiving, Web-based Browsing and Search Tool Requirement".

Usenet's origins are rooted in a similar social and technical environment. Beginning in 1979, it was developed and used by early computer and network adopters, specifically by users of the open Unix operating system (Kelty, 2012, Hauben, 2002). Usenet carries the image of a breeding-ground for the internet technical, cultural and political culture (Hauben & Hauben, 1997; Rheingold, 1993). Beyond these representations, though, it has been difficult to assess the heritage value of Usenet because of the complexity and diversity of its uses, even if committed Usenet thinkers have stated its status of public good early on, a place of collective and reciprocal knowledge contribution (Hauben, 2002). However, with its international spread, its heritage extends well beyond the local and national interests of archive institutions. The intricate tree-structure of its system, a distribution of themes and sub-themes at many levels, makes its representation difficult, let alone on a single web page. Technically speaking, Usenet remains at the same time one global system and a series of local distribution sub-systems: users subscribe to the newsgroups of their choice, and Usenet providers do not all offer the entirety of the newsgroup hierarchy. The fact that one can never know the wholeness of Usenet is actually part of its folklore: as reported in one of its famous FAQs, like in the tale of the elephants and the blind men, you can understand its parts but never its whole.[6] For a long time, most servers distributing Usenet messages set up expiration dates that would allow the automatic deletion of messages all over the network after a few weeks, because of computer resource management limitations. No automated, standardized and open software was offered for the management and archiving of Usenet: it was left to users or administrators to dump newsgroup discussions manually into textfiles structuring discussions like an email history; a few online indexes would provide addresses to download archived newsgroups (Hauben, 2002) with File Transfer Protocol (FTP) and later, the Web. Finally, in spite of the absence of a general sociological assessment of Usenet users, it is safe to say that they have been and are still very diverse in their social backgrounds and purposes (Donath, 2009; Fisher, 2003; Pfaffenberg, 2003; Tepper, 1997).

The web is a turning point in Usenet's history and memory (Paloque-Berges, 2012, 2013a, 2013b). The legend of 1993's "Eternal September" narrates, in a mythical fashion, the massive change of quality and quantity in Usenet users when commercial web providers and portals opened the gates of Usenet to a crowd of newcomers. With the perceived disappearance of Usenet's golden age—leading to its symbolic death[7]—the work of building memory and heritage began. The general migration of experienced internet users to the web played its part: web pages became the media of choice to gather and distribute information on Usenet, with many guides, FAQs and other didactic generic publications. Webpages were mixed with a folkloric, homogenized representation of the "netiquette", the "netizen", even the "net.wars" (Grossman, 1998; Hauben & Hauben, 1997; Rheingold, 1993)—a representation often enchanted and nostalgic. Usenet was deemed the ancestor of internet culture, with inheritors everywhere in web forums, rightful heirs in terms of CMC.

CMC web archiving as service: Heritagization as an economic strategy

Commercial Usenet providers were born with the web: it was there they advertised their Usenet services, and also offered web portals for Usenet access. Déjà News Research Service was one of them, known for offering the first massive access to Usenet archives as an incentive to users' subscription. Started in 1995, this initiative was typical of the early dot.com era, when young companies started to play with web information systems. It is arguable that Déjà News used Usenet archives to test three innovative purposes. First, they promoted their search engine—at the dawn of the economy of web search. Second, they offered a web interface allowing users for the first time to not only search for Usenet messages, but also browse and retrieve analytics from their records. Third, it is highly probable they experimented with opinion mining on the archive data—particularly from 1999 to 2001, when the company rebranded itself as Déjà.com, a shopping service set up on a professional oriented service called the "Déjà communities". When the bubble burst and Déjà. com met its demise, the shopping technology was sold to the young eBay who was itself interested by experiments in opinion mining for recommendation systems.

After Déjà.com fell to the bubble, the News Research service and the associated Usenet archive were sold in 2001 to another young web company: Google. In their turn, Google made the archive accessible for searching and browsing (this time freely) within their new web forum service called Google Groups. This acquisition seemed to feed into Google's strategy to become a major player in the web economy after the dot.com bubble. As for Déjà News, I argue that three strategies were at play—and might still be, although Google doesn't communicate on the topic. First, Usenet archives are data, and thus provide material for experimenting with techniques of search, data mining and recommendation.[8] Second, beyond the information layer, it gives users access to the social material of CMC, communication and opinions, attracting new users to Google Groups at a time when Google was already thinking about service diversification. Third, Google positioned (and continues to position) itself as a cultural referent for the history and memory of one of the most popular pre-web locus of network encounters; as a treasure of internet's past, the Usenet archive attracted experienced users to Google.[9]

Google's heritage strategy was more crucial and more advanced than Déjà News', as it was built on a diversified SaaS approach for the web. As part of the legitimization process, Google designed a hypertext timeline featuring a curated series of discussions retrieved from the archives, providing entry points to the complex world of Usenet.[10] The timeline cleverly mixes events of global history (like the appearance of Aids, or the Chernobyl catastrophe and many others heavily discussed "hot topics"), with computing and computer networks' history—especially projects getting a kick start on Usenet (like Linus Torvalds' call for participation for the Linux project, or Tim Berners-Lee's announcement of the WWW code becoming public). Toward the end of the timeline, standing at the convergence of the world's memory and the latest digital economy innovations, Google asserts its own place in history (carefully obscuring Déjà News' pioneering initiative) (Figure 14.1). Google, assuming this referential position in its own making of history, also positions itself on the map of the web, getting larger by the minute in the early 2000's. Google is where old and new internet users converge.

```
|
|
-------- May 1995 First mention of DejaNews
|
-------- Dec 1995 Announcement of the AltaVista launch
|
|
-------- Mar 1998 First mention of Google
|
-------- May 1998 First mention of Mac OSX
|
-------- Feb 2001 Google acquires Deja archive
|
----- 11 Dec 2001 Google offers 20-year Usenet Archive
```

Figure 14.1: The six last entry points of the original 2001 page, "The 20 Year Usenet Timeline" from the Internet Archive Foundation archive.

Critical responses to Usenet's web archive

This legitimization process has had mixed results. In the mid-1990's, Déjà News' archival initiative was first met with enthusiasm. But early on users started to voice concern about a profitable service experimenting with users' information for its own vested interests, in contradiction with Usenet's culture of public sharing—especially considering it went through a long period of public funding, with support from the American National Science Foundation infrastructure and agreeing with its non-commercial "Acceptable Use Policy" prior to 1995 (Hauben, 2002). In addition to techniques like "nuking" messages out of Usenet archives, critical users added a piece of code to message headers' metadata (called the X-No-Archive) in order to block Déjà News' indexing. It is thus interesting to see how the information system experiments of young dot.com companies was met with users' counters ranging from criticism to technical retaliation.

Likewise, users of the Google Usenet archive were enthusiastic at first, and became critical with time—as shown in the results from a 2013 study (see note 9). Usenet old-timers, and internet early adopters in general, were first in showing interest and praising the archives. I call their celebratory discourses "ego-searches" (finding one's contributions in the past conversations) and "alter-searches" (finding common references of events known to Usenet's community). These reflexive practices helped build the collective cultural memory of Usenet. Among them, though, some raised concerns of the same kind that Déjà News encountered. They criticized the initiative for unearthing and bringing out information about individuals, a concern towards the risks associated with displaying personal data and opinions; as well as for copyrighting individuals' contributions. Google soon provided a feature for the removal of messages, as an early example of experimental device to solve "right to be forgotten" issues. The ambivalent status of Usenet conversations—public, in that newsgroups were openly accessible, but private in the sense that the vast majority of Usenet was composed of small, confidential groups—was thus revealed. Compliance with the rights of individuals remains one of the first and most fundamental impediments to building accessible web archives, as objections are raised against commercial as well as scientific exploitation of digital data.[11] In addition to these ethical issues, the social identity of Usenet itself was thought to be put at risk, with users having less and less possibility "to affect the corporate decision making process" and with concern about the responsibility of "safeguarding the public nature of the archives" (Hauben, 2002: 65 and 67).

In time, users have increasingly criticized Google's archival SaaS. The interface was deemed illegible, with little to no tools for helping with searching, browsing, and retrieving messages—notwithstanding a series of confusing system redesigns (more on this later). The search functions in particular were constrained with numerous failures and flaws due to the redesigns—an issue underlined as highly ironical "for a search company", according to one recent journalistic coverage of the case.[12] In the end, users complained that Google left the Usenet archive to decay into "digital ruins"—an insult added to the initial injury that was the ambiguity of a "corporation doing a library's job" (see note 12). Apart from helping with message removal, Google's communication policy about the Usenet archive has been non-existent, with online contact forms leading to nowhere and left without answer—in blatant contradiction with Usenet's culture of user dialogue and cooperation (Hauben, 2002).

What these user responses show is how the web archiving and accessibility of Usenet inscribe social issues into the technical complexity of records and uses of born-digital documents. Users thus engaged in producing a counterpart view of how to think and build the memory of the internet on the web.

A VERNACULAR ARCHIVE: LAYERED EXPERIENCES OF CRITICAL RE-APPROPRIATION

Usenet archives have thus evolved along with the technical, economic, cultural and social transformations of the web. But as such, they have gone through a process of socialization but not standardization. As such, they retain vernacular value, in that they are re-appropriated and re-invented by internet users.

Adding a new layer to Google's Usenet archive

Users did not only critically talk about Google's initiative; some were also committed to a critical re-use of Google's archive. For instance, one Usenet old-timer created an alternative interface in order to offer a comprehensive view of Usenet's complex branching structure on one single page, with top-domain newsgroup names linking to content kept in the Google Groups.[13] Another Usenet veteran, Norman Yarvin, has been deploying a similar vernacular appropriation called "Yarchive" that sums up all the critical issues about the web archival of Usenet—and the answers amateur archivists can bring by creating their own. First and foremost, issues regarding programs, formats and protocols: the archive keeper justifies his choices at length, like keeping the original message format while at the same time adapting to the hyperlink structure of the web by linking unique messages to full conversations as archived in the Google Groups. Yarvin also tackles issues of copyright—taking the most common path in internet re-publishing practices: publish first, take down later (if someone asks); as well as economy issues, adopting Google's AdSense service. Finally, he spends time with issues of cultural representation: "Yarchive" is a curation of messages considered by Marvin as quasi-publications, "posted by people who have a well-deserved reputation for a high level of accuracy". The list of archived messages, fact-checked by the amateur archivist here taking the role of an editor, carries the ambivalence of Usenet itself: at first, it reads as a coherent sum of knowledge about science and technology, but looking closer, heterogeneity stands out. What binds everything together is the encyclopedic ethos of Usenet culture of leveling topics of interest like "Jokes", "Physics" and "Air Conditioning". Veterans' imaginary of Usenet as a coherent community, despite its obvious hybridity, is a strong incentive and driving force behind vernacular archiving.[14]

Heritage as data: New ways to explore internet's past

Usenet is still alive today, even though its uses have been completely redefined. Even if many commercial services exist, Usenet still has a sense of abstruseness prompting its user base to self-organize in order to better inform the community, like in the old days. For example, the community forum Reddit, a direct inheritor of Usenet, maintains a "subreddit" (a topic-dedicated board) dedicated to its ancestor. It is not used primarily for memory purposes such as nostalgia but for everyday functional questions.[15] But, involved in practical issues of handling and maintenance, users are faced with the ambivalence between heritage and service exposed earlier. References to alternative web services offering free Usenet archives with a search engine, like Narkive, come with suspicion from users regarding their underlying motives, at a moment where data has become the official currency of the social web economy— whether these web archives impose ads or maintain opacity on who they are and why they are doing this.

Considering Usenet archives as data also opens to a new and rich potential for the appropriation of internet heritage, as shown by the Usenet collections at the Internet Archive Foundation (IAF). Indeed, in a context of defiance towards Google's (and other web services) handling of Usenet archives, users turned to IAF for a non-profit, permanent, responsible, and explicitly heritage-oriented preservation. Numerous pleas have been deposed on the archive.org forum, with reference to Google Groups Usenet digital ruins.[16] Archive.org has actually been maintaining a Usenet Archive since 2011, a relatively small file of Usenet archives collected between 1981 and 1991 by the administrators of a server hosted at the Zoology department at University of Toronto. Since then, IAF's archivists have expanded their Usenet archives. First, they set up a partnership with one of the biggest current Usenet provider, Giganews, for archives going back as early as 1993. Second, they received an anonymous donation called "The Usenet Historical Collection", comprised of archives most likely retrieved from the Google Groups stock—as hinted by the metadata, to which I will come back.[17] Third, they added a portion of their shareware collections (managed by Jason Scott's Archive Team) dedicated to newsgroups archives burnt into share CDs called *Netnews offline* in the mid–1990's. These four collections are gathered in a dynamic web page called "Usenet archive", fed by at least two collections that are still expanding (Giganews and Historical).[18] It is notable that this web page is also categorized in the "Data collection" category of archive.org. Indeed, these archives take the shape of "dump" files, meaning they are an exhaustive and plain copy of data from a file system without any transformation of the data comprised in the original textfiles. Contrary to initiatives led by web services like Google Groups, this allows users to actually manipulate the archives beyond simple content search, for academic or heritage research purposes.

Indeed, IAF's Usenet archive dataset has been appropriated. I argued before that Usenet's web archives were highly socialized, engaging users to participate in the building of history and memory by searching and discussing Déjà News and Google Groups' collections, or by experimenting with web editing techniques. With Usenet archives as data, this process goes even further. For instance, one technically proficient user analyzed the IAF dataset in order to challenge Google's claim that they had found the earliest Usenet message posted.[19] According to Ian Milligan, who has been experimenting with data analysis on the IAF's Usenet archives, such collections of born-digital archives open a "third wave of computational history" (2012): "All of this is to start thinking about how we can use this unique source as a social, cultural, and even political record of the past."[20]

Creative recreation: Conflating past and present uses

In the margins of historians and academic researchers appraising the value of such material for historical and sociological studies, other initiatives open new perspectives in the reflexive use of CMC web archives.

Explicitly artistic or cultural archival projects explore in creative ways the layered complexity of these born-digital archives embedded in web information systems, particularly when they provide an exhibition system. *WWWTXT. Revisit the early Internet (1980–94)*, a project by researcher, archivist and artist Daniel Rehn, emphasizes curation: hosted on the micro-blogging service Tumblr, it collects, selects, and displays messages relevant to computer network sub-cultures found in archives of old internet communication systems like Usenet. *Olduse: a real-time historical exhibit*, by Joey Hess, an open source programmer from the hosting company Branchable, emphasizes emulation: using the UTZOO dataset (and soon expanding to Usenet Historical File), he recreates the experience of receiving Usenet messages in real-time in an emulated newsgroup reader, from 1981 on.

It is notable that such projects prompt users to marvel at the fact that time has passed, but that nothing has changed! Indeed, I have found that many reactions on Reddit, Metafilter and other forum-type websites (which assume, as underlined before, a strong Usenet heritage and consider themselves as heirs) are a variation on one assessment: the way we express ourselves and communicate today on the social web is the same as before, notwithstanding technological changes. This is an interesting case of temporal shortcut drawn from layering Usenet archives with web data management: it helps with assessing anthropological continuities within a temporality of fast technological evolution.

Further, this can be compared with Megan Sapnar Ankerson's study of how nostalgia is a powerful incentive for users of the Wayback machine on archive.org. She analyzes the device as a time travel machine that turns "chronotourism" into a critical process: revealing hidden corners of internet history, forgotten in official historiographies.[21] Such nostalgic "time travel" layers, do have analytical interest beyond metaphors, in their layered materiality, as I will show in the following.

PROPOSALS FOR MULTI-LAYERED ANALYSIS

When exploiting Usenet's archives for my own research on the histories of computer network's early user communities, I crafted a multi-layered analysis especially aimed at studying born-digital text material (textfiles).[22] I chose to embrace not only content, but also software structures and encoding standards—an approach familiar to infrastructure studies and critical code studies. As such, I focused on different layers of source material found in electronic conversations, from content to header metadata. The embedding of textfiles in web-based archives is the top layer allowing reading the material in a web navigator. I argue that these layers have value both in terms of discursive content analysis and in software and infrastructure analysis.

The web interface as medium and obstacle

The first meaningful layer of web-hosted Usenet archives is of course the web itself. While it is not necessary to elaborate all of the web's technical layers, I will highlight the elements that frame the archives in a limiting or enriching manner for research. I will concentrate on the two instances of web archiving that can be used—and are indeed—by researchers: the access interfaces of the Google Groups (GG) service and of the Internet Archive Foundation (IAF) web pages with 'textfiles dumps'.

GG offers a system for searching the Usenet archives, but rather than facilitating access, it raises many obstacles.

1. Lacking explicit heritage endorsement. Coming to GG's front page today, there is no indication that Usenet archives are actually there, contrary to before 2013 where the Usenet archival mission was explicitly stated. A search for "Google Usenet archive" on Google's main page actually outputs descriptive metadata in the search results indicating its former mission, a

description absent from the GG page. Minimal information is given in a support page that is hard to find if you are not looking for it (Figure 14.2).

2. Indiscriminate search results. Searching into the GG engine outputs posts from GG and Usenet indiscriminately. In practice, both GG and Usenet messages are dynamically archived, meaning that they are incremented as activity is produced. This embedding has three major consequences. First, as hinted before, GG makes no effort at showing the complex branching tree structure of Usenet's newsgroups. The only indication is a minimal "Group: (nameofthegoup)" mention next to the result. Second, it is virtually impossible to look specifically for Usenet messages if the user is not familiar with Usenet syntax—for instance, adding an asterisk after a root name will output all the sub newsgroups embedded under it. Thus, a prior knowledge of Usenet's complex hierarchy of thematic groups is crucial to finding relevant material (Figure 14.3). Finally, depending on the search criteria, the engine might very well output different results every time used, so there is no stability of search. Considering that a lot of newsgroups have never been closed and have been living on spam since at least a decade, the amount of noise is highly problematic. Before 2013, a series of search tools were available to limit search with temporal criteria, as well as chronological tables with numbers of messages per month and per year, and links to access them. The difficulty to search and navigate diachronically in the archive has increased over the years and has made in depth search virtually impossible. A good metaphor for this obstacle is the adoption of the infinite scrolling feature in 2013: for groups riddled with spam, users have to scroll forever before accessing meaningful content.

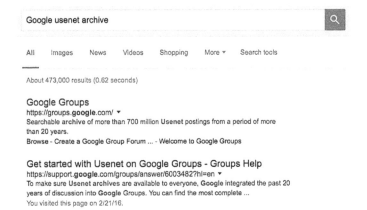

Figure 14.2: A March 2016 Google search showing that GG's metadata still indicates hosting Usenet archives.

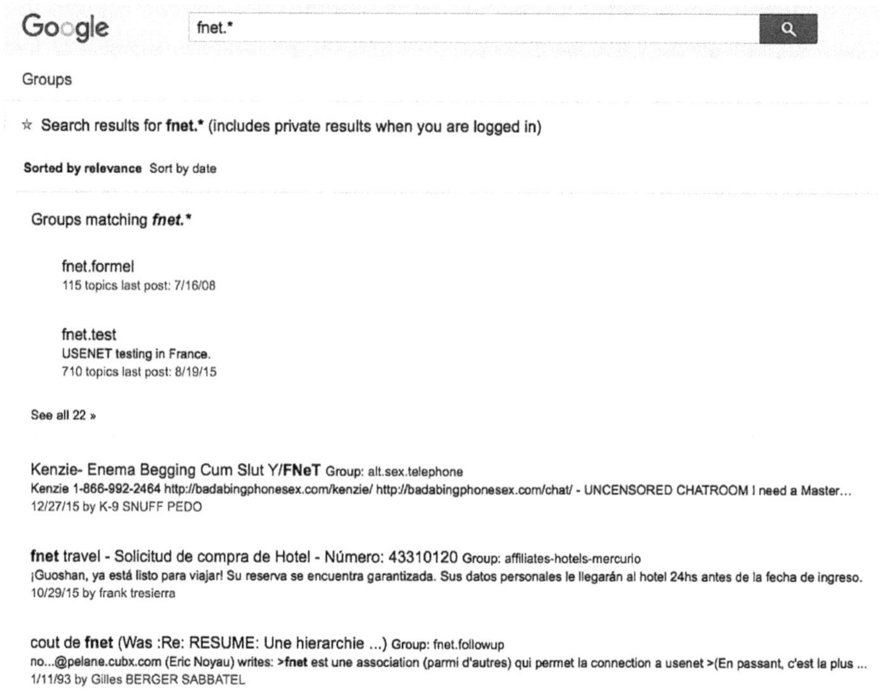

Google   fnet.*   🔍

Groups

☆ Search results for **fnet.*** (includes private results when you are logged in)

Sorted by relevance Sort by date

Groups matching *fnet.***

fnet.formel
115 topics last post: 7/16/08

fnet.test
USENET testing in France.
710 topics last post: 8/19/15

See all 22 »

Kenzie- Enema Begging Cum Slut Y/**FNeT** Group: alt.sex.telephone
Kenzie 1-866-992-2464 http://badabingphonesex.com/kenzie/ http://badabingphonesex.com/chat/ - UNCENSORED CHATROOM I need a Master...
12/27/15 by K-9 SNUFF PEDO

fnet travel - Solicitud de compra de Hotel - Número: 43310120 Group: affiliates-hotels-mercurio
¡Guoshan, ya está listo para viajar! Su reserva se encuentra garantizada. Sus datos personales le llegarán al hotel 24hs antes de la fecha de ingreso.
10/29/15 by frank tresierra

cout de **fnet** (Was :Re: RESUME: Une hierarchie ...) Group: fnet.followup
no...@pelane.cubx.com (Eric Noyau) writes: >**fnet** est une association (parmi d'autres) qui permet la connection a usenet >(En passant, c'est la plus ...
1/11/93 by Gilles BERGER SABBATEL

Figure 14.3: Searching for "Fnet.*" on GG's engine outputs Fnet-rooted newsgroups, but also irrelevant non-Usenet groups.

3. Complicating the retrieval of data. Beyond these impediments, the GG service does not allow the automated crawling, indexing or retrieving of the archive. Any attempts to do so are blocked for obvious reasons regarding the commercial and security interests of Google information systems. An unsuspecting user attempting to copy a Usenet message by hand from the main interface system will find that HTML and CSS codes from the web formatting layer are included and they will need to clean the data afterwards. A discrete option to access the original textfiles is given, however, proving crucial for studying both the content (body data) and header information (metadata) of the electronic messages.

IAF's web interface has been redesigned recently as well, which makes the logic of the composite collection described before a little hard to understand. Similarly, the search function is quite opaque. The crucial improvement from GG's approach is the ability to access massive plaintext dataset ('textfiles dumps') by downloading them directly from IAF's servers or as torrent files. The archivists at IAF have created a system for bundling up folders automatically from their dump archive. These folders are created by a search on any term (and thus the folder produced will contain any Usenet messages from the IAF archives where the string of character is present). Zip folders also exist for specific newsgroups. The preservation choice of IAF does not provide a comprehensive view of what was Usenet and what part of Usenet they preserved; the user still feels one's way along intuitively. Finally, looking at the "Historical Usenet Collection" data, it is quite clear that its anonymous "generous donor" did extract them from the Google Groups, as showed in the dump metadata. It is not too risky to interpret this collection as a result of a hack, in line with the IAF's general casualness regarding copyright and born-digital material as well as its willingness to circumvent technical barriers to preservation–as illustrated in the "panic downloads" practices of their Archive Team. This strategy backs up the idea that IAF provides vernacular archives fostering hands-on uses and re-uses, and thus carries a cultural, collective and popular conception of heritage (Paloque-Berges, 2014).

Format as analytical resource and structure

Going back to research uses, I will showcase how accessing plaintext messages is crucial to a layered and in-depth analysis. I rely on an (*infra*)structural approach to decoding and understanding electronic messages—and I will focus here more specifically on the importance of formatting.

Formats determine the encoding of characters (from digital bits to text) and the structuring of messages across many software layers, producing a readable document. There are many electronic messages formats, but in our case, archived Usenet messages still rely on the simplest form of text encoding, the ASCII format. Designed and standardized in the early 1960's, it was aimed at helping the transmission and readability of text through machine communication. In the context of the digital, where the criterion of originality is absent from archival process, ASCII code carries some kind of authenticity. Without guarantee of stabilization, it offers a view of the life of data across space and time:

- the original data content;
- the   palimpsest nature of the message when included in a mail exchange: for instance traces of answering back and forth at the level of content (messages quoting previous messages for the purpose of answering) and at the level of code (traces of formatting as messages have been read and answered through different mail software);
- the   paratextual side of messages, with header metadata showing signs of its circulation through time and technology.

ASCII encoding provides a view of the rudimentary structuring of electronic messages and how users appropriated these simple text format (also called plaintext) to make their messages as telltale as possible. As anthropologist Jack Goody has shown, the materiality of writing has shaped the way we think (1977): some "technologies of intelligence", as he calls them, for instance tabular forms, have domesticated the mind into thinking in abstract ways. It can be argued that the ASCII encoding format has helped early computer network users "domesticate" the cognition and sociality of computer-mediated communications. Coincidentally, the Wikipedia article uses the same kind of metaphors as Goody when arguing that ASCII allows electronic messages to "survive 'in the wild', in part by making them largely immune to computer architecture incompatibilities".[23] As such, directly analyzing the plain ASCII text is a good approach for studying several layers of CMC archives: its archeology and paleography, showing the conditions and constraints through which the document has been structured and documented. As such, looking at ASCII text has methodological value for studying born-digital archives in general as time-traveling artifacts, starting with the source code of web pages.

Let us have a look at two messages (Figures 14.4 and 14.5). Both are extracted from a dump of the IAF's "Usenet Historical Collection" and more specifically from the "Eunet.general" newsgroup, a general information group for European users connections to Usenet and internet opened in the mid-1980s.[24] I chose these two messages in particular because their content and format show the transition between the pre-web internet era (1990) and a moment when the web has become widespread (1995); as well as traces of the evolution of computer networks information system for displaying and organizing electronic text. I will illustrate my layered methodology for the purpose of sociotechnical historical communication analysis.[25] In each case, I emphasize the role of format and code in the analytical process.

```
From -2507831815941689301
X-Google-Language: ENGLISH,ASCII-7-bit
X-Google-Thread: fec63,50afad2cb1f946ef,start
X-Google-Attributes: gidfec63,public
X-Google-ArrivalTime: 1990-09-14 08:56:17 PST
Path: gmdzi!unido!mcsun!inria!bull.bull.fr!echbull!integ.ec.bull.fr!yan
From: ███@integ.ec.bull.fr
Newsgroups: eunet.general
Subject: lodging in England (Hull)
Keywords: student Hull
Message-ID: <454@echbull.bull.fr>
Date: 14 Sep 90 15:56:17 GMT
Sender: news@bull.bull.fr
Reply-To: ███@integ.ec.bull.fr (███████████████)
Organization: Bull SA Echirolles
Lines: 19
Posted: Fri Sep 14 16:56:17 1990

I'm not sure this is the right group; please don't *flame* ...

I am acting for a colleague whose son, a French university student, needs
lodging in Hull (UK). He prefers room with family, near Cottingham Rd, and
is willing to babysit, etc.

Anyone who could help can Email to:

        ████████████@ec.bull.fr

Thanks a lot to everybody.
```

```
==============================================================================
███████████████      Email: ███@integ.ec.bull.fr         \  / /\  |\  |
Bull SA Unix Center    or: ███████████@ec.bull.fr        \/ /_\ | \ |
Echirolles - France  Phone: +33 76 39 77 85              __/ /    \|  \|
==============================================================================
```

Figure 14.4: Message from "Usenet historical collections"'s EUnet dump, posted September 14, 1990 on the eunet.general newsgroup.

```
From -992430432073587172
X-Google-Language: ENGLISH,ASCII-7-bit
X-Google-Thread: 10bda7,e23bd3821a670ef0,start
X-Google-Attributes: gid10bda7,public
[…]
From: oracle1@shell02.ozemail.com.au (Craig Massey)
Subject: Oracle of Man
Date: 1995/12/09
Message-ID: <4aateq$eun@shell02.ozemail.com.au>#1/1
X-Deja-AN: 121385891
organization: OzEmail Pty Ltd - Australia
newsgroups: fido.eur.genealogy,eunet.news,eunet.general,es.rediris.fallored,
es.news.admin,es.eunet.spanish-tex,edm.usrgrp,dungeon.forsale,dk.foredrag,

Whatever your Newsgroup interest may be,

The fact that you are using the Internet, means that you are part of the
greatest explosion of information technology (IT) in the history of mankind.
Computer developments are well documented but the future of artificial
intelligence is limited only by our imagination.

P▓▓▓▓▓▓▓▓▓, owner of one of the largest IT companies in Australia,
has written a compelling book which is raising controversy and arguments
throughout the world. His disturbing and unnerving prediction is that we
are now close to a breakthrough in the race to give computers a conscious
intelligence. This will give them the ability to interface with human beings.
This giant leap forward brings the incredible possibility of being able to
"download" our whole psyche. This will include our personality, intelligence
and knowledge transfering into Technological Life Forms" or "TLF's", to give
ourselves eternal life.

For further information, please visit our Web page on

http://www.oracle_of_man.aust.com
```

Figure 14.5: Message from "Usenet historical collections"'s EUnet dump, posted December 12, 1995 on several Europe-related newsgroups.

INFRASTRUCTURAL ANALYSIS

The metadata on Usenet messages is rich with infrastructural information at the hardware and software levels. It reveals a great deal about who, when, from where, by which means, this message was sent through a computer network, and what this network was like at a given point in time and space.

For instance the field "Path" indicates the message routing source and relays until finally reaching its destination, while the field "Organization" indicates where the source machine is precisely located (Figure 14.4). Usenet was built upon a network of Unix machines (with UUCP protocol designed in 1976, redesigned as NNTP to join the internet protocol family in 1986), which explains the strange syntax of this route. This network is distributed, offering a store-and-forward solution for the transmission of messages: each machine (named and defined with the exclamation point, a symbol of the UUCP protocol) relays the message, indicating the actual topology of the network. In this case, the relationships between the French computer research academic hotspot INRIA and the industrial hardware manufacturer BULL are illustrated in the computer, institutional and social network outlined by these UUCP addresses.

At the level of the Usenet software, the field "newsgroups" exhaustively shows what thematic groups were targeted by the sender (Figure 14.5). In this case, the sender targets diverse and seemingly random groups, which is telltale of a spammer's method—massively deployed on Usenet from the mid-1990's and exponentially. Sending this promotional message to a series of "Eunet" themed groups can be interpreted as an attempt, from a non-European sender, to guess the newsgroups where the message will be spread widely in Europe.

Metadata fields are potential markers if one would like to operate a network relational analysis with digital tool methods—methods currently applied frequently to social networks datasets like, for instance, Twitter (which, in spite of their brevity, are framed indeed with metadata, from "author" to "date" and "hashtag"). Ian Milligan, in the aforementioned scholar blogpost (see note 20), is one of the researchers applying these new methods to Usenet "old" material: he showcases experiments in "topic modeling", based on the "newsgroup" field, but also prospects to reconstruct a regional network (the Canadian networks) based on other metadata fields. This methodological perspective allows to adopt a "distant reading" approach currently promoted in the Digital Humanities,[26] dedicated to show general tendencies: in the case of Usenet, the evolution of one or several newsgroups in time, in space, the type of members and their occupational identities, the comparison between the informational and infrastructural cartographies of message circulation are many research issues that could be investigated.

INTERACTION ANALYSIS

The epistolary model for studying asynchronous exchanges through a computer network is still valid, but should be updated with the format layers added by the medium. As such, it is still important to understand who writes, to whom, how they open and close their message—in reference to formal and social norms.

The sender in Figure 14.4, an employee at BULL, is an experienced Usenet user following the netiquette. Knowing that posting to the wrong group is a breach of rules, he proceeds with caution; the ASCII formatting of the word "*flame*" (Usenet jargon for online dispute), with a pair of asterisks indicating bold emphasis, is indicative of his awareness. In contrast, the second sender directly breaches the rule of multi-postings without a relevant reason to do so, in a typical spammers' fashion. New information to be taken into account is comprised in the email address and signature, giving out occupational data as well as indications of the user's technical proficiencies. The signature of the first sender is typical of Usenet folklore (with ASCII visual art), following the netiquette standards. On the contrary, the sender in Figure 14.5 is anonymous, replacing the typical signature with a link, revealing the promotional nature of their interaction. Finally, not depicted here but of utmost importance for interaction analysis are marks left by answering or quoting someone in an asynchronous conversation. Usually marked with angle brackets (> or >>, incremented with the number of times the message has been quoted), a variety of other markers exist, from simple quotation marks to generic or personalized automatized introduction ("x writes: ...", "x once wrote: ...", "according to x, ...").

Digging into interaction issues offers a refinery of data at the level of content useful to do analysis in at least two methodological orientations. One is the microanalysis of how actors interact, discuss, argue, collaborate, etc., and feeds into studies in history, sociology or anthropology that favor close-readings and bottom-up research perspectives. To our knowledge, none have been performed on Usenet metadata apart from ours, but it should be noted that considering the materiality of electronic messages, has been adopted punctually, explicitly or implicitly in works tackling the history of the internet (for instance Brunton, 2013; Hafner & Lyon, 1998; Hauben & Hauben, 1997), its sociology and anthropology (Baym, 1995; Donath, 2009; Fisher, 2003; Pfaffenberg, 2003; Tepper, 1997), its language, enunciation and discourse (Marcoccia, 2001, 2004; Mourlhon-Dallies & Colin, 2004). These works, of different fields and methods, all ask how Usenet interaction define or re-define social organizations in the technological context of the internet and thus the inscriptions left in born-digital documents by these interactions. If 1990's cybercultural studies tended to rely on the idea that online communities such as Usenet renewed social structures, later studies qualifies these stance, showing how preexisting social structured were imported online—for instance, the import of scholar enunciation rituals in the context of newsgroups (Mourlhon-Dallies & Colin, 2004). A neighboring approach, with different theoretical postulates, is the Science and Technology and Society perspective (STS) applied to online controversies in mailing-lists or newsgroups (for instance Paravel and Rosental, 2003). These studies are complementary close-reading to the methods evoked earlier, and are particularly cogent to shed light on actor-network strategies. Among studies I have reviewed, however, I haven't seen any emphasis on format aspects and its significance to understand the meaning of interaction—most of them tackling manifestations or signs of interaction metadata.

TEXT-AS-DOCUMENT ANALYSIS

Mostly absent here, some metadata labels inform on the most formal and technical dimensions of electronic messages: general format (here plaintext, but in the 1990's the HTML encoding is coming with webmails), encoding for specific newsreaders or software environments, linguistic parameters, etc. Some traces of this formatting are present in the "X-Google-Language" field, evidence that the text was reformatted for the purpose of web access.

Plain ASCII characters are also used to formalize structure like tables, bullet lists, partitions, even visual art etc., as in the case of Figure 14.4's email signature. The extent to which a discourse analysis of plaintext messages will be impacted by the formatting frame depends on the research question being asked. I have underlined the use of asterisks for emphasis, a common habit in plaintext writing for experienced computer users. What is more interesting in this case is the use in Figure 14.5 of a rudimentary hypertext element: web links have been making an appearance in newsgroups messages since at least 1993, when the web became public. The use of referential hyperlinks introduces a telling reflection of the writing texture of the web.

Here again, format elements are seldom taken into account in text-oriented analysis conducted on Usenet (in linguistics, socio-linguistics, or communication studies). One notable example is the work of French linguist and communication scholar Michel Marcoccia, who operates multi-level analysis on forums like Usenet: linguistic, discursive, and documentary. In order to study conversation in this context (relevant to interaction analysis), he suggests that it is important to look at the way forum text is structured as a dynamic, collective document, not only automatically by forum software, by the users themselves—which produces methodological challenges for the researcher trying to build her corpus: where does the conversation content end in relation to format that can be used expressively and structurally by users? (Marcoccia, 2001, 2004).

ARCHIVAL ANALYSIS

Finally, in order to perform an analysis focused on the document as archive, some elements can help pinpoint the nature of the object and of its preservation, even re-use. Right away, we see traces of the penultimate web archiving of the message, that is, Google's, that we already interpreted as the result of a hack. The "From -…", "X-Google-Language", "-Thread" and "-Attribute" fields testify that the original dump archives have gone through a re-archiving process to fit the Google Groups system of search and retrieval.

The web archivist's process (whether amateur or professional) of intervening, gathering, and re-publishing these documents is key here.[27] The default metadata structure can be a first step in a process of formalization for re-use purpose, whether for a simple informational search or for a more analytical research. Two key elements are at stake. First, the identification of the message as a single unit, that can be based on the original "Message ID" field that as generated when the message was sent. Second, fields and markers can be the basis of a formal structuration with standardized markup language. I experimented with this structuration for testing corpora standardization (Paloque-Berges & Kembellec, 2014), but the issue of structuration for plain search as well as deeper research has not been resolved to this day on a large enough scale for a serious heritage valorization of Usenet.[28]

CONCLUSION

Ultimately, CMC web archives include layers of the digital past and present internet, as exemplified by the genealogy of web-based archives of Usenet newsgroups from the 1990's. As objects of digital cultural and technical memory, their value lies in the traces they bear of earlier CMC interactions and conditions. They testify of pre-web computer network experiences, and also the way users discovered, built and appropriated web technologies—for their own vernacular memory-making. As such, Usenet archives are a critical resource—metaphorically, materially and methodologically—for internet and web alternate histories. I showed how users critically handle this layering, training their own sense of digital time, history and memory in confrontation and appropriation with archives managed and published by Google or the Internet Archive Foundation. I also demonstrated how researchers can frame their analyses with a layered perspective. Assessing the multiple, material layer of these archives provides insight against the opacity of black boxed web archiving services. A layered methodology offers a novel perspective on information systems' legacy: it reveals details about the changing environment of born-digital documents. The materiality of web archived CMC heritage bear marks left by these systems. If we pay attention to their layered existence and the possibilities that these layers offer, not only for analysis but also re-appropriation, they provide a contrarian position to the perspective that materials are locked-in and their legacies are limited to a particular service or platform (Erickson & Kelty, 2015).

The main challenge regarding Usenet archives for historians and social scientists is their accessibility, fragmentation and non-exhaustivity: not only are there holes in the archives, a traditional historiographical problem, but there are also several collections with concurrent data and information systems. These are exciting challenges indeed, and archivists, paleographists, anthropologists should be working along aforementioned researchers to solve auxiliaries and cultural issues related to the new science of born-digital archives.

REFERENCES

Abbate, J. (1999). *Inventing the Internet*. Cambridge, MA: MIT Press.

Baym, N. K. (1995). The emergence of community in computer-mediated communication. In S. Jones (Ed.), *Cybersociety: Computer-mediated communication and community* (pp. 138–163). Thousand Oaks, CA: Sage.

Brunton, F. (2013). *Spam: A shadow history of the Internet*. Cambridge, MA: MIT Press.

Caplan, L. (2016). Method without methodology: Data and the digital humanities. *E-flux Journal, 72*. Retrieved from http://www.e-flux.com/journal/72/60492/method-without-methodology-data-and-the-digital-humanities/.

Chanier, T., Poudat, C., Sagot, B., Antoniadis, G., Wigham, C. R., Hriba, L., Longhi, J. & Seddah, D. (2014). The CoMeRe Corpus for French: Structuring and Annotating Heterogeneous CMC Genres. *JLCL – Journal for Language Technology and Computational Linguistics, 29*(2): 1–30.

Donath, J. S. (2009). Identity and deception in the virtual community. In M. A. Smith & P. Kollock (Eds.), *Communities in cyberspace* (pp. 29–59). Abingdon: Routledge.

Erickson, S., & Kelty, C. M. (2015). The durability of software. In I. Kaldrack & M. Leeker (Eds.), *There is no software, there are just services* (pp. 40–52). Lüneburg: Meson Press.

Fisher, D. (2003). Studying information spaces. In C. Lueg & D. Fisher (Eds.), *From Usenet to CoWebs: Interacting with social information spaces* (pp. 3–20). New York, NY: Springer.

Flichy, P. (2007). *The Internet imaginaire*. Cambridge, MA: MIT Press.

Gitelman, L. (2006). *Always already new: Media, history and the data of culture*. Cambridge, MA: MIT Press.

Goody, J. (1977). *The domestication of the savage mind*. Cambridge, MA: Cambridge University Press.

Grossman, W. (1998). *net.wars*. New York, NY: New York University Press. Retrieved from http://nyupress.org/netwars.

Hafner, K., & Lyon, M. (1998). *Where wizards stay up late: The origins of the Internet*. New York, NY: Touchstone.

Hauben, R. (2002). Commodifying Usenet and the Usenet archive or continuing the online cooperative Usenet culture? *Science Studies, 15*(1), 61–68.

Hauben, M., & Hauben, R. (1997). *Netizens: On the history and impact of Usenet and the Internet*. Hoboken, NJ: Wiley-Blackwell.

Kelty, C. M. (2008). *Two Bits: The cultural significance of free software*. Durham: Duke University Press Books.

Marcoccia, M. (2001). L'animation d'un espace numérique de discussion: l'Exemple des forums Usenet. *Document numérique, 5*, 11–26.

Marcoccia, M. (2004). L'analyse conversationnelle des forums de discussion: Questionnements méthodologiques. *Cahiers du Cediscor, 8*, 23–37.

Mazzini, F. (2014). Cyber-cultural history: Some initial steps toward a cultural history of digital networking. *Humanities, 3*(2), 185–209.

Milligan, I. (2012). Mining the "Internet Graveyard": Rethinking the Historians' Toolkit. *Journal of the Canadian Historical Association, 23*(2), 21.

Mourlhon-Dallies, F., & Colin, J. Y. (2004). Les rituels énonciatifs des réseaux informatiques entre scientifiques. *Cahiers du Cediscor, 8*, 161–172.

Niu, J. (2012). An overview of web archiving. *D-Lib Magazine. The Magazine of Digital Library Research, 18* (3/4). Retrieved from http://www.dlib.org/dlib/march12/niu/03niu1.html.

Latzko-Toth, G., & Proulx, S. (2013). Enjeux éthiques de la recherche sur le Web. In C. Barats (Ed.), *Manuel d'Analyse Du Web* (pp. 32–52). Paris: Armand Colin.

Paloque-Berges, C. (2012). La mémoire culturelle d'Internet: Le folklore de Usenet. *Le Temps des médias, 18*, 111–123.

Paloque-Berges, C. (2013a). Un patrimoine composite: Le public Internet face à l'archivage de sa matière culturelle. In J.-F Tétu, N. Pélissier, L. Idjeraoui Ravez, P. Stefanescu & I. Dragan (Eds.), *Traces, mémoire et communication* (pp. 279–286). Bucarest: Presses de l'Université de Bucarest.

Paloque-Berges, C. (2013b). Une pédagogie documentaire par le folklore: Analyse des modes d'emploi d'Internet au temps de la "frontière électronique". *Documentaliste-Sciences de l'Information, 50*(4), 64–71.

Paloque-Berges, C. (2014). Le rôle des communautés patrimoniales d'Internet dans la constitution d'un patrimoine numérique: Des mobilisations diverses autour de l'auto-médiation. In B. Dufrêne & E. Barbier (Eds.), *Patrimoine et humanités numériques* (pp. 277–290). Berlin: Lit. Verlag.

Paloque-Berges, C., & Kembellec, G. (2014). Nouvelles sources numériques et logiques d'open corpus: L'intérêt d'archiver et de partager des courriers électroniques. *Cahiers de la Sfsic, 9*, 239–244.

Paravel, V., & Rosental, C. (2003). Les réseaux, des objets relationnels non identifiés? *Réseaux, 118*(2), 237–270.

Pfaffenberg, B. (2003). A standing wave in the web of our communications: Usenet and the socio-technical construction of cyberspace values. In C. Lueg & D. Fisher (Eds.), *From Usenet to CoWebs: Interacting with social information spaces* (pp. 21–40). New York, NY: Springer.

Quarterman, J. S. (1990). *The Matrix: Computer networks and conferencing systems worldwide*. Englewood Cliffs, NJ: Prentice Hall.

Rheingold, H. (1993). *Virtual Community – Homesteading on the Electronic Frontier*. Cambridge, MA: MIT Press.

Tepper, M. (1997). Usenet communities and the cultural politics of information. In D. Porter (Ed.), *Internet culture* (pp. 38–54). Abingdon: Routledge.

Turner, F. (2006). *From counterculture to cyberculture*. Chicago, IL: University of Chicago Press.

Wellman, B. (2001). Computer networks as social networks. *Science, 293*(5537), 2031–2034.

Zimmer, M. (2016). The Twitter archive at the Library of Congress: Challenges for information practice and information policy. *First Monday, 20*(7). Retrieved from http://firstmonday.org/article/view/5619/4653.

NOTES

1. This research was supported in part by the French ANR Young Research program "Web 90: Heritage, Memories and History of the Web in the 1990s" (ANR-14-CE29-0012).
2. Comments from a Reddit user in reaction to finding Usenet archived in the Google Groups web service (posted on May 24, 2012) https://www.reddit.com/r/usenet/comments/19rfj0/20_year_archive_on_google_groups.
3. I would like to extend special thanks to Kevin Driscoll for not only his careful copy-editing of this chapter, but also his thoughtful comments and complementary references.
4. Linguists in particular were early in creating corpora of born-digital language interactions. For instance in France, a national Research Infrastructure was dedicated to building reference corpora for 'Network Mediated Communication' in accordance with international standards (Chanier et al., 2014).

5. Since the web's success in fostering and expanding internet user communities, Usenet has been downgraded to a shadowy part of the computer inter-networks. Invaded by spam, it is used since the end of the 1990s mainly for exchanging 'binary files' within social networks of computer hackers and pirates (Brunton, 2013).

6. FAQ 'What is Usenet? A Second Opinion', started by Edward Vielmetti in 1991 (last version is 1999) http://www.faqs.org/faqs/usenet/what-is/part2.

7. Reddit, one of Usenet self-proclaimed Usenet heirs, entertains its cultural heritage by feeding into the myth of Usenet's death, as testified by the topic 'Why Usenet died' created in July 2015 by experienced user 'dredmorbius', owner of a personal subreddit ('lairs') https://www.reddit.com/r/dredmorbius/comments/3c3xyu/why_usenet_died/.

8. AdSense was placed in the Google Groups, and thus in the Usenet archives, for a few years but is gone since a 2013 big redesign.

9. An earlier study by the author of a Slashdot forum discussion (the earliest self-proclaimed Usenet heir as a web forum) and other technology-oriented online media receiving the news of Google's archiving of Usenet in 2001, showed that the main quality seen in the Usenet archive was the abundance of information and opinions—a 'cornucopian high-tech harvest' to quote one of them (Paloque-Berges, 2013b).

10. Originally standing on its own web page entitled "The 20 Year Usenet Timeline" https://web.archive.org/web/20011212191924/http://www.google.com/googlegroups/archive_announce_20.html, the timeline has been retrograded to a list of ' Memorable Usenet Moments'» and embedded in a crude help page dedicated to the Google Groups Usenet archive https://support.google.com/groups/answer/6003482?hl=en.

11. According to internet research ethics, this problem falls under the category of 'contextual integrity': a researcher should aim at keeping this integrity when facing the problem of uncovering public or private data (Latzko-Toth & Proulx, 2013).

12. Matthew Braga, "Google, a Search Company, has Made its Internet Archive Unsearchable" (Feburary 13, 2015) http://motherboard.vice.com/read/google-a-search-company-has-made-its-internet-archive-impossible-to-search. See also the monitoring of Reddit users on the case https://www.reddit.com/r/usenet/comments/1ihw3k/why_are_google_neglecting_their_usenet_archive/.

13. Ryan Baumann, "Early Usenet History and Archiving." Ryan Baumann—/etc (blog), (February 23rd, 2015) https://ryanfb.github.io/etc/2015/02/23/early_usenet_history_and_archiving.html.

14. Yarchive.net, by Norman Marvin, since 2003—last update: 2011 http://yarchive.net/.

15. A search for "Usenet archive" returns around a hundred results on Reddit, most of which (67 to this day) are falling under the Usenet subreddit category https://www.reddit.com/search?q=%22Usenet+archive%22.

16. Search for "Usenet" on the IAF's forums produced around 60 results to this day https://archive.org/search.php?query=forumPost%3A1%20AND%20usenet.

17. The Google Groups service doesn't allow data crawling and automated massive retrieval, and effectively blocks all attempts at harvesting their collections—which explains why the 'Usenet Historical Collections' donor remains anonymous. 'The Usenet archive', a website maintained by an 'early Usenet user' (Mazzini, 2014), provides a searchable archive of Usenet, but is quite opaque in its mission and motives. Favoring the textfile format, it is possible to see that the data was extracted from the Google Usenet archive—and it is probable that the owner is the same donor mentioned in the case of IAF's 'Usenet historical collection' http://www.thesusenetarchive.com.

18. https://archive.org/details/usenet.

19. See the Wayback machine archive of this now defunct page http://web.archive.org/web/20010413040236/http://starbase.neosoft.com/~claird/news.lists/rootnewsgroup_archives.html.

20. Quote from a blog post entitled "Exploring the USENET Archive: Early Thoughts" (March 6, 2013) https://ianmilligan.ca/2013/03/06/exploring-the-usenet-archive-early-thoughts/.

21. Ankerson's recent study have been presented at two 2015 international conferences: "Web History as Time Travel: Digital Nostalgia & Collaborative Filtering in Public Engagement with the Internet Archive's WayBack Machine" (RESAW, Web Archives as Scholarly Sources: Issues, Practices and Perspectives, 8–10 June, Aarhus University, Denmark; "Take me back! Web History as Chronotourism of the Digital Archive" (TTOW, Times and Temporalities of the Web, 1–3 December, ISCC, Paris, France).

22. Erickson and Kelty (2015) analyze software as a 'layered environment' (a concept for thinking critically about Software as Service) but do not offer a layered-analysis methodology per se.

23. http://ascii-world.com/history; http://en.wikipedia.org/wiki/Plain_text.

24. Names were redacted for the purpose of anonymity. Brackets have been added to cut a long list of Google metadata header code. The dump from which these message were extracted has been generated in February 2016 by a search for the keyword 'Eunet' within IAF's 'Usenet Historical Collections' https://archive.org/details/usenethistorical?and[]=eunet.

25. The reader should keep in mind that what is laid out below are only samples of potential analysis drawn from my research corpora, and do not explicit the epistemological postulates, methodological framing, and contextual material on which they rely for further case studies.

26. For a relevant criticism of some of Digital Humanities methodological and epistemological limits, I would like to refer the reader to Caplan (2016).

27. I have not been able to get in touch with those responsible with the 'Usenet historical collection' at IAF in order to understand their rationale.

28. The ePADD email history archiving and visualization software developed at Stanford University Libraries is extremely advanced but do not handle multiple authors email corpora such as Usenet or mailing-lists.

Contributors

Marguerite Barry
Marguerite Barry, PhD, is Assistant Professor at the School of Information and Communication Studies, University College Dublin. Her research focuses on digital media discourses, conceptualisations of 'interactivity', technology and wellbeing and ethics in technological design. Her work is published in *Interacting with Computers, New Media & Society, Proceedings of CHI*, the *International Communication Gazette* and *Participations*.

Paolo Bory
Paolo Bory is PhD candidate in Media Studies at USI—Università della Svizzera italiana in Lugano, Switzerland. His research focuses on the analysis of media and social imaginaries and on the histories of digital media and digital networks. One of his last papers on these topics has been recently published on the international journal *New Media & Society*.

Niels Brügger
Niels Brügger is Professor in Internet Studies and Digital Humanities, Aarhus University, Denmark, Head of the Centre for Internet Studies, and of NetLab. His research interests are web historiography, web archiving and digital humanities. Within these fields he has published monographs and a number of edited books as well as articles and book chapters. Recent books include *Web History* (ed., Peter Lang, 2010), *Histories of Public Service Broadcasters on the web* (co-ed. with M. Burns,

Peter Lang, 2012), *The web as history: Using web archives to understand the past and the present* (co-ed. with R. Schroeder, UCL Press, 2017), and he is co-founder and Managing Editor of the newly founded international journal *Internet Histories: Digital Technology, Culture and Society* (Taylor & Francis/Routledge).

Anwesha Chakraborty

Anwesha Chakraborty is a final year PhD candidate at the University of Bologna. Her dissertation explores various aspects of the museum as a scientific institution: its history, its export to other cultures, its present communication strategies in different contexts. Her most recent work is an exhibit review of the new permanent gallery at the Museo della Scienza in Milan, which has appeared in the journal *Technology and Culture*.

Jean Marie Deken

Jean Marie Deken is Archivist and Manager of the Archives, History and Records Office and Research Library groups of the SLAC National Accelerator Laboratory of Stanford University. Her research interests include archival administration, and electronic data and records preservation and management. She is the author of *Stanford Linear Accelerator Center, Celebrating 40 Years: A Photo History* (2002); contributing Editor to W. K. H. Panofsky, *Panofsky on Physics, Politics and Peace* (Springer: 2007); and a contributing author to *Many Happy Returns: Advocacy and the Development of Archives* (SAA, 2011). Her work has appeared in *Archival Outlook*, and *symmetry*.

Anne Helmond

Anne Helmond, PhD, is Assistant Professor of New Media and Digital Culture and Program Director of the MA New Media and Digital Culture at the University of Amsterdam. She is a member of the Digital Methods Initiative where she focuses her research on developing methods to study (the historical development of) social media platforms and apps. Her research interests include software studies, platform studies, app studies, infrastructure studies, algorithms and web history. Anne's work has been published in highly-ranked peer-reviewed journals such as *New Media & Society, Theory, Culture and Society, Social Media + Society, First Monday*, and *Computational Culture*.

Michel Hockx

Michel Hockx is Professor of Chinese Literature and Director of the Liu Institute for Asia and Asian Studies at the University of Notre Dame. His research focuses on modern and contemporary Chinese literary communities, the way they organize themselves, the media through which they distribute their products, and their relationship with the state. His most recent book publication is *Internet Literature in China* (Columbia University Press, 2015).

Paul Koerbin

Paul Koerbin is the Assistant Director for Web Archiving and Government Publications at the National Library of Australia. He has been involved with the development and operation of the NLA's 'PANDORA' web archiving program since its inception the late 1990s. He contributed to the development of one of the first workflow systems for selective web archiving and led the development of the Australian Government Web Archive released in 2014. He had a major role in preparing the NLA's input to the drafting of electronic legal deposit legislation in Australia which came into effect in February 2016. He holds a graduate quali-fication in library and information studies from the University of Tasmania and a PhD in ethnomusicology from Western Sydney University.

Ditte Laursen

Ditte Laursen, Head of department, PhD, The Royal Library Denmark. Her inter-ests as a researcher and curator include digital archives, social interaction in, around, and across digital media, and users' engagement with museums and libraries. She is author or co-author of numerous publications on these topics, all published in international peer-reviewed journals and anthologies.

Elisabetta Locatelli

Elisabetta Locatelli, PhD, is adjunct professor of 'Media and social networks' at Università Cattolica del Sacro Cuore and researcher at OssCom, (Research Center on Media and Communication of Università Cattolica del Sacro Cuore). Her main research interests are about social media use; social shaping of technology; ethics of research on social media. Among the most important publications are the mon-ography *The Blog Up: Storia sociale del blog in Italia* (Franco Angeli, Milano, 2014) and articles in *Social Media + Society* and *Comunicazioni Sociali. Journal of Media, Performing Arts and Cultural Studies*.

Per Møldrup-Dalum

Per Møldrup-Dalum, Master of science, The State and University Library Denmark. Research interests includes how quantitative methods can be used in the liberal arts, how computational resources can assist in exploring the human mind as it is expressed through its intellectual artefacts.

Federico Nanni

Federico Nanni is a final year PhD candidate at the University of Bologna. His research is focused on considering web materials as primary sources for studying the recent history of academic institutions. His works have been published (or will appear) in relevant digital humanities journals, such as *Digital Humanities Quarterly*, the *International Journal of Humanities and Arts Computing* and *D-Lib*.

Simone Natale

Simone Natale is Lecturer in Communication and Media Studies at Loughborough University, UK. His research focuses on the imaginary related to media and technology. He is the author of *Supernatural Entertainments: Victorian Spiritualism and the Rise of Modern Media Culture* (Penn State University Press, 2016) and of articles published in numerous journals, including the *Journal of Communication*, *New Media & Society*, *Communication Theory*, and *Media, Culture and Society*.

Sybil Nolan

Sybil Nolan is a lecturer in publishing and communications at the University of Melbourne. She was a newspaper journalist for 15 years before going into book publishing. In between, she taught journalism at RMIT University, Melbourne from 1997 to 2003, and in that capacity led the creation of the first online newsroom there. Her 2003 paper "Journalism online: the search for narrative form in a multilinear world" is recognized as one of the first scholarly articles to consider the impact of blogging on journalism, and has been extensively cited, and set in online journalism subjects.

Camille Paloque-Berges

Camille Paloque-Berges holds a PhD in Communication and Information sciences and is currently a research engineer at the History of Techno-Sciences lab (HT2S) at Conservatoire National des Arts et Métiers in Paris, France. She researches, within the history of computing, how computer-centric occupational communities communicate and engage in networks, as well as born-digital internet heritage. Recent publications are in *Routledge Companion to Global Internet Histories*, or in *Histoire@Politique*, n° 30. She has co-edited *Histoires et cultures du libre* (with C. Masutti, 2013) and is the author of *Poétique des codes sur les réseaux informatiques* (2009).

Matthew Weber

Matthew Weber is an Assistant Professor in the School of Communication and Information, and Co-Director of Rutgers' NetSCI Network Science research lab. Matthew's research examines organizational change and adaptation, both internal and external, in response to new information communication technology. His recent work focuses on the transformation of the news media industry in the United States in reaction to new forms of media production. Matthew's work has been published in numerous leading academic outlets including *American Behavioral Scientist*, *Management Communication Quarterly*, *Journal of Communication* and *Communication Theory*.

Peter Webster

Dr. Peter Webster is founder and managing director of Webster Research and Consulting. He specialises in two fields: the contemporary history of British Christianity, and the digital turn in scholarship as it affects libraries, archives and their academic users. He has published widely on both these topics, with a particular interest in the archived web. His study of Michael Ramsey, archbishop of Canterbury, was published in 2015. Before founding Webster Research and Consulting, he was engagement and liaison manager for the UK Web Archive at the British Library, and program officer for the International Internet Preservation Consortium.

General Editor: **Steve Jones**

Digital Formations is the best source for critical, well-written books about digital technologies and modern life. Books in the series break new ground by emphasizing multiple methodological and theoretical approaches to deeply probe the formation and reformation of lived experience as it is refracted through digital interaction. Each volume in **Digital Formations** pushes forward our understanding of the intersections, and corresponding implications, between digital technologies and everyday life. The series examines broad issues in realms such as digital culture, electronic commerce, law, politics and governance, gender, the Internet, race, art, health and medicine, and education. The series emphasizes critical studies in the context of emergent and existing digital technologies.

Other recent titles include:

Felicia Wu Song
  Virtual Communities: Bowling Alone, Online Together

Edited by Sharon Kleinman
  The Culture of Efficiency: Technology in Everyday Life

Edward Lee Lamoureux, Steven L. Baron, & Claire Stewart
  Intellectual Property Law and Interactive Media: Free for a Fee

Edited by Adrienne Russell & Nabil Echchaibi
  International Blogging: Identity, Politics and Networked Publics

Edited by Don Heider
  Living Virtually: Researching New Worlds

Edited by Judith Burnett, Peter Senker & Kathy Walker
  The Myths of Technology: Innovation and Inequality

Edited by Knut Lundby
  Digital Storytelling, Mediatized Stories: Self-representations in New Media

Theresa M. Senft
  Camgirls: Celebrity and Community in the Age of Social Networks

Edited by Chris Paterson & David Domingo
  Making Online News: The Ethnography of New Media Production

To order other books in this series please contact our Customer Service Department:

(800) 770-LANG (within the US)

(212) 647-7706 (outside the US)

(212) 647-7707 FAX

To find out more about the series or browse a full list of titles, please visit our website:

WWW.PETERLANG.COM